Excavations at King's Low and Queen's Low

Excavations at King's Low and Queen's Low

two Early Bronze Age barrows in Tixall, North Staffordshire

by Gary Lock, Dick Spicer, Winston Hollins
and members of the
Stoke-on-Trent Museum Archaeological Society

with written contributions by Anne Andrews, Angela Boyle, Philippa Bradley, Dana Challinor, Frank Chambers, Jenny Foster, Alex Gibson, Les Higgins, Rose Longden, Peter Northover, Alan Outram, Derek Outram, Alison Sheridan, Andrew Shortland, Heather Sugden, Mike Tite and Ian Wilshaw

Archaeopress
Gordon House
276 Banbury Road
Oxford OX2 7ED

www.archaeopress.com

ISBN 978-1-905739-66-0

© Archaeopress, contributing authors,
and Stoke-on-Trent Museum Archaeological Society 2013

All rights reserved. No part of this book may be
reproduced, stored in a retrieval system, or transmitted,
in any form or by any means, electronic, mechanical,
photocopying or otherwise, without the prior
written permission of the copyright owners.

Designed and typeset by Chris Hulin, Oxford Book Projects
Printed in England by 4edge, Hockley

In memory of Dick Spicer
1947–2000

Contents

	List of figures, tables and plates	viii
	Preface	x
1	**Introduction and background**	**1**
1.1	Introduction *Gary Lock*	1
1.2	A third barrow? *Gary Lock*	1
1.3	The naming of King's Low and Queen's Low *Rose Longden*	3
1.4	The environmental setting *Helen Sugden and Alan Outram*	4
1.5	The archaeological setting *Gary Lock*	4
2	**The excavations**	**14**
2.1	King's Low *Gary Lock*	14
2.1.1	The excavations	15
2.1.2	The cross *Anne Andrews and Rose Longden*	33
2.2	Queen's Low *Winston Hollins*	36
2.2.1	The excavations	36
2.2.2	The kerbstones *Derek Outram*	46
3	**People and the environment**	**49**
3.1	An environmental history of the River Sow region, Stafford *Heather Sugden and Alan Outram*	49
3.2	The King's Low pollen *Frank Chambers and Ian Wilshaw*	59
3.3	The cremated human bone *Angela Boyle*	60
3.4	The King's Low wood charcoal *Dana Challinor*	62
4	**The material culture**	**65**
4.1	The pottery *Alex Gibson*	65
4.1.1	Pottery reconstructions *Derek Outram*	71
4.2	The worked flint *Philippa Bradley*	73
4.3	The faience beads	79
4.3.1	Description and discussion *Alison Sheridan*	79
4.3.2	Technical analyses *Mike Tite and Andrew Shortland*	82
4.3.3	Comments based on experimental faience *Les Higgins*	84
4.4	Copper alloy artefacts	86
4.4.1	The King's Low bracelets *Jenny Foster*	86
4.4.2	Technical analyses *Peter Northover*	87
5	**King's Low and Queen's Low: a wider discussion** *Gary Lock*	**90**
5.1	Background and antiquarian interest	90
5.2	Barrows in the landscape	91
5.3	The construction and use of barrows	94
Appendices		
1	King's Low context description list *Gary Lock*	99
2	Queen's Low context description list *Winston Hollins*	102
	Bibliography	**107**

List of figures, tables and plates

Figures

Fig. 1.1	The location of King's Low and Queen's Low, Staffordshire, together with the general area of the environmental core in the valley of the River Sow	2
Fig. 1.2	Neolithic sites within a 20-mile radius of King's Low and Queen's Low (courtesy of Staffordshire HER, produced by Suzy Blake)	5
Fig. 1.3	Neolithic finds within a 20-mile radius of King's Low and Queen's Low (courtesy of Staffordshire HER, produced by Suzy Blake)	6
Fig. 1.4	Bronze Age barrows within a 20-mile radius of King's Low and Queen's Low (courtesy of Staffordshire HER, produced by Suzy Blake)	7
Fig. 1.5	Bronze Age barrows in the Staffordshire Peak District (courtesy of Staffordshire HER, produced by Suzy Blake)	8
Fig. 1.6	Bronze Age sites within a 20-mile radius of King's Low and Queen's Low (courtesy of Staffordshire HER, produced by Suzy Blake)	9
Fig. 1.7	Bronze Age finds within a 20-mile radius of King's Low and Queen's Low (courtesy of Staffordshire HER, produced by Suzy Blake)	10
Fig. 1.8	Iron Age sites within a 20-mile radius of King's Low and Queen's Low (courtesy of Staffordshire HER, produced by Suzy Blake)	11
Fig. 1.9	Iron Age finds within a 20-mile radius of King's Low and Queen's Low (courtesy of Staffordshire HER, produced by Suzy Blake)	12
Fig. 2.1	King's Low: before excavation showing felled larch trees	14
Fig. 2.2	King's Low: the excavated areas	15
Fig. 2.3	King's Low: the main north-south section	16–17
Fig. 2.4	King's Low: the main west-east section	18–19
Fig. 2.5	King's Low: the approximate size of the Phase 1 and Phase 2 barrows, the main contexts and the distribution of the Grooved Ware sherds and Collared Urn KL11	20
Fig. 2.6	King's Low: Test Pit 3 section, Area A	20
Fig. 2.7	King's Low: a schematic section across the central area showing the main contexts described in the text, not to scale	23
Fig. 2.8	King's Low: Pit (245 = 445), Area D, at an early stage of excavation	24
Fig. 2.9	King's Low: Collared Urn KL10 during excavation	25
Fig. 2.10	King's Low: charcoal within Context (53)	25
Fig. 2.11	King's Low: the distribution of cremated human bone, 1,692 pieces in total, scattered by rabbit activity (drawn by John Pouncett)	27
Fig. 2.12	King's Low: section drawings for Areas R and N	30
Fig. 2.13	King's Low: section drawings for Areas M and F, the latter showing the stone cross and its socket hole	31
Fig. 2.14	King's Low: the stone cross during excavation	32
Fig. 2.15	King's Low: the stump of the cross at the start of the excavation, 1986	33
Fig. 2.16	King's Low: the decorated head of the cross photographed c.1954 by Mr. D. Mayer	34
Fig. 2.17	Sepulchral stone showing the Figure of St. Saeran, Llanynys church, Denbighshire (photograph by Dave and Maureen Thomas)	35
Fig. 2.18	Queen's Low: the view before excavation in 1993	36
Fig. 2.19	Queen's Low: topographic survey	37
Fig. 2.20	Queen's Low: resistivity survey	37
Fig. 2.21	Queen's Low: the excavated areas	38
Fig. 2.22	Queen's Low: looking north across the excavated area showing the sandstone natural with incised plough marks	39
Fig. 2.23	Queen's Low: excavation Areas B, F, E and SX showing the main features of the kerb	40
Fig. 2.24	Queen's Low: excavation Areas G, H and WX showing the main contexts	41
Fig. 2.25	Queen's Low: the south-eastern kerb stones viewed from above	42
Fig. 2.26	Queen's Low: the inside face of the kerb	42
Fig. 2.27	Queen's Low: north-south section of the eastern baulk of Area E	42
Fig. 2.28	Queen's Low: a schematic section showing the main contexts in the area of the kerb stones, not to scale	43
Fig. 2.29	Queen's Low: Context (18), white sand disturbed by ploughing in two directions, where the northern continuation of the kerb would have been	46
Fig. 2.30	Queen's Low: kerb stone with cup mark (drawn by Derek Outram)	47
Fig. 2.31	Queen's Low: kerb stone, possible saddle quern (drawn by Derek Outram)	47
Fig. 2.32	Queen's Low: marked kerb stone, probably a modern plough mark (drawn by Derek Outram)	47
Fig. 3.1	The locations of the pollen test pits and the pollen core on the River Sow floodplain (RSF), Stafford	49
Fig. 3.2	The generalised influx of pollen to floodplain environments (based on Scaife and Burrin 1994)	50
Fig. 3.3	The relative percentages of identifiable molluscan species	51
Fig. 3.4	The relative percentage pollen diagram from the River Sow floodplain, Stafford. The percentages are based on the total land pollen sum (excluding aquatic pollen and spores)	52

Fig. 3.5	Pollen concentration diagrams for the River Sow floodplain, Stafford	53–55
Fig. 4.1	a) King's Low Collared Urn, KL10, (drawn by Katie Banks); b) neck and collar decoration (photograph by Dave Thomas)	66
Fig. 4.2	King's Low pottery: a) KL1, SF5514; b) KL3, SF6381; c) KL3, SF6383; d) KL5, SF5049; e) KL7, SF7160; f) KL15, SF7025; g) KL19, SF3016 (drawn by Derek Outram)	67
Fig. 4.3	King's Low Collared Urn sherds, KL11: a) SF6541; b) SF6393; c) SF6330; d) SF6503; e) SF6025; f) SF6495; g) SF6339 (drawn by Derek Outram)	68
Fig. 4.4	Queen's Low pottery: a) QL1, SF823; b) QL1, SF7253; c) QL8, SF 49; d) QL8, SF350; e) QL8, SF62; f) QL8, SF676; g) QL10, SF7299; h) QL10, SF301; i) QL13, SF130; j) QL13, SF130 (drawn by Derek Outram)	70
Fig. 4.5	A possible reconstruction of the Collared Urn KL11 from King's Low: a) the conjoining sherds; b) the reconstruction (drawn by Derek Outram)	72
Fig. 4.6	a and b A possible reconstruction of the position of rim sherds of Collared Urn QL7 from Queen's Low (drawn by Derek Outram).	73
Fig. 4.7	A possible reconstruction of the Collared Urn QL7 from Queen's Low: a) the conjoining sherds; b) the reconstruction (drawn by Derek Outram)	75
Fig. 4.8	The worked flint, a) to s) from King's Low, t) from Queen's Low; a) SF653; b) SF6470; c) SF3632; d) SF228; e) SF2144; f) SF3550; g) SF7109; h) SF6334; i) SF3353; j) SF14; k) SF6218; l) SF328; m) SF317; n) SF1600; o) SF5043; p) SF3970; q) SF1442; r) SF83; s) SF3572; t) SF167 (drawn by Noel Boothroyd)	76–77
Fig. 4.9	The faience beads: left, the Queen's Low quoit-shaped bead (SF283); right, the King's Low spherical bead (SF479) (drawn by members of SOTMAS)	80
Fig. 4.10	SEM-CP image of the highly weathered surface of the QL bead, showing the characteristic structures derived from the weathering due to water	83
Fig. 4.11	High vacuum SEM image of the un-weathered under-surface of a small stub mounted sample of the QL bead	83
Fig. 4.12	The King's Low bracelets, (drawn by Derek Outram)	86

Tables

Table 3.1	The numbers of identifiable molluscs recovered, River Sow floodplain, Stafford	51
Table 3.2	The lithology of pollen core sediments	51
Table 3.3	Pollen taxa in a sample from King's Low, Context 51 (as percentage of total land pollen sum of 250 grains)	59
Table 3.4	Summary of cremation data from King's Low and Queen's Low	60
Table 3.5	Weight of cremated bone within anatomical categories and size ranges, King's Low and Queen's Low.	62
Table 3.6	Summary of large charcoal samples, King's Low	63
Table 4.1	The worked flint assemblage composition	73
Table 4.2	The worked flint: retouched forms	75
Table 4.3	The worked flint: core typology	78
Table 4.4	SEM-EDS analysis of the King's Low and Queen's Low beads, with some Scottish beads for comparison	83
Table 4.5	Typical values obtained from the analysis of bricks made from clays of various geological deposits	84
Table 4.6	Analysis of the copper-based metalwork from King's Low	88

Plates

Plate 2.1	King's Low: an example of podsolisation showing the leached out A horizon above, the enriched B horizon below and a zone of hard-panning in between.	21
Plate 2.2	King's Low: typical rabbit damage at depth within the mound showing filled in runs and nests between areas of orange mound material.	21
Plate 2.3	King's Low: stake hole (1044), a) as seen before excavation, b) the lower half in section, c) nearly the full length in section; stake hole (1051), d) the full length in section.	22
Plate 2.4	King's Low: Context (51).	26
Plate 2.5	King's Low: a composite plan photograph showing the main contexts in parts of Areas B and D	28
Plate 2.6	King's Low: Contexts (51) and (53) with turf staining	26
Plate 2.7	King's Low: turves shown in section	29
Plate 2.8	King's Low: the Phase 1 turf mound, Area D	29
Plate 2.9	Queen's Low: the kerb, looking west	44
Plate 2.10	Queen's Low: cremation within a hole cut into the bedrock just inside the line of the kerb, Context (48), a) before excavation, b) after excavation	45
Plate 2.11	Queen's Low: kerb stone with cup mark	48
Plate 2.12	Queen's Low: kerb stone, possible saddle quern	48
Plate 3.1	The King's Low cremation	61
Plate 3.2	The charred plank fragment, Context (51/53) (1017)	64
Plate 4.1	King's Low Collared Urn, KL10, (photographed by Dave Thomas)	74
Plate 4.2	A possible reconstruction of the Collared Urn KL11 from King's Low (made by Les Higgins).	74
Plate 4.3	A possible reconstruction of the Collared Urn QL7 from Queen's Low (made by Les Higgins).	74
Plate 4.4	The faience beads: left, the Queen's Low quoit-shaped bead (SF283); right, the King's Low spherical bead (SF479) (photographed by Ian Cartwright)	85
Plate 4.5	Bracelet 1 from King's Low, (photographed by Dave Thomas)	85

Preface

King's Low was excavated during the summers of 1986 to 1992, and Queen's Low 1993 and 1994, under the auspices of the Stoke-on-Trent Museum Archaeological Society (SOTMAS). The excavations and post-excavation have been funded by SOTMAS and many members of the society have formed the workforce for all activities. Gary Lock and Dick Spicer directed the work with Winston Hollins co-ordinating much of the post-excavation.

King's Low stands within an area of commercial woodland and we are indebted to Tilhill Economic Forestry and Economic Forestry Group PLC, especially Mr. David Owen, for permission to work there. Queen's Low stands within farmland and we thank Mr Robert Madders of Lower Hanyards Farm and Mr Nigel Bostock of Tixall Garden Farms for similar permission.

A considerable number of SOTMAS members have been involved in the excavation and post-excavation work and we would like to thank them all. The following deserve special mention: Dave Thomas for photography; Les Higgins for pottery and faience reconstructions; the Outram family, Helen and Derek for pottery reconstruction, the young Alan for tireless work on site and dealing with the finds at Queen's Low. Thanks also to Floss Wilkins for all drawings, unless otherwise acknowledged, and to Chris Hulin for invaluable advice.

We would also like to thank David Barker and Deb Ford of the City Museum and Art Gallery, Hanley, Stoke-on-Trent for support in various ways, for displaying some of the material from the excavations and for providing a home for the site archive.

1 Introduction and background

1.1 Introduction
Gary Lock

King's Low and Queen's Low are situated in the parish of Tixall to the north-east of Stafford, Staffordshire (Fig. 1.1). At the time of investigation King's Low (Staffordshire HER PRN 851, SJ 3954 3237) was still extant and lies within Blackheath Covert whereas Queen's Low (Staffordshire HER PRN 855, SJ 3963 3238), about one kilometre to the east, was virtually ploughed-out and within a field of rough pasture.

The barrows are located on Tixall Heath, the northern most point of Cannock Chase and just within the Cannock Chase Area of Outstanding Natural Beauty. The topography of the immediate area is gentle with King's Low standing at 90 m OD and Queen's Low at 122 m OD, this is the 'central lowland belt' of Staffordshire with the Cannock hills to the immediate south (Pallister 1976). The barrows lie approximately 2.5 km to the south of the River Trent and its floodplain and one kilometre to the south of King's Low is the River Sow which flows eastward to join the Trent in approximately 4 km. Like much of the rest of Cannock Chase, the barrows lie within an area of superficial glacial and periglacial deposits[1] derived during the Pleistocene Ice Age and overlying Keuper Marls and sandstones. The surface deposits are a mixture of tills and glacio-fluvial sands and gravels with river terrace deposits in the valley of the Sow. The gravels are a mixture of pebbles and cobbles formed from a variety of rock types, most being of various quartz-rich rocks such as quartzite, vein quartz and red, brown or black chert and flint clasts. The nature of these indicates that these glacial deposits were laid down by the late Devensian Irish Sea Ice which brought debris into the Stafford area, not only from the floor of the Irish Sea, but from as far north as the Lake District and the Southern Uplands.[2]

1.2 A third barrow?
Gary Lock

There is a possibility of there originally being a third barrow on Tixall Heath although the early sources seem to confuse this with the finding of two, now missing, urns in the area. The second edition of William Camden's survey of Britain states that:

> On Tixall heath are two barrows, called the King's and Queen's Low. Two urns found on this heath in the last century were lately in the custody of Walter Lord Aston (Camden 1806, 511).

Camden's monumental work incorporated much material gathered by other people and for the presence of King's Low and Queen's Low he acknowledges Thomas Pennant. In Pennant's account of his journey from Chester to London in 1780 he writes: 'On leaving Tixal, I went through the park, and part of a common of the same name, on which are two *tumuli;* one called the king's, the other the queen's *Low;* but no reason is assigned for the names'.[3] There is no mention of a third barrow although by the early 19th century Clifford and Clifford write the following:

> these urns have not been preserved nor is the account very accurate , for only twenty years ago three lows were visible, one of which has since been levelled by the plough but not until it had been dug into but without making any discovery (Clifford and Clifford 1817, 86-87).

Erdeswick's Survey of Staffordshire (1844) offers a slightly different account:

> Tixall Heath is distinguished by two remarkable Tumuli: one named the King's and the other the Queen's Low. About a century ago, two urns were found near them, supposed to have been of Roman workmanship (page 70).

So, Camden mentions the lost urns being found but ascribes them to 'the heath' rather than either King's or Queen's Low specifically, Pennant does not mention the urns at all nor a third barrow and by 1817 Clifford and Clifford imply that the urns were by then lost and did not come from digging into the third mound anyway, a view supported by Erdeswick. The conclusion is that the original location of the two lost urns is unkown, as is the location of the third barrow. As part of the background work for this excavation a survey of aerial photographs covering ploughed and pasture fields and a fieldwalking survey through nearby woodland produced no evidence of a third barrow.

The only other recorded finding of pottery from the two barrows is a note in Hanley Museum by Robinson: 'two amorphous pottery sherds from the barrow at Blackheath Covert (Tixall parish). Private possession on loan to Stafford Museum (L90b, c)'. The date of finding is recorded as 'unknown' and the sherds are now in Hanley Museum

---

1 http://maps.bgs.ac.uk/geologyviewer_google/googleviewer.html (accessed February 6th 2012).
2 Geological information provided by Bob Roach.
3 Vision of Britain at http://www.visionofbritain.org.uk/text/contents_page.jsp?t_id=Pennant_C2L (accessed February 7th 2012).

Excavations at King's Low and Queen's Low

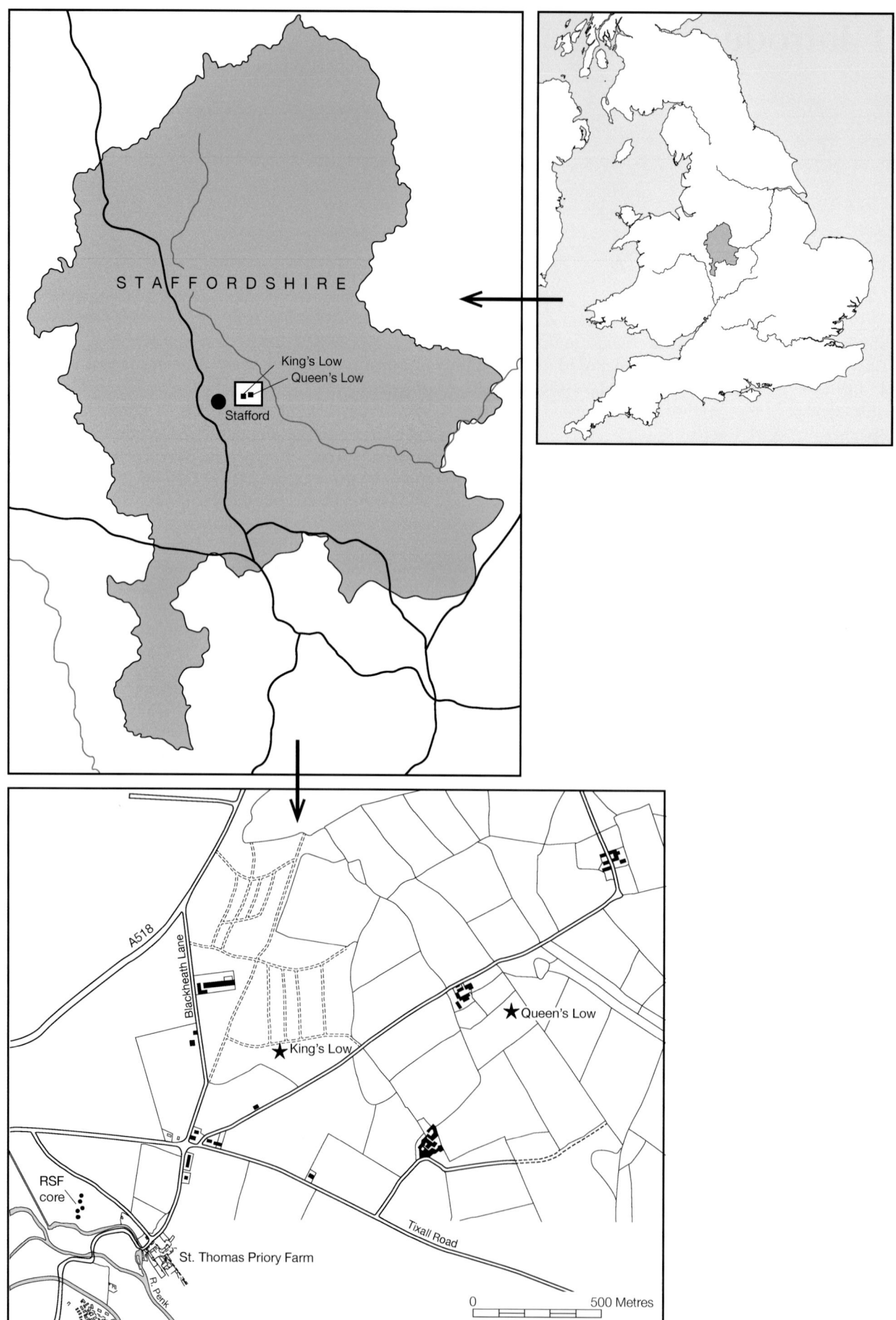

Figure 1.1 The location of King's Low and Queen's Low, Staffordshire, together with the general area of the environmental core in the valley of the River Sow (see Chapter 3.1).

(Accession number K38.1978) and have been confirmed as Early Bronze Age, undecorated.

1.3 The naming of King's Low and Queen's Low
Rose Longden

In order to try and establish the age of the names of the two barrows a selection of map and other documentary evidence was consulted.

Map evidence

All of the following maps were consulted in the Stafford Record Office.[4]

The early maps of Staffordshire are too small in scale to indicate any detailed landmarks. Robert Morden's map of 1722, as used in Camden's *Britannia*, does show a curious barrow-like hill at the location of King's Low although it is not annotated. The other maps which were checked are Staffordshire Estate and Tithe maps and awards as follows:

Baswich (1778) ref: D/240/B/1/50
Baswich (1809) ref: D615/M/6/10
Baswich (late 17th century) ref: D603/H/3/9
Ingestre (1802/1813) ref: D240/E(A) 2/134
Tixall (1753) ref: D240/E(A) 2/253
Tixall (1749) ref: D240/E(A) 2/252
Tixall (early 19th century) Upper and Lower Hanyards ref: D240/E(A)2/272

None of the above indicate the existence of King's Low and Queen's Low.

The William Yates map of 1775[5] was the first systematic survey of the county at the scale of 1 inch to the mile. It does not indicate the barrows at all but it does show the general area which is now called Blackheath Covert named as St. Thomas' Heath. It also shows what appears to be a large pool less than one mile to the south towards the River Sow, named as Kingston Pool (discussed further below). This is also represented on John Speed's map of Stafford from 1611 where it is called the King's Pool.

The earliest map which locates the two barrows and names them as 'King's Low' and 'Queen Low' is the 1831/32 Henry Teesdale map.

The Ordnance Survey First Edition map of the area (ref: 37.12), dating to 1881 and 1901, is marked 'Tumulus' and 'Stone Cross Remains' at the position of King's Low although it is not named. The 1901 and 1923 map (ref: 38.9) indicates the position of a 'Tumulus' where Queen's Low is situated, but again it is not named.

The conclusion from the map evidence is that Teesdale's map of 1831/2 is the earliest to name the two barrows.

Documentary evidence

There is no mention of the barrows in Robert Plot's 1686 survey of the natural history and antiquities of Staffordshire, although he does mention a considerable number of other Lows in the county. As mentioned above, by the early 19th century Camden's second edition of *Britannia*, probably using the evidence from Pennant's 1780 publication, is using the names King's Low and Queen's Low which then become established and used in subsequent texts and Teesdale's and future maps.

The map evidence, however, does not indicate why the two barrows are called King's and Queen's Low nor for how long before 1831/2 they are likely to have been known by these names. It has already been mentioned above that not far from King's Low was a pool known as King's Pool or Kingston Pool. What we can see from Teesdale's map is that close to the area of the mounds there is an area called King's Pool. Cockin (2000, 231) suggests that medieval pools in this area were owned by the Crown and in King John's reign tenants could hold the pools on condition that the King could keep all the pike and bream that he caught there. According to the Chartulary of St. Thomas (Parker 1887, 191) the site of King's Pool or the area near it was know in medieval times as 'Kinesbroc'. If we deconstruct this name, 'broc' means marsh, marshy ground, any watery area or pool (Ekwall 1960) and the first part of the work 'Kines' could be a derivation of the word King. On the outskirts of Stafford is the ancient parish of Kingston (or Kingstone) which means a royal manor or King's tun (*ibid*.), although the word can also be spelt 'Kyneston'. It is a possibility, therefore, that Kines in Kinesbroc, means King's and the medieval area known as Kinesbroc means King's marshy area or pool. There is a possibility, therefore, that the name King's Low does takes its name from that of the area close to it (i.e. King's Pool or Kinesbroc in medieval times). The word 'Low' is Old English, usually translated as 'hill' but such 'features in the West Midlands were in fact tumuli, many of them associated with Anglo-Saxon pagan burial' (Hooke 1983, 45), indicating that King's Low could mean King's barrow or hill.

But as Clifford and Clifford point out (1817, 87) no one really knows why these barrows were given the names of King's Low and Queen's Low. The Reverand T. Loxdale, a 19th century antiquarian, calls them 'the kings' and queen's lows' but states that 'there is no room for a conjecture in what age it might be'.[6] Despite now knowing the approximate age of the mounds we are still no nearer to knowing the origins of their names.

Although Clifford and Clifford state that the origin of the name King's Low is 'now forgotten' they do make a guess at the origin of Queen's Low suggesting it takes its name from the adjoining fields called 'Quinsleys'. This, they propose, is assigned to the time of Elfreda, the daughter of Alfred, Queen of Mercia who may have fought a battle in the area (*ibid.* 87). Obviously local people, historians and antiquarians of the 19th century and before were unaware of the real age of the barrows and may not have realised that they belonged to a period long before Elfreda of the 10th century. But of course, it doesn't mean that Clifford and Clifford's reasoning as to why it was named so is wrong as people may have attributed the mound to this Queen, unaware of its antiquity. 'Quins' may be a derivative of Queen and 'ley' means a forest clearing or meadow

---

4 http://www.staffordshire.gov.uk/leisure/archives/homepage.aspx (accessed 7th February 2012).
5 Collections for a History of Staffordshire, 4th Series, Volume 12.
6 Stafford Record Office, Microfilm 50.

(Paffard 1996, 7). So Queen's Low could have taken its name from Quinsleys, but equally it could have been the other way round and the fields could have been named after the barrow if that was named first.

Whatever the origins of the name 'Queen's Low', whether associated with Elfreda or not, it does not explain why the other barrow is called King's Low. But Clifford and Clifford include a footnote, a poem of Henry of Huntingdon an ancient historian, in which he styles Elfreda as 'both king and queen' so if the area was considered a battle place of Elfreda in the past, where she 'ordered heaps of earth … to be raised over the bodies of the slain' (Clifford and Clifford 1817, 87) then both barrows could have been named after her. Alternatively, it could be argued that if there were two barrows quite close together and one is called Queen's Low after her, naming the other as King's Low would infer a pair of barrows of the same age and same origins.

1.4 The environmental setting
Helen Sugden and Alan Outram

In Ch. 3.1, below, Helen Sugden and Alan Outram present a detailed report on the environmental development of the area based on molluscs and pollen from a core taken from the River Sow floodplain approximately one kilometre away from King's Low. The following summarises their conclusions:

A slow flowing fluvial environment depositing fine sediments and supporting reeds and sedges existed in the late-glacial/early Holocene. A relatively sparse landscape in terms of vegetation existed locally, including birch, grasses and herbs, characteristic of the early Holocene. Peat began to form *in situ* in parts of the floodplain, and subsequent drying allowed the colonization of these by pine, particularly at the floodplain edges and on higher ground. Pine persisted as the dominant tree type although fires, some possibly created by humans, allowed the expansion of oak and hazel within this woodland. Locally, areas of wet heath and reeds were colonized by alder *c.* 6000 BP and climatic warming and increased wetness reduced local pine populations and promoted the growth of lime on the floodplain margins. A series of small scale, temporary clearances occurred from *c.* 3000 BP onwards in the mid-late Bronze Age and thereafter the local woodland re-colonized. Further clearance may have occurred in the Iron Age and Romano-British periods for which there is evidence from the nearby King's Pool pollen core (Bartley and Morgan 1990). However, this is not readily substantiated in the River Sow pollen record. There is a strong possibility that a hiatus covering this period occurs in the pollen profile with a sharp decrease in arboreal pollen. From the early medieval period clearance is extensive, and evidence of cereal cultivation arises. Such clearance, as expected, continues into the present.

In terms of the extent of human impact on vegetation within the region, particularly that which is contemporaneous to King's Low and Queen's Low, there is a suggestion in the River Sow and King's Pool evidence that initial human interference occurs in the Mesolithic. However, the first substantial clearance shows in the King's Pool analysis as reductions in arboreal pollen types and increases in anthropogenic indicators dating from 4170 BP (uncal) onwards. Pollen has also been extracted from the ground surface immediately under the King's Low barrow from which 'considerable human induced disturbance must be inferred (Chambers and Wilshaw, Ch. 3.2). However, the pollen profile from the River Sow floodplain shows nothing so significant as to be interpreted as human disturbance of the landscape until *c.* 3000 BP (uncal).

The later timing of the clearance in the River Sow diagram does not however contradict the above. The contrast between the three sites in the timing and extent of human impacts is explained by Limbrey's (1983) hypothesis that pollen relating to woodland clearances is often masked by surrounding forest, particularly at the floodplain edge. Hence clearance patterns may be indistinct or absent in pollen diagrams from floodplains as these areas tend to be latterly and inconsistently exploited.

Thus the accumulated evidence seems to suggest that human clearance of the landscape occurred in the region on drier ground from the Early Bronze Age. This clearance continued in a sporadic and intermittent fashion through to the Later Bronze Age. At this time, the pollen evidence from the floodplain suggests that human use of the environment temporarily encroached onto the wetter ground, perhaps indicating the expansion of human activity in the area leading to the use of more marginal land.

1.5 The archaeological setting
Gary Lock

This section places King's Low and Queen's Low, Tixall, within the context of known archaeological sites and finds for the Neolithic to Iron Age periods as recorded in the Staffordshire Historic Environment Record.[7] It is meant to act as a pointer to the detailed information within the HER and only provides a visual snapshot of the density of finds and sites within a 20-mile radius of King's Low and Queen's Low together with HER PRNs (Primary Reference Numbers). Some of the sites shown are discussed in more detail in Chapter 5 below with references, where a more extensive discussion of King's Low and Queen's Low is presented within the context of barrow studies from the antiquarian to modern periods.

There are no recorded Neolithic sites close to Tixall (Fig. 1.2), the nearest being the concentration of Neolithic and Early Bronze Age funerary and ritual sites further east in the valley of the River Trent and at its confluence with the River Tame. Here are three likely cursuses identified by aerial photography and varying amounts of excavation (a small one at Catholme (00204) and at Alrewas (00207)) although at Barton-under-Needwood (00208) the site is unlikely. Part of the same Catholme complex is a hengi-form monument (00203), together with a causewayed enclosure (00209), while a less likely henge is suggested by aerial photography at Shenstone in the valley of

---

7 We would like to thank Suzy Blake of the Staffordshire HER for producing the figures presented here, Figures 1.2 to 1.9, together with reports for all of the shown PRNs. Also thanks to Janet Cooper for liaising with the HER.

1 *Introduction and background*

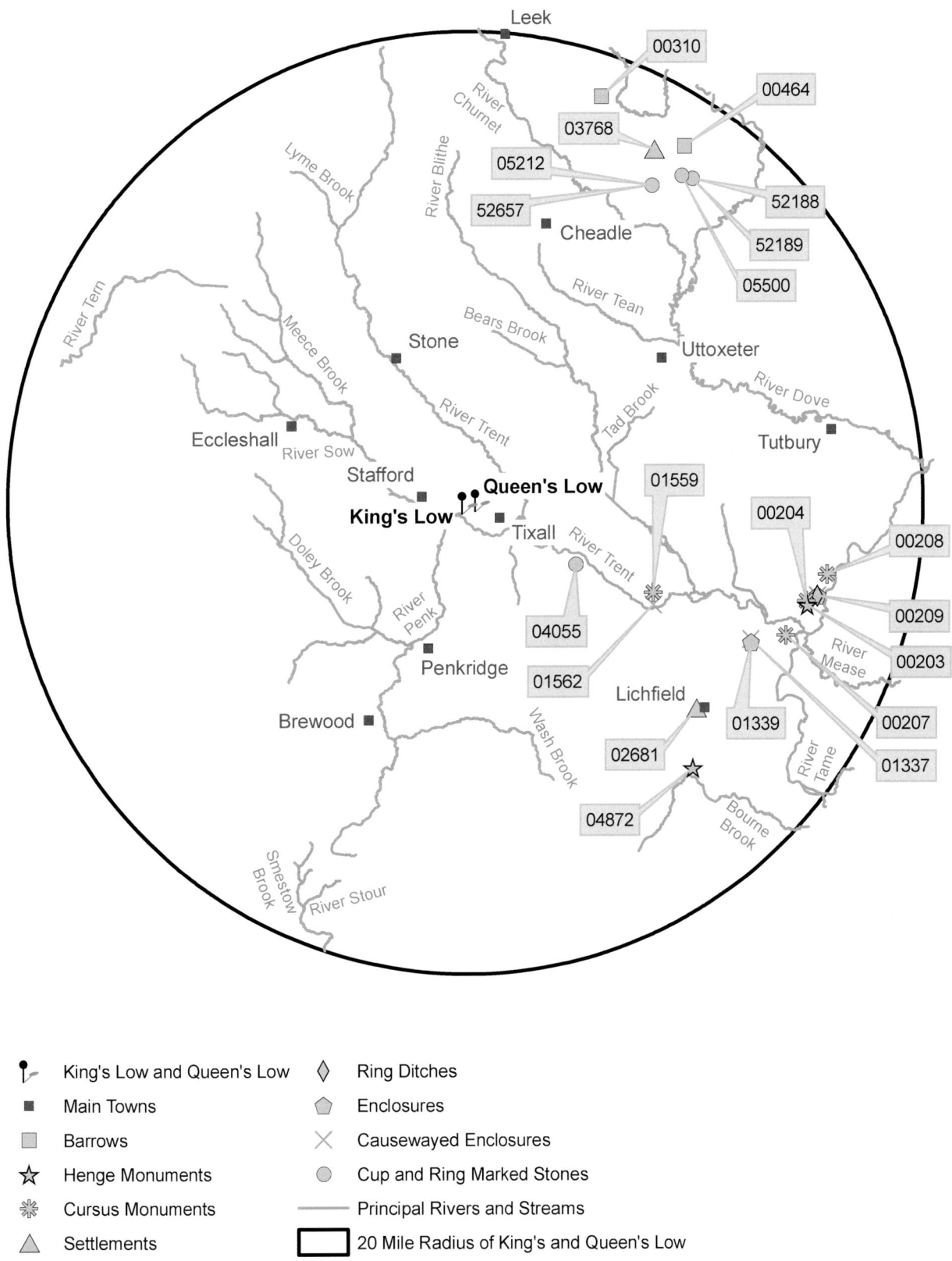

Figure 1.2 Neolithic sites within a 20-mile radius of King's Low and Queen's Low (courtesy of Staffordshire HER, produced by Suzy Blake).

Excavations at King's Low and Queen's Low

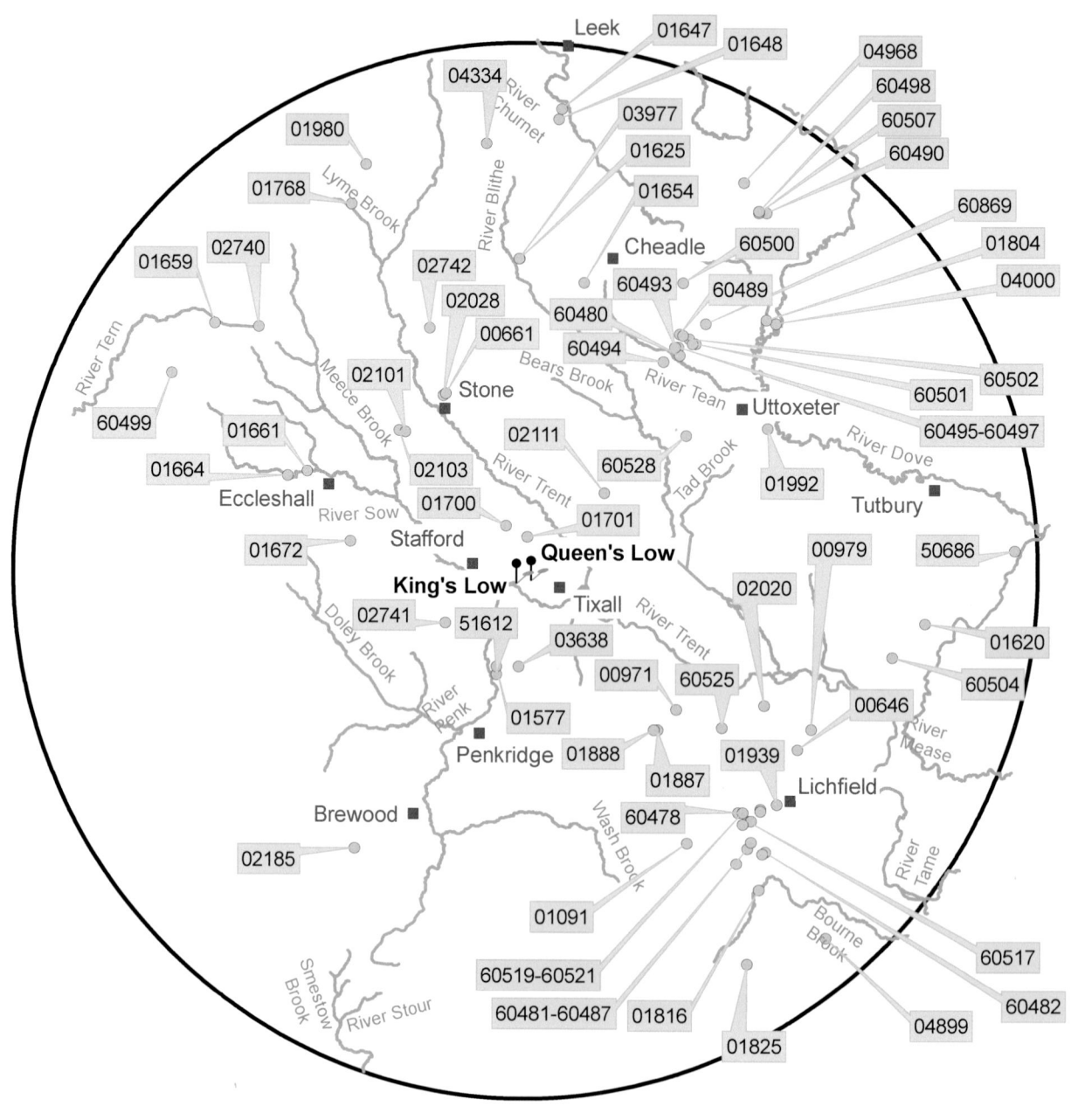

Figure 1.3 Neolithic finds within a 20-mile radius of King's Low and Queen's Low (courtesy of Staffordshire HER, produced by Suzy Blake).

1 *Introduction and background*

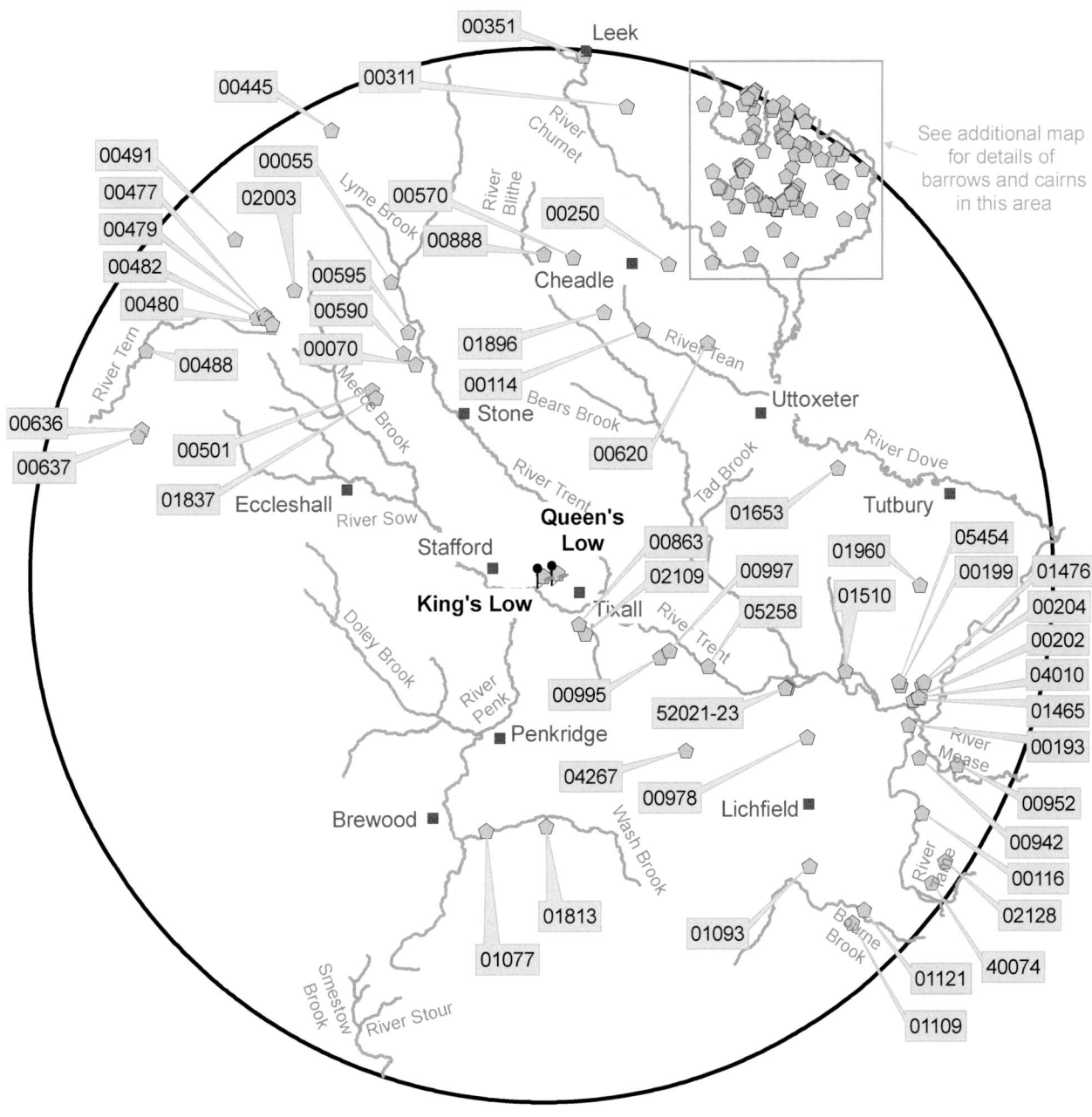

Figure 1.4 Bronze Age barrows within a 20-mile radius of King's Low and Queen's Low (courtesy of Staffordshire HER, produced by Suzy Blake).

Excavations at King's Low and Queen's Low

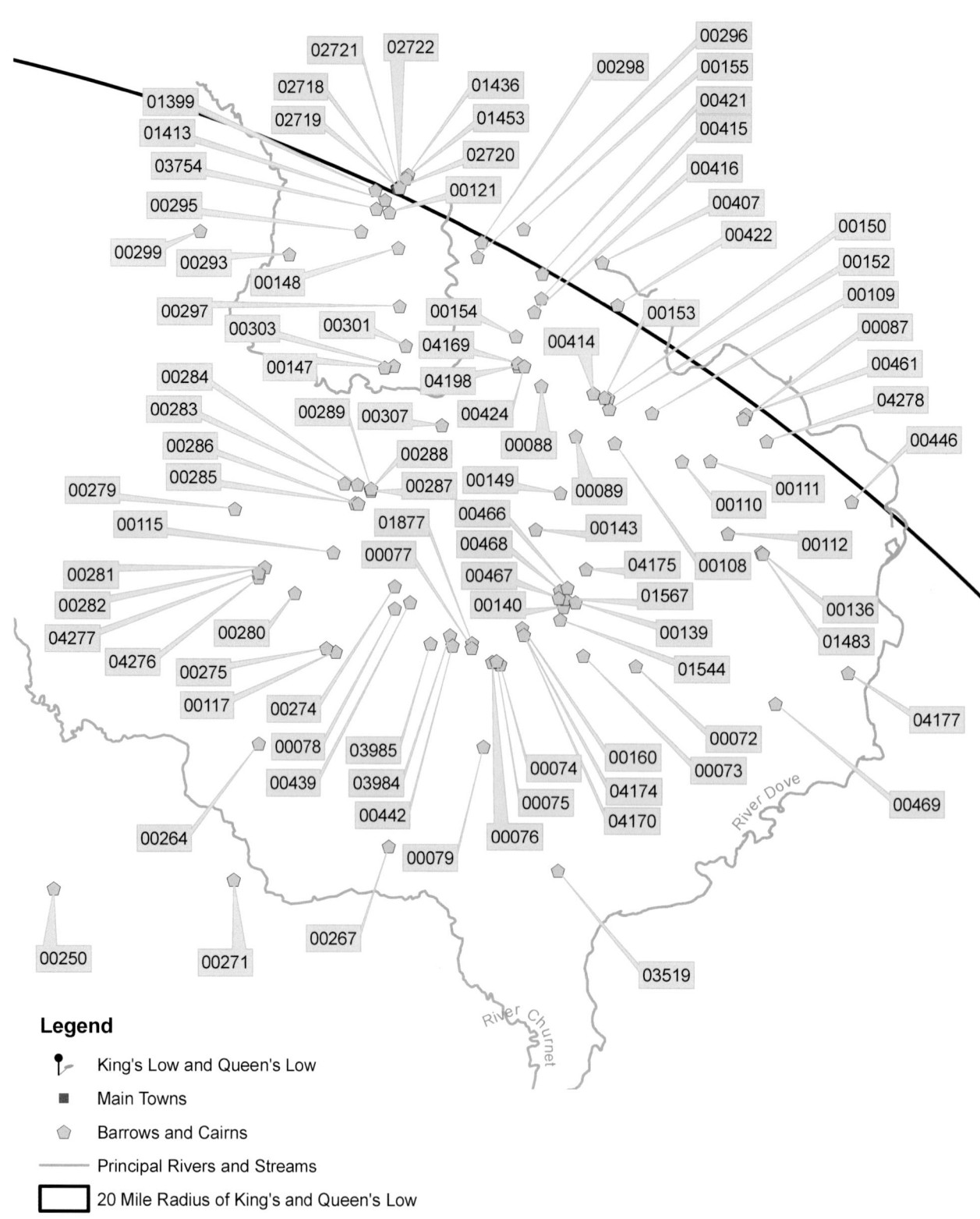

Figure 1.5 Bronze Age barrows in the Staffordshire Peak District (courtesy of Staffordshire HER, produced by Suzy Blake).

1 Introduction and background

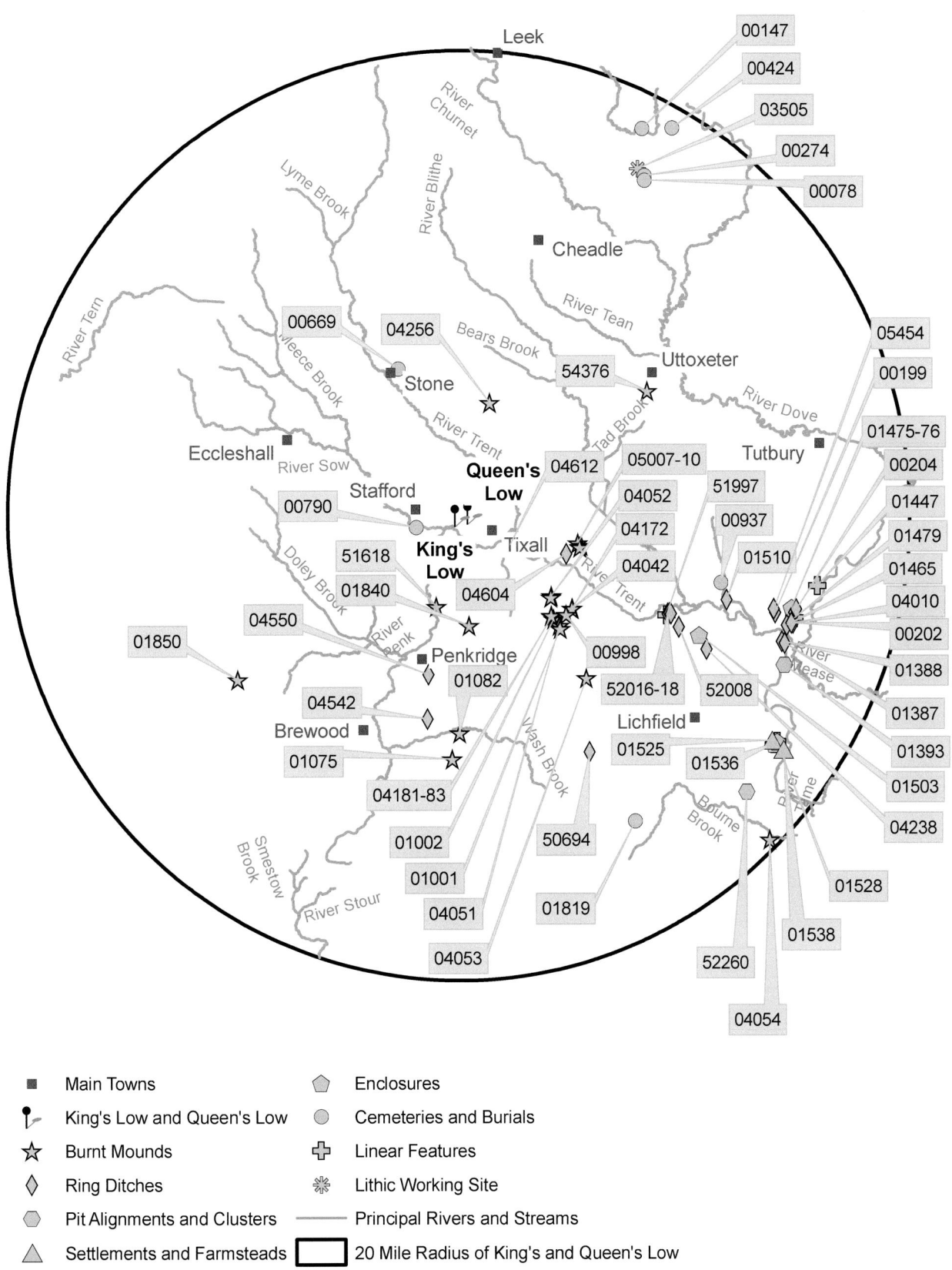

Figure 1.6 Bronze Age sites within a 20-mile radius of King's Low and Queen's Low (courtesy of Staffordshire HER, produced by Suzy Blake).

Excavations at King's Low and Queen's Low

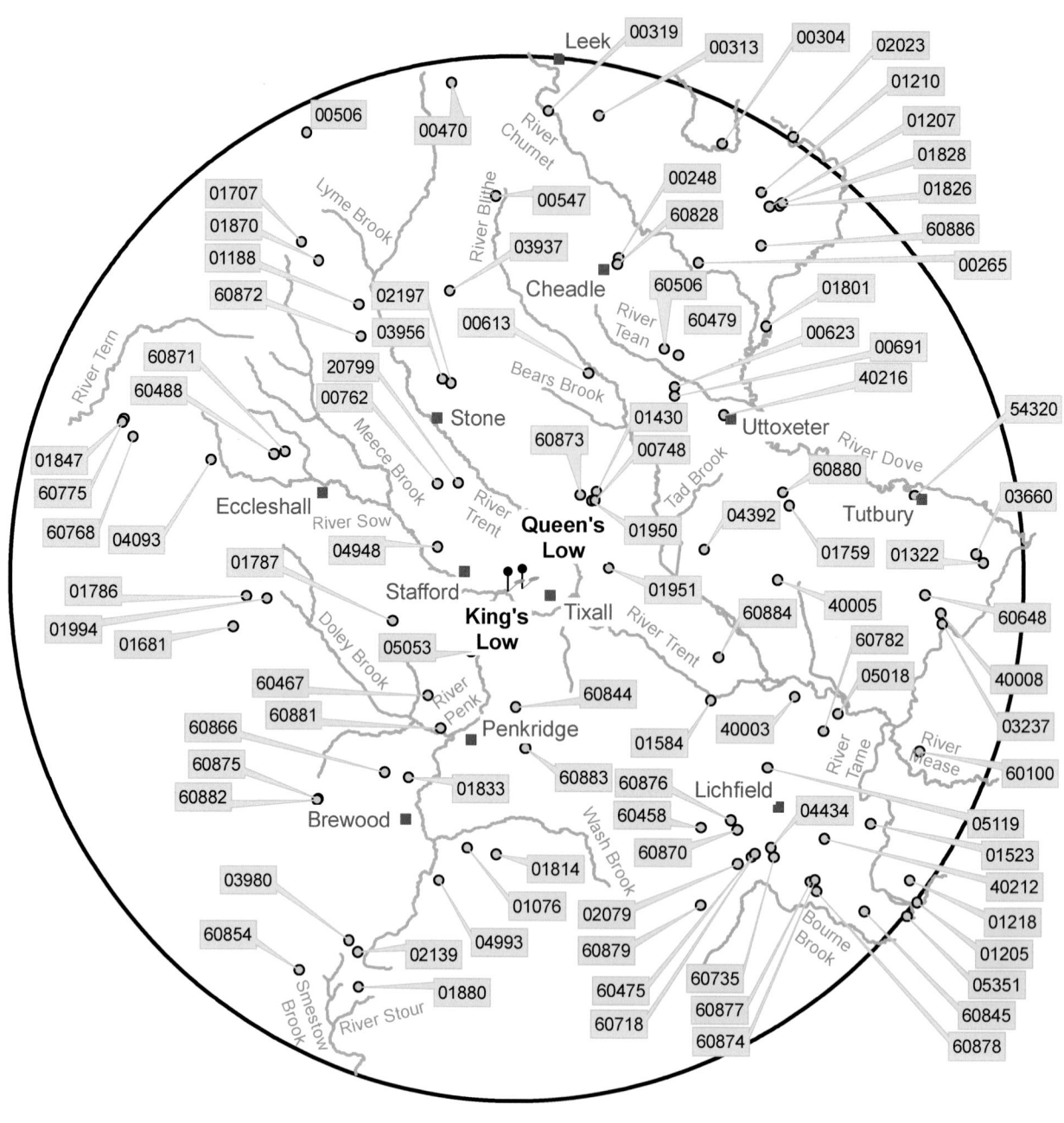

Figure 1.7 Bronze Age finds within a 20-mile radius of King's Low and Queen's Low (courtesy of Staffordshire HER, produced by Suzy Blake).

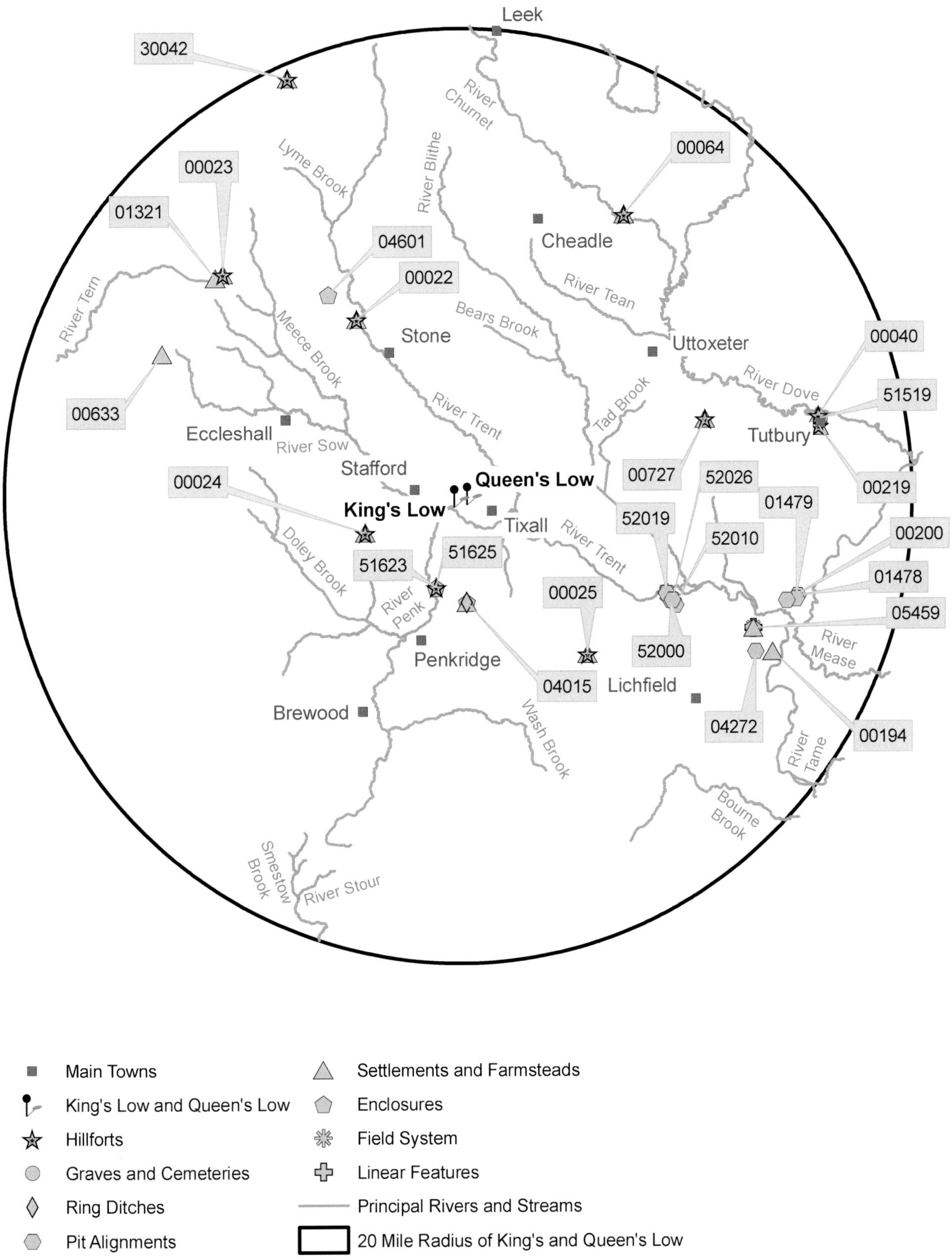

1 *Introduction and background*

Figure 1.8 Iron Age sites within a 20-mile radius of King's Low and Queen's Low (courtesy of Staffordshire HER, produced by Suzy Blake).

Excavations at King's Low and Queen's Low

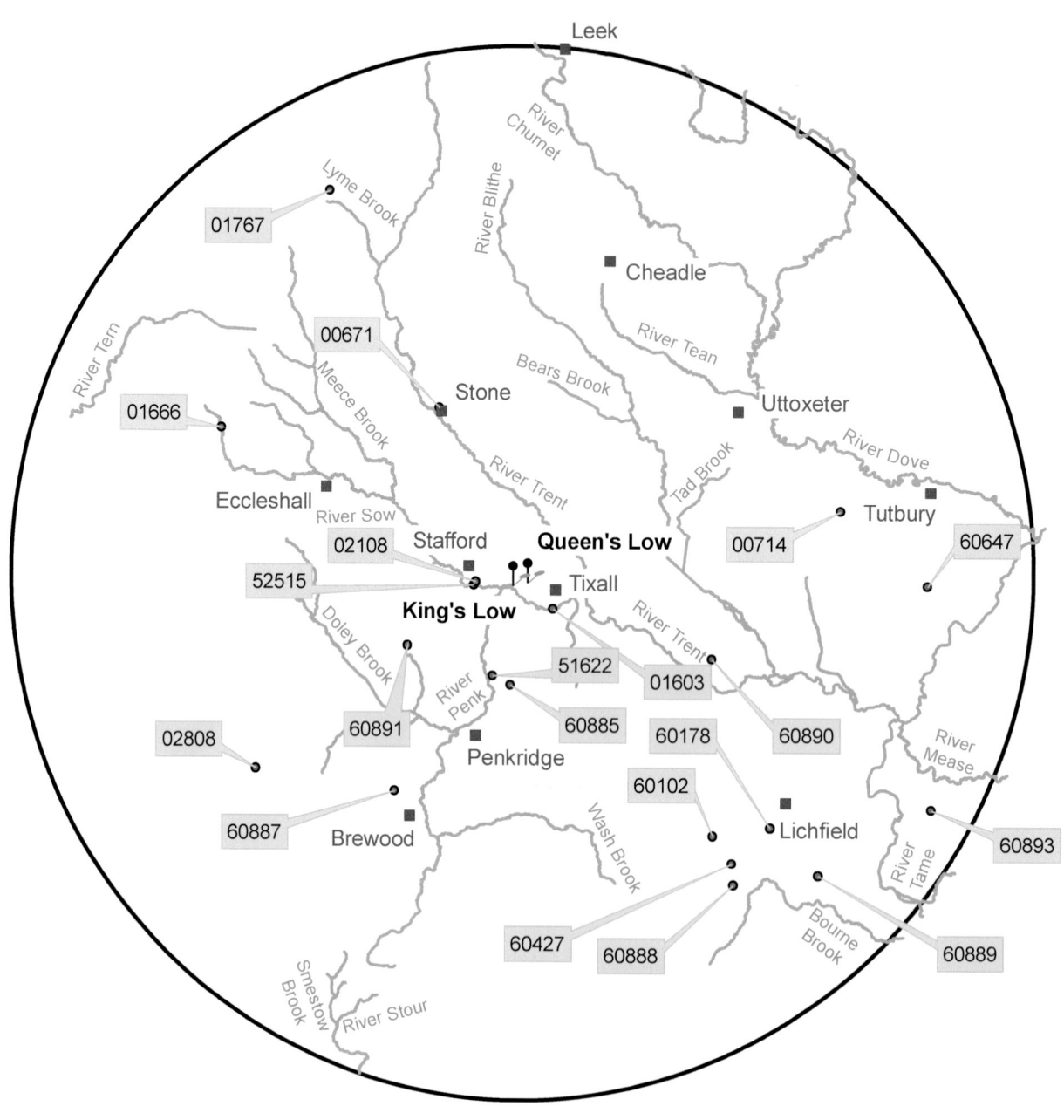

Figure 1.9 Iron Age finds within a 20-mile radius of King's Low and Queen's Low (courtesy of Staffordshire HER, produced by Suzy Blake).

Bourne Brook (04872). A cropmark complex at Mavesyn Ridware, also in the Trent valley, includes a possible cursus (01599) and causewayed enclosure (01562) while a possible enclosure is north of Fradley (01339). There are only two possible Neolithic settlements in the area, one comprising pits, pottery and lithics verified by excavation within Lichfield (02681), the other suggested by field walking finds at Cotton in the Peak District (03768). Funerary evidence is limited to possible Neolithic barrows in the Peak District (00310 and 00464) and ring ditches within the Catholme complex (00209). The distribution of Neolithic finds in many ways reflects that of the sites, being concentrated within valleys together with the upland areas of the Peak District (Fig. 1.3). The finds are mainly surface finds with very few from excavations, individual artefacts which are usually lithic tools and flint scatters. The two closest to King's Low and Queen's Low are two miles away at Hopton, a stone axe-hammer (01700) and a flint scatter (01701).

The distribution of Bronze Age sites is dominated by barrows and ring ditches, again showing concentrations along valleys, especially the River Trent and its tributaries, and within the upland Peak District (Figs 1.4, 1.5 and 1.6). Other than barrows and ring ditches, the concentration of burnt mounds to the south-east of King's Low and Queen's Low is striking although these are likely to be Middle to Late Bronze Age rather than Early. Of the eight 'cemeteries and burials' shown (Fig. 1.6), seven are likely to have been associated with barrows and one has been re-designated as Romano-British (00937). Settlement evidence is also likely to be Middle and Late Bronze Age such as the crop-mark enclosures at Fisherwick (01525, 01538, 01536 and 01528), King's Bromley (01503) and Barton-under-Needwood (01475) and the linear features and possible pit alignments associated with the continuing complex of cropmark and excavated evidence at the Trent Tame confluence (01447, 01393). Bronze Age finds in the area are 98 in total (Fig. 1.7), mainly an assortment of copper-alloy artefacts found as stray finds or reported as metal detecting finds via the Portable Antiquities Scheme.

Of the ten Iron Age hillforts shown on Figure 1.8, seven are relatively well preserved while Tutbury Park (00219), Marchington (00727) and the excavated length of late Iron Age gully-built stockade at Acton Trussell Roman villa (51623) are doubtful as hillforts. The closest to King's Low and Queen's Low is Berry Hill (00024), a univallate enclosure approximately five miles away to the south-west of Stafford. Possible Iron Age farmstead enclosures are known from aerial photography (04601 and 04015) as well as part of the Alrewas complex which also includes possible pit alignments and field systems (05459), and associated with the Acton Trussell villa. As with earlier periods the Trent valley is particularly rich in cropmark evidence, not least a series of possible pit alignments at Catholme (0020, 01478 and 01479), and further to the west at Kings Bromley (52000, 52010 and 52019). Three of these cropmark complexes also include evidence that has been interpreted as possible Iron Age field systems (52019, 52026 and 05459) associated with enclosed farmsteads. As is usual for the Iron Age period burials are not common and only one record is in the HER, three disturbed inhumations at Tutbury (51519) inconclusively assigned to this period. Iron Age finds from the area, 20 in total (Fig. 1.9), are a mixture of stray finds and metal detected finds including eight silver and gold coins, a gold torc (00714) and an enamelled copper-alloy terret ring (01603). In waterlogged deposits in Stafford, only three miles from King's Low and Queens Low, were found three worked timbers (52515) and nearby two antler picks (02108) all assigned to the Iron Age. Iron Age pottery (51622), associated with the pre-Roman occupation, was excavated at Acton Trussell five miles away from Tixall. As with the earlier periods, the importance of the river valleys in the Iron Age is shown by the distribution maps although it is unsure whether this is due to the success of aerial photography and the associated amount of archaeological work in these areas or whether it reflects prehistoric occupation density. The decrease in evidence from the Bronze Age to the Iron Age in the upland areas of the Peak District is clear.

2 The excavations

Both King's Low and Queen's Low were excavated by hand and recorded using standard single context recording methods. Context recording sheets were based on the Oxford Archaeological Unit system current at the time (Wilkinson 1992). Plans were drawn at a scale of 1:20 and sections at 1:10, plans were composite rather than single context.

2.1 King's Low
Gary Lock

In the early 1970s large areas of Blackheath Covert, including the entire surface area of King's Low, were cleared of old indigenous trees and planted with larch trees as a commercial crop (Fig. 2.1). The stumps of much larger and older trees were visible on the barrow which, together with intensive rabbit activity, formed sufficient threat to the site to warrant excavation. In 1908 the VCH recorded King's Low as being circular, 120 feet (36.5 m) in diameter and 9 feet (2.7 m) high (Page 1908). By the early 1960s Gunstone's field visit records it as 28 paces diameter (presumably one pace is approximately one metre) and 4 feet (1.2 m high), indicating a considerable reduction in both diameter and height (Gunstone 1965, 49). At the time of excavation it was still approximately the same size as recorded by Gunstone with no surface evidence for any previous excavation.

King's Low has suffered from podsolisation, a geo-chemical process typical of heathlands and soils beneath coniferous forests in acidic conditions. This process involves the eluviation, washing out, of certain minerals especially Iron and Aluminium Oxides, from the A Horizon and the deposition and accumulation of these deeper down in the B Horizon, the zone of illuviation (Pl. 2.1). The actual depths of the A and B Horizons depends on local circumstances including past land use and hydrology, although the general characteristics are the same. The leached out A horizon is typically ash-grey in colour and rich in quartz and silica which are not removed. The interface between the eluvial and illuvial zones may have an Iron Pan, a dark/black layer of re-deposited iron which can be extremely hard, as indeed was the case at King's Low (in the text and illustrations below the leached material is Context (3) and hard-panning is (13 and 3/13). Below this is a zone of red/orange material, sometimes mottled, sometimes with layer-like deposits, where iron and aluminium are re-deposited. Depending on ground water conditions and water-logging, associated gleying and mottling may occur.

The implications of podsolisation for archaeology and excavation in particular are serious, as encountered at King's Low. The process can remove, or at least mask, original stratigraphy and characteristics such as colour and texture that differ between contexts can be completely

Figure 2.1 King's Low: before excavation showing felled larch trees.

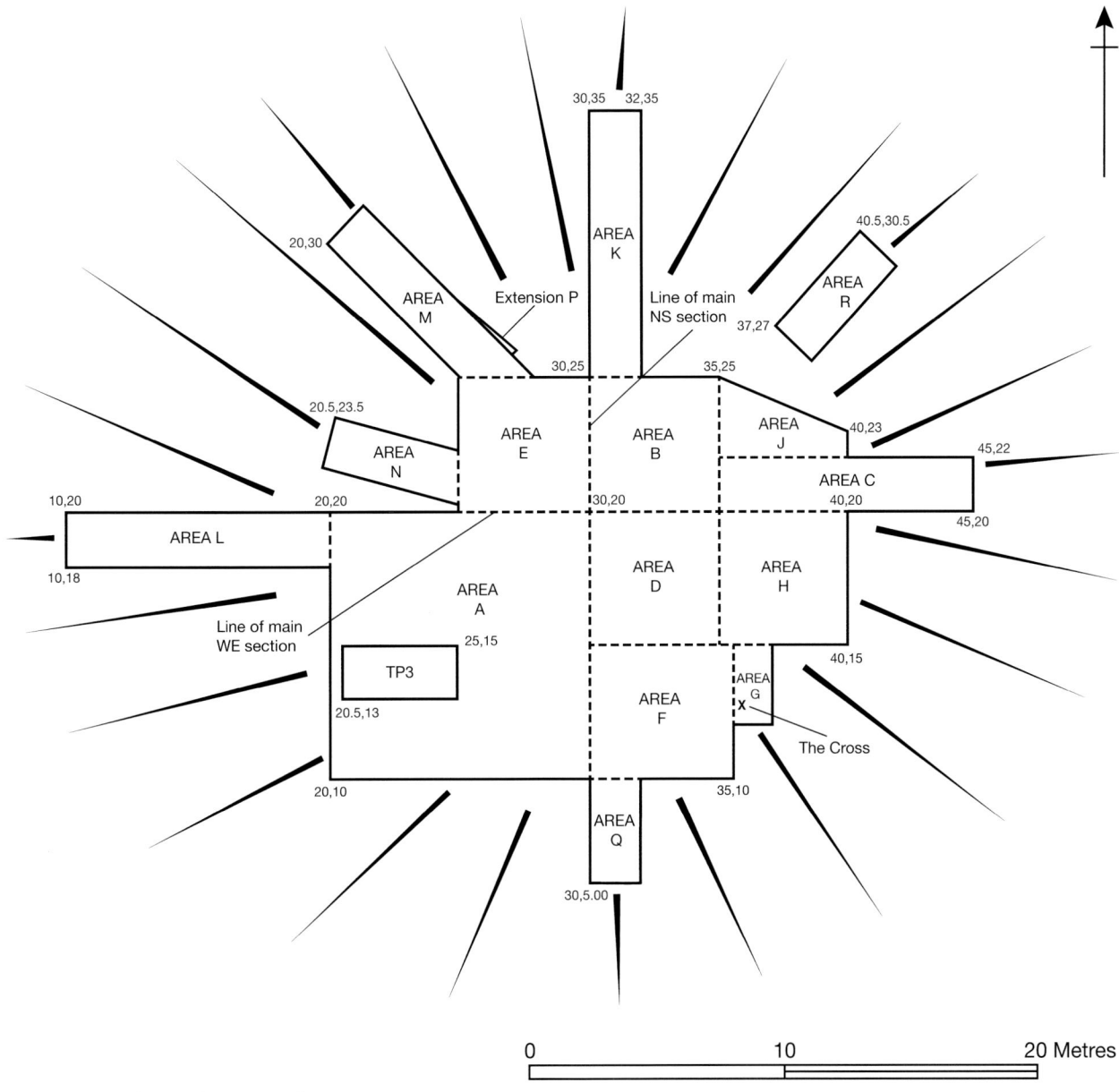

Figure 2.2 King's Low: the excavated areas.

altered. As well as this, an artificial stratigraphy is imposed through the layering of the A and B Horizons, with much of the material in the upper horizon appearing as a homogenous grey layer, while Iron panning and the B Horizon take on the appearance of stratigraphy although it is entirely due to natural processes. In addition, little organic/vegetable matter survives and pollen is severely degraded with charcoal being the only exception.

King's Low was also severely damaged by rabbit activity, both currently active burrows as well as a network of old, filled in runs. As well as destroying contexts and relationships, this also had the effect of spreading material throughout the mound making many of the finds re-deposited, most severely hit being the cremated bone (from secondary and perhaps tertiary burials), pieces of which were found throughout the mound (see below). It was very clear during the excavation that large areas of rabbit disturbed material in the upper parts of the mound gave way to identifiable filled in individual rabbit burrows in the lower levels, often containing finds (Pl. 2.2). The combination of podsolisation and rabbit activity made the excavation, recording and interpretation of King's Low a difficult process.

2.1.1 The excavations

The complexity of the deposits due to the natural variable sandy nature of the material, severe disturbance by rabbits and roots and alteration through podsolisation and other geo-chemical processes, has resulted in over recording as a cautionary measure. The developmental sequence described below uses single context numbers which often represent an amalgamated group of contexts determined to be stratigraphically equivalent during the excavation and post-excavation. The details of all groups and contexts are in Appendix 1.

The areas of excavation, A to R (Fig. 2.2), were opened alphabetically although several were in the process of being excavated at the same time in order to maintain horizontal continuity across the areas. The two main sections through the barrow, north-south and west-east, are shown in

Excavations at King's Low and Queen's Low

NS1 Area K

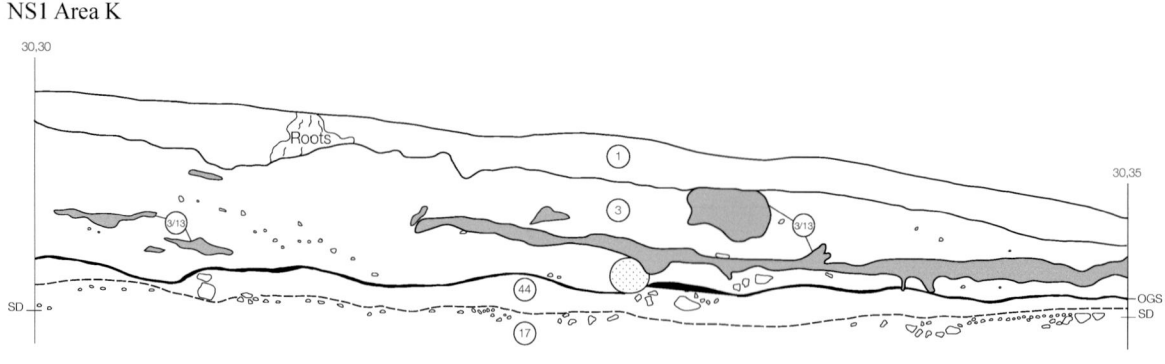

NS2 Area K

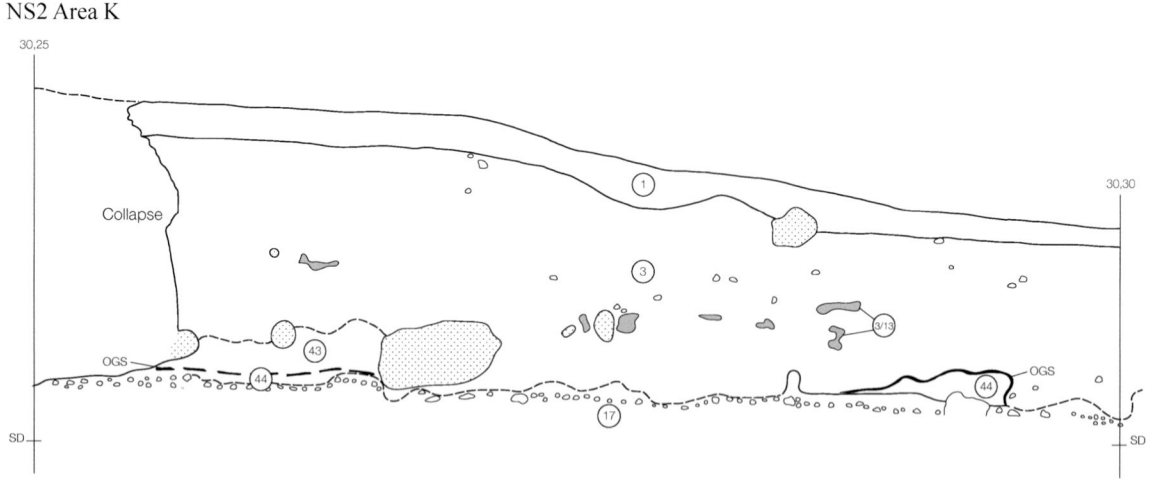

NS3 Area B

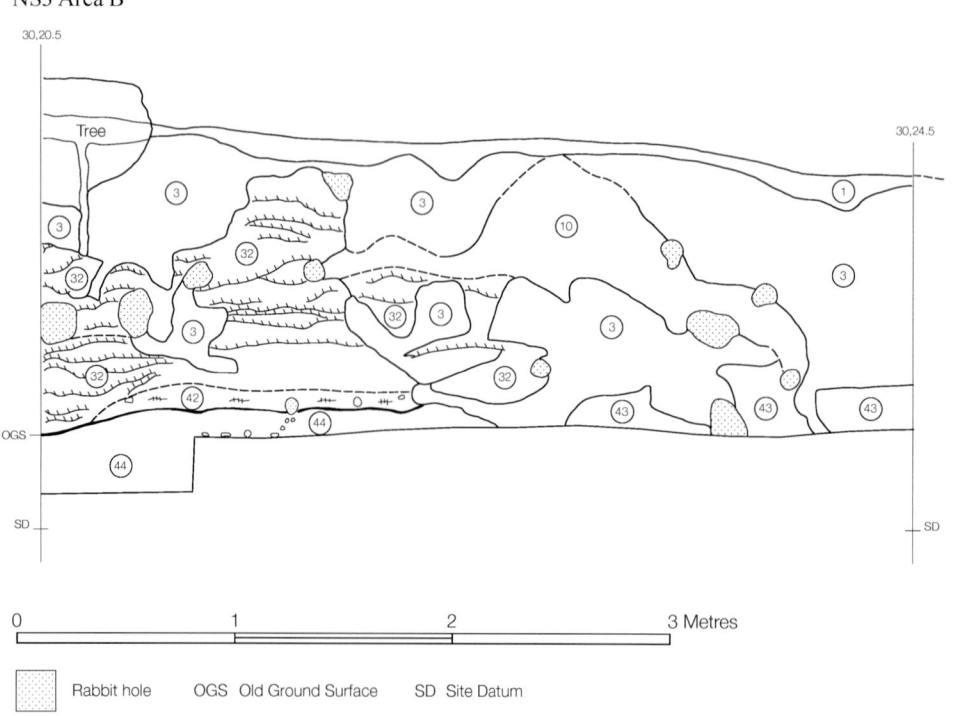

Figure 2.3 King's Low: the main north-south section.

Figures 2.3 and 2.4. Figure 2.5 shows the estimated sizes of the barrow for different phases and the extent of the main contexts as they survived when excavated. Preservation was better in the southern half of the barrow and the estimated sizes, therefore, are based mainly on deposits excavated in those areas with the assumption that the barrows were originally approximately circular.

Again, because of the nature of the deposits, it was decide not to draw detailed scale plans and instead a system of vertical photography was established consisting

2 The excavations

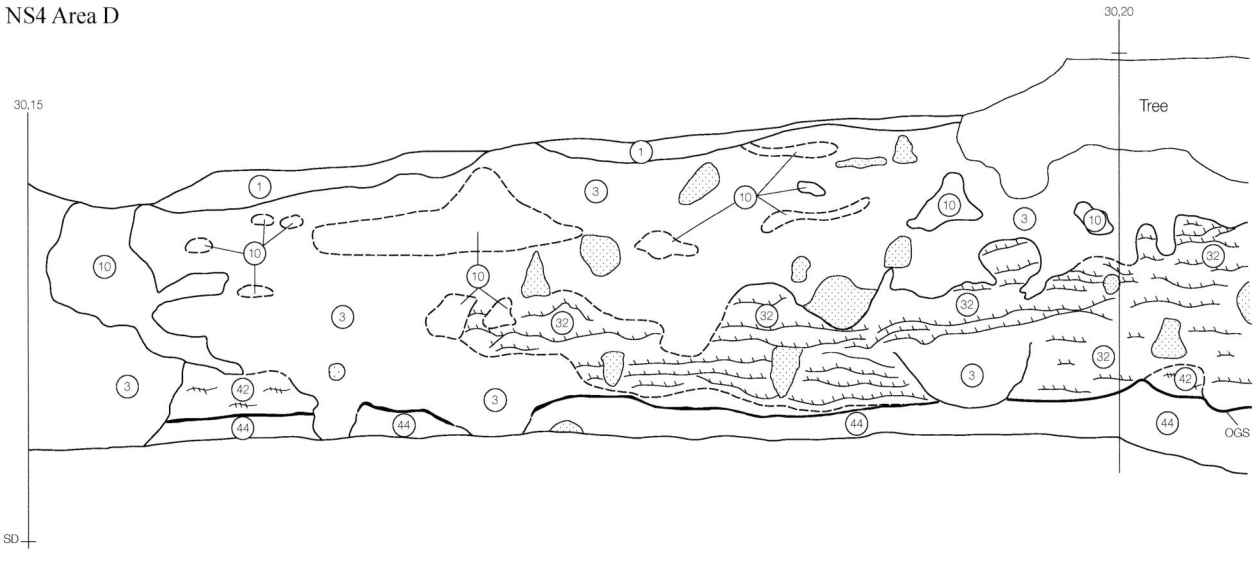

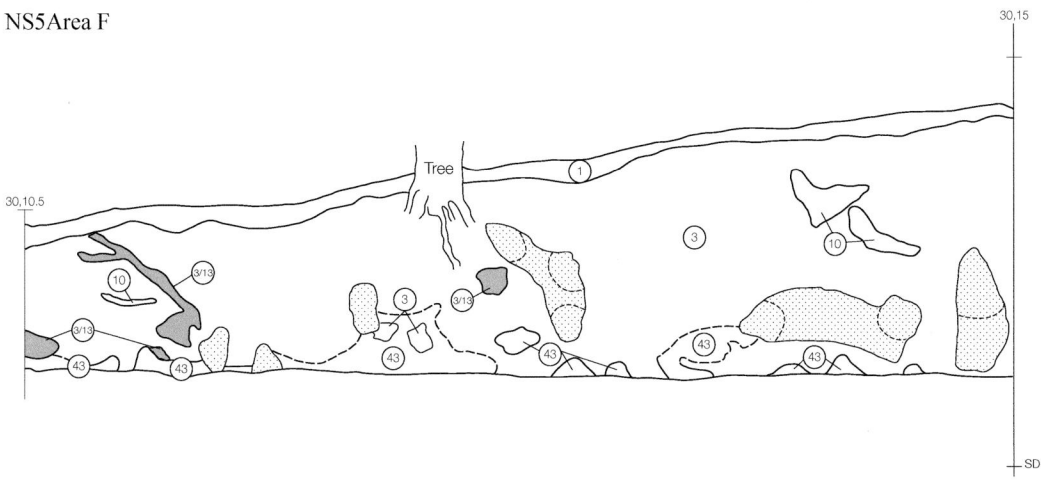

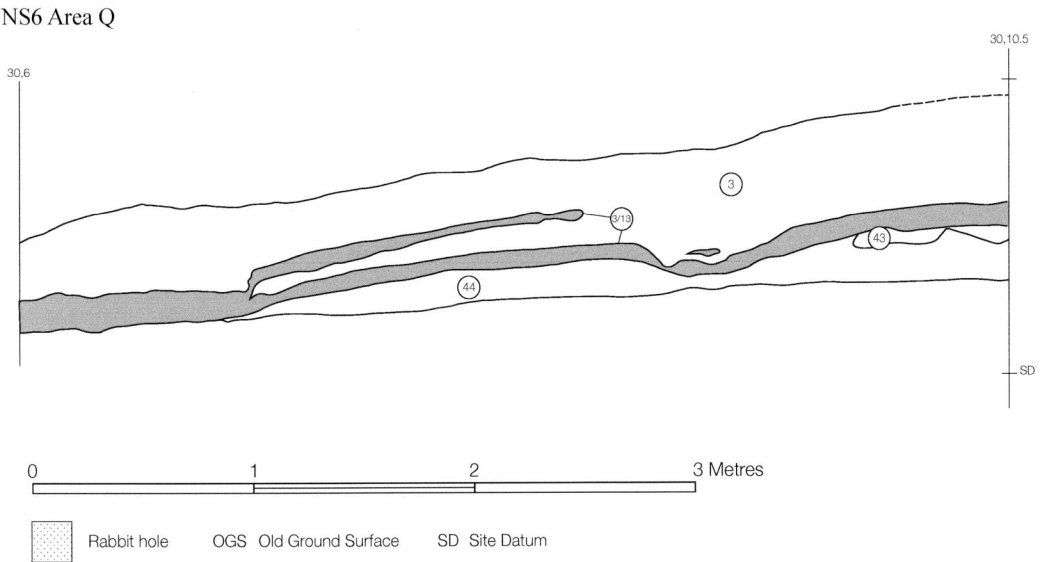

Figure 2.3 cont.

of a wooden frame holding the camera a set distance above the ground. The surface to be photographed was gridded into 1 metre squares using nails, each photograph covered 1 metre and they were then joined together to produce a continuous surface. For most of the excavation it was not possible to excavate stratigraphically and a spit method was used with the removal of between c. 5 cm and c. 10 cm per spit with photographs being taken every spit together with heights. The very few cut features, such as pit (245) were excavated by sectioning.

17

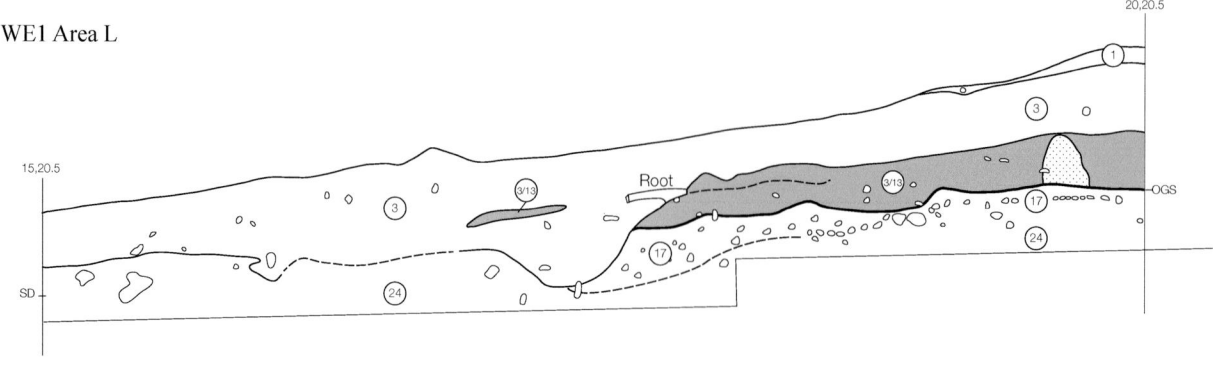

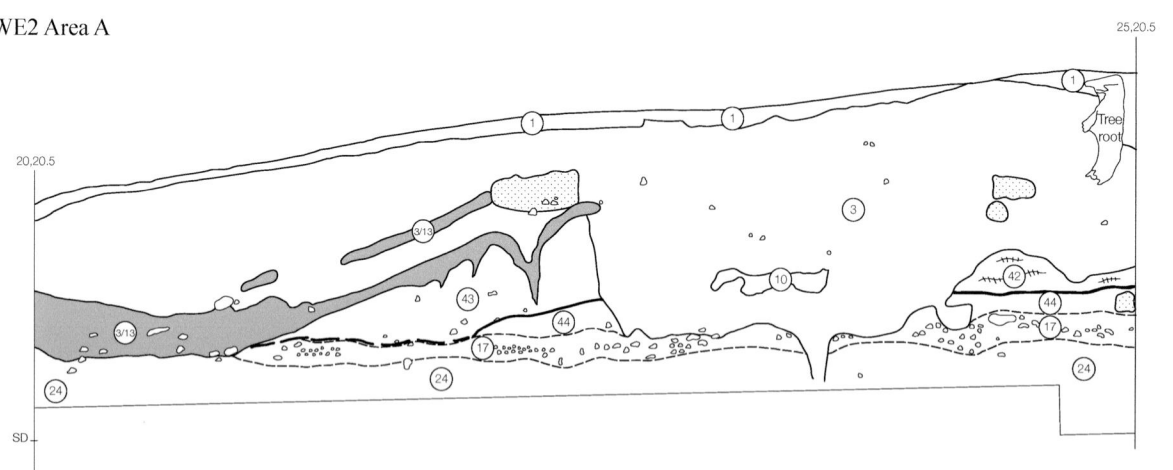

Figure 2.4 King's Low: the main west-east section.

The natural across the whole site comprises glacial sands and gravels, very mixed with pockets of clay. It was possible to distinguish between Context (24), deep undisturbed natural mainly firm red/orange sand with occasional clay patches, pebbles and deeper down sandstone fragments broken off from the bedrock below. Above this was Context (17) a bright orange/red hard sand containing many water-worn cobbles and pebbles up to a maximum size of c. 20 cm. In places these formed almost continuous 'surfaces' although the density decreased towards the bottom of the layer. Both (17) and (24) were continuous across the whole site although not excavated everywhere (the sequence was confirmed at depth within Test Pit (TP) 3 in Area A (Fig. 2.6)).

2 The excavations

WE4 Area D

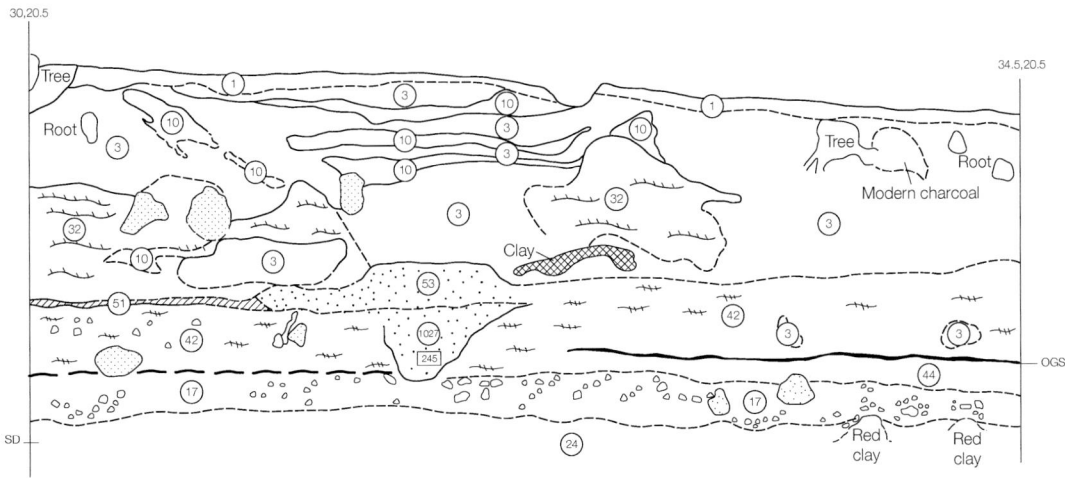

WE5 Area H

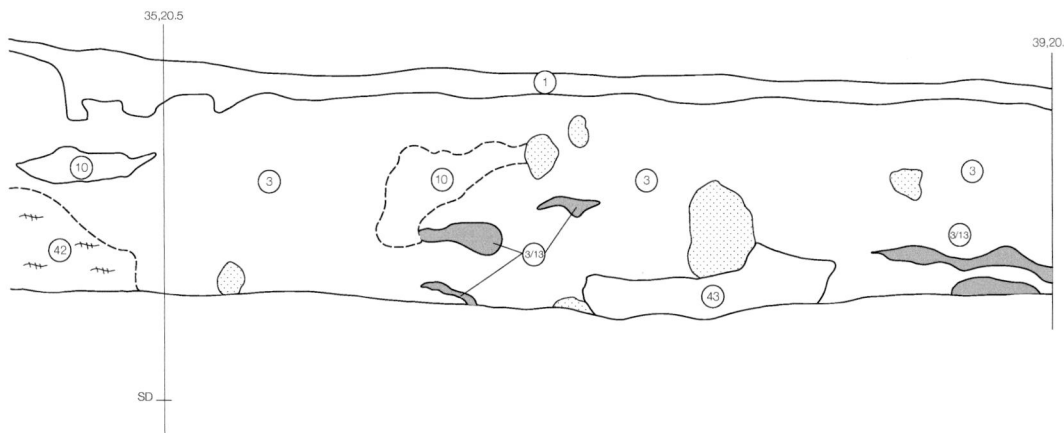

WE6 Area C (Reversed)

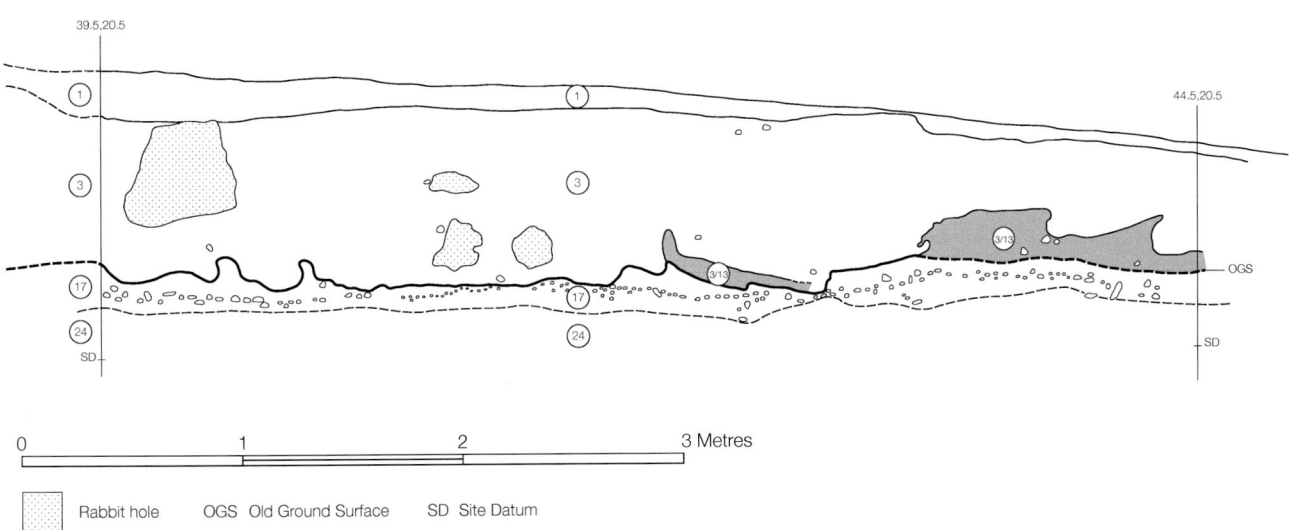

Figure 2.4 cont.

The next layer, Context (44) only survived in patches, albeit sizeable in places. This was clean orange sand with charcoal flecks and occasional concentrations, the top of which is considered to be the late Neolithic/early Bronze Age ground surface (OGS). Here we differentiate between two different OGS (indicated in Figures 2.3 and 2.4). The first is the top of Context (44), the surface upon which barrow deposits were directly lain, typically Context (42) for the first phase barrow and Context (43) for the second phase extension. In places, particularly towards the centre of the barrow, Context (44) has been removed and the lowest barrow deposits lay directly on deeper subsoil, Context (17), thus the top of (17) is OGS2. There is no indication of a ditch for either the Phase 1 or Phase 2 barrows

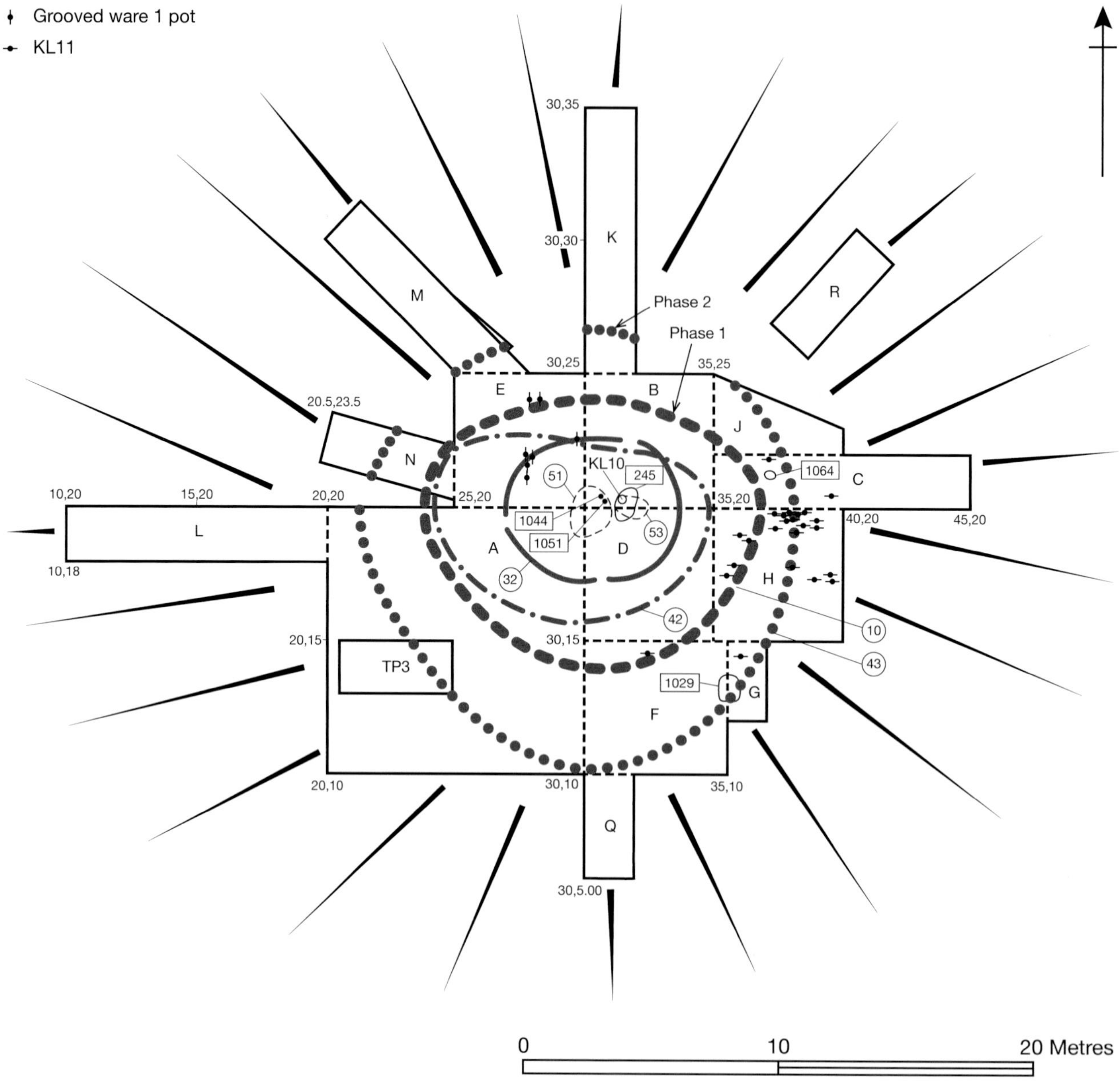

Excavations at King's Low and Queen's Low

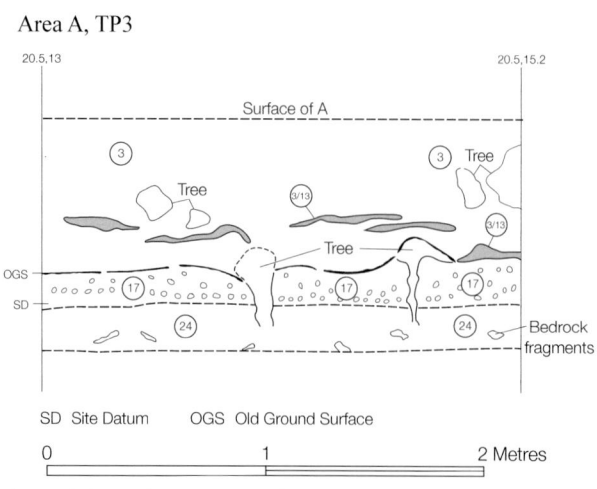

Figure 2.5 King's Low: the approximate size of the Phase 1 and Phase 2 barrows, the main contexts and the distribution of the Grooved Ware sherds and Collared Urn KL11.

so material for the mounds was probably scraped from the surrounding surfaces, this is discussed further below.

Figure 2.6 King's Low: Test Pit 3 section, Area A.

Pre-barrow activity in the area is indicated by the presence of a small number of lithics (Ch. 4.2) and pottery (Ch. 4.1). Sporadic Mesolithic activity is represented by three diagnostic microliths and other possibilities, one of which (SF6470) occurs in sub-soil Context (44), the others being incorporated into mound material. This is also the case for an Earlier Neolithic leaf-shaped arrowhead (SF2144) and Beaker material including two fine barbed and tanged arrowheads (SF3550 and SF7109) and two thumbnail scrapers (SF6334 and SF3353). Similarly with the pre-barrow ceramics which includes at least 18 sherds of Later Neolithic Grooved Ware mainly in upper mound materials although several sherds did occur in Contexts (51) and (53), basal layer of the Phase 1 barrow (discussed below). A minimum of 5 Beaker vessels are represented, albeit all very fragmentary, all within upper barrow material. The scattered locations of this mixed assemblage supports the idea that the mound material was collected from the surface in the immediate area incorporating within it

2 The excavations

Plate 2.1 King's Low: an example of podsolisation showing the leached out A horizon above, the enriched B horizon below and a zone of hard-panning in between.

Plate 2.2 King's Low: typical rabbit damage at depth within the mound showing filled in runs and nests between areas of orange mound material.

Plate 2.3 King's Low: stake hole (1044), a) as seen before excavation, b) the lower half in section, c) nearly the full length in section; stake hole (1051), d) the full length in section.

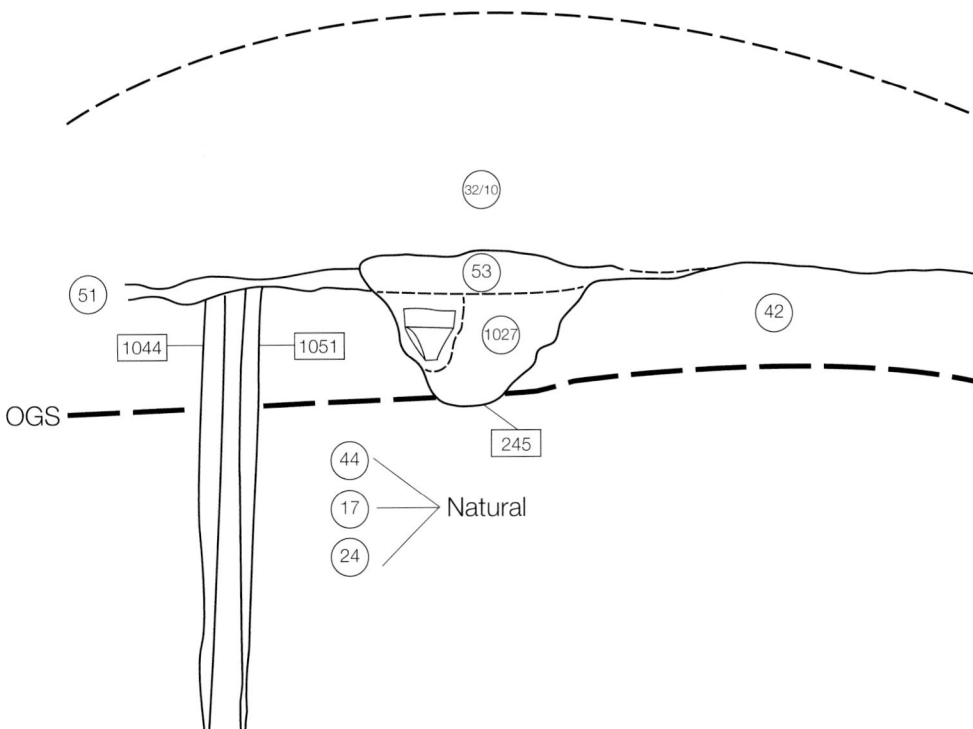

Figure 2.7 King's Low: a schematic section across the central area showing the main contexts described in the text, not to scale

pottery and lithics although the presence of the two high quality barbed and tanged arrowheads does raise the possibility of a Beaker burial in the vicinity. There is a concentration of Grooved Ware sherds from the same vessel (KL3 in the catalogue) in Area E (Fig. 2.5), suggesting perhaps a near complete pot that was broken as the later mound was constructed.

There is also limited pollen evidence that relates to pre-barrow activity in the immediate area (Ch. 3.2) indicating a high level of ribwort plantain which is an indicator of human-induced disturbance, perhaps pastoralism within a damp grassland environment. Although the sample is from Context (51), an early layer in the Phase 1 barrow, if as argued above this material has been collected locally and re-deposited it can still be taken as a reliable indicator of localised environmental conditions.

The first barrow-related activity is represented by Context (42), a uniform pink/orange sand with occasional dark orange lines, perhaps indicating occasional incorporated turves, together with flecks and small pieces of charcoal. This is only present within the central area of the barrow (see Fig. 2.5), an area of approximately 10 metres in diameter. This sand has been scraped up from the surrounding area to form a low platform perhaps only 20 cm high, probably originally flat but now greatly disturbed. The dark orange lines show the inclusion of occasional small pieces of turf, and perhaps complete cut turves although many less in number and density than in Context (32) described below, together with a single flint and sherd of pottery, both un-diagnostic.

On the surface of (42) a series of activities took place associated with the burial of a sub-adult, 9–11 years old, sex undetermined (Ch. 3.3). The sequence of events is summarised in the schematic section of Figure 2.7, with the first being located centrally where two pointed stakes (1044 centred at 30.8, 20.2 and 1051 centred at 30.95, 20.19) (Fig. 2.5), were driven into the ground through (42) spaced about 10 cm apart. The former was c. 5 cm diameter at the top and the latter 3.5 cm, both narrowing with depth and ending in a sharpened point. Both were remarkably vertical, (1051) had a displacement of only 10mm at the bottom-most point, both penetrated through natural layers (17) and (24) for c. 0.8 m, ending at the interface with the underlying sandstone bedrock and giving a total depth of c. 1 m (Pl. 2.3a–d). Both were sectioned for their full depth and both were filled with grey sand with black organic-looking material in the bottom and around the edges in places, electron microscopy has suggested tiny fragments of bone and charcoal in the fill.

The problem with this interpretation of (1044) and (1051) being stake holes is that due to the characteristics of the natural, i.e. hard and stony, it is extremely difficult to hammer a stake in to the depth of nearly a metre, as demonstrated by our attempts to replicate this. The alternative is that these holes were dug and didn't contain a stake at all (and then filled?) which seems equally implausible due to their small diameter, consistent circularity and considerable depth.

The two stake holes were overlain by layer (51) suggesting that by then the stakes themselves were broken off at ground level although the time span between the two activities is unknown so the stakes could have rotted. Layer (51), averaging 1.5 cm thick, survives only in the central area (Fig. 2.5), and consists of hard red sand with occasional purple/brown patches, it has an even consistency and contains charcoal pieces, some up to 5 cm in size with considerable concentrations (Pl. 2.4). Embedded within (51) were 9 un-diagnostic sherds of pottery and 10 flints including SF3970 an Early Bronze Age backed blade which had been burnt. This is a layer of turf which was

23

Figure 2.8 King's Low: Pit (245 = 445), Area D, at an early stage of excavation.

either placed over the surface of (42) as the basal layer of the turf mound to follow, or the surface was exposed for long enough for the turf to grow. Considering the limited extent of (51) it seems more likely that it was laid only over the central area of the (42) platform and that the construction of the platform, the stakes and the events that followed were continuous activities over a relatively short period of time.

The next sequence of events are the burning of the body and the burial of the cremated remains in a Collared Urn. It is impossible to say whether the funeral pyre was actually on the platform (42) and turf layer (51) although Challinor (Ch. 3.3) suggests that this may be so, or at least that the pyre was nearby. Analysis of the large amounts of charcoal in the area suggest that the pyre was probably constructed from a single large oak tree. There was a noticeable lack of branch and shrub material within the charcoal which may indicate that only the larger pieces were removed from the pyre and placed in this area, in which case the pyre was located elsewhere. One large piece of charcoal (1017) was part of a radially split plank which could have been part of a coffin or from the pyre construction. This and one other specimen provided two radiocarbon dates:

GrN-17440. KL1016. 3370±35 BP. 1750–1598 (0.90 at 2 sigma).

GrN-17441. KL1017. 3365±40 BP. 1751–1527 (0.99 at 2 sigma).

Samples of cremated bone were tested for radiocarbon dating but were so extensively burnt that no carbon remained.

An irregular shaped pit (245=445) was dug through the platform (42) averaging 0.8 m west to east, 1.2 m north to south and approximately 30 cm deep (Fig. 2.8). The Collared Urn (KL10 = SF5113) was positioned within the fill of the pit and not directly on the pit bottom. It was impossible to tell whether the pot was positioned directly against the north western edge of the pit or whether a smaller approximately hexagonal hole was cut through the pit fill (1027) and the pot fitted tightly within this, a possibility suggested by dark material around the pot itself (Fig. 2.9).

The urn was filled with the cremated bone of the burnt individual which had been carefully collected from the pyre and placed in the urn. Boyle comments on how little of the cremated bone was missing (Ch. 3.3) and it was noticeable that very little charcoal was mixed with the bone in the urn, both points emphasising the care taken in the filling of the vessel. The fill (1027) of (245), below and around the pot, was mottled brown/orange sand containing charcoal lumps up to 3 cm in size, and lumps of clay. Over the top of the hole and merging with turf layer (51) although standing higher than it as a slight mound c. 10 cm high, was deposit (53) (Pls 2.5 and 2.6). This was patchy grey/purple/silver sand, with hard dark red lines, patches of charcoal and grey ashy material containing charcoal pieces, some large and with heavy concentrations of smaller pieces (Fig. 2.10). This represents pyre material, either *in situ*, partially *in situ*, or if moved and dumped then probably from not far away, although pieces of charcoal were spread throughout the

2 The excavations

Figure 2.9 King's Low: Collared Urn KL10 during excavation, note the dark material around the pot which may suggest a smaller hole was dug to contain the pot.

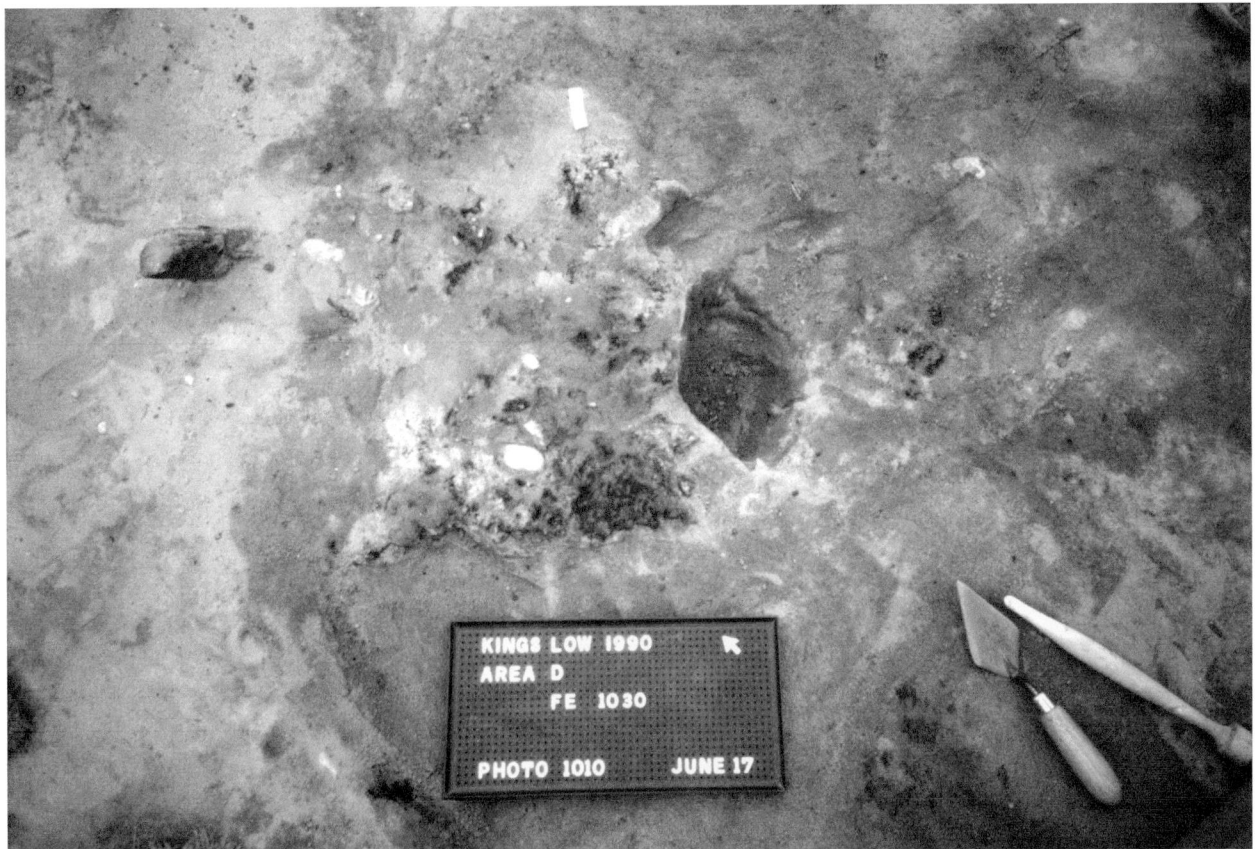

Figure 2.10 King's Low: charcoal within Context (53).

Excavations at King's Low and Queen's Low

Plate 2.4 King's Low: Context 51.

Plate 2.6 King's Low: Contexts (51) and (53) with turf staining.

2 The excavations

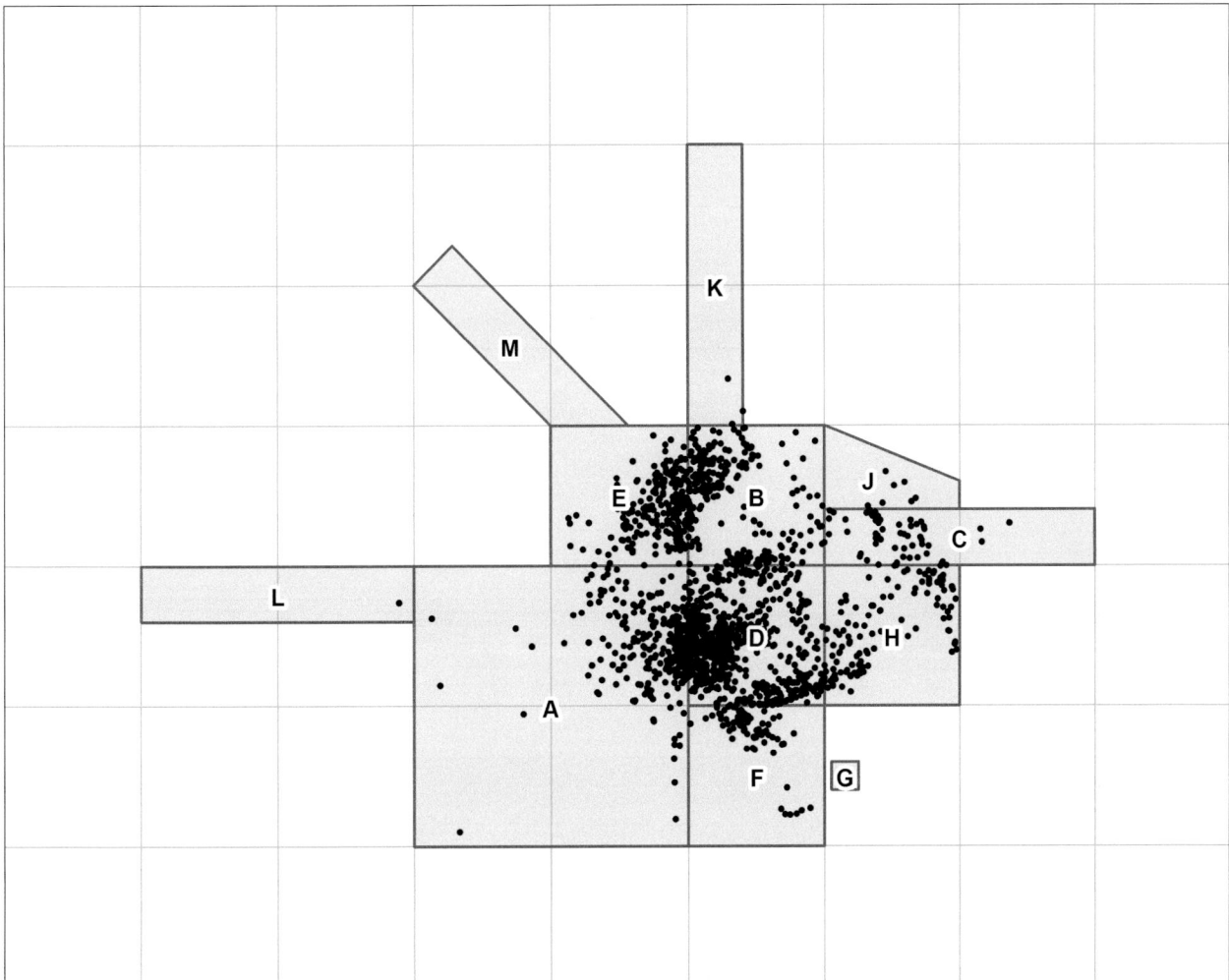

Figure 2.11 King's Low: the distribution of cremated human bone, 1,692 pieces in total, scattered by rabbit activity (drawn by John Pouncett).

mound by rabbit action the main area of concentration is (51) and (53) (Fig. 2.5). Layer (53) contained 7 sherds of undiagnostic pottery, and 17 flints including SF5043, a backed knife, all possibly associated with the burial in some way. The only artefacts that showed evidence of burning, and therefore being pyre goods, were SF3970, a backed blade found within the turf layer (51) and SF1442 a fabricator or rod, found in the general area but in rabbit disturbed upper mound (3). The spherical faience bead (SF479), although again found higher up the mound and in rabbit disturbed Context (3), had been exposed to heat (Sheridan, Ch. 4.3.1) and was very probably on or with the body during cremation. Found in a similar context were two fragments of heated, wrought sheet bronze, SF3900 and SF2283, probably early Bronze Age and associated with the cremation (Northover, Ch. 4.4.1).

The building of the First Phase barrow proper is the next event and comprised the stacking of turves and sand over the platform (42), layer (51) the burial pit (245) and its capping (53) containing the remains of the pyre. Turves were cut, probably from nearby, and stacked to form a circular mound approximately 13 m to 14 m in diameter, about the same size or just slightly bigger than the platform (42) (Fig. 2.5). Context (32), the turf mound, was a very colourful sand with pink/orange/peach patches showing dark red lines in section and as dark red outlined patches in plan. Around the lines the material had a soft 'creamy' texture with 'greasy' silver/purple patches. Throughout (32) were small pieces and flecks of charcoal. Above (32) is Context (10), a red/orange mottled and patchy sand with a soft 'creamy' texture, this is probably (32) degraded by both rabbit action and geo-chemical action and can be considered as part of the same original mound. The height of the Phase 1 barrow is impossible to reconstruct but Context (10) survives in patches to about 1.8 m above OGS. Distinctive blocks of (32) were found 'floating' in (10). In both section and plan individual turves can be distinguished. The deep red lines are probably due to the redeposition of iron minerals leached from the mound above as part of the podsolisation process, and it appears that this occurred within the actual grass layer on the top of each turf and gradually faded out through the soil part of the turf below the grass suggesting that some, if not all, of the turves appear to have been stacked grass-side down (Pl. 2.7). In plan many of the turves were approximately rectangular c. 35 cm by 20 cm in size (Pl. 2.8).

That the turves were cut from the surrounding area is supported by a variety of artefacts contained within them from different periods of activity already indicated. In Context (32) a broken rod microlith, SF3632, and in Context (10) a retouched piercer (SF228), are both Mesolithic. There are also various sherds including SF6523, a

Plate 2.5 King's Low: a composite plan photograph showing the main contexts in parts of Areas B and D, North is to the top and each individual photograph is 1m square.

2 The excavations

Plate 2.7 King's Low: turves shown in section.

Plate 2.8 King's Low: the Phase 1 turf mound, Area D.

Excavations at King's Low and Queen's Low

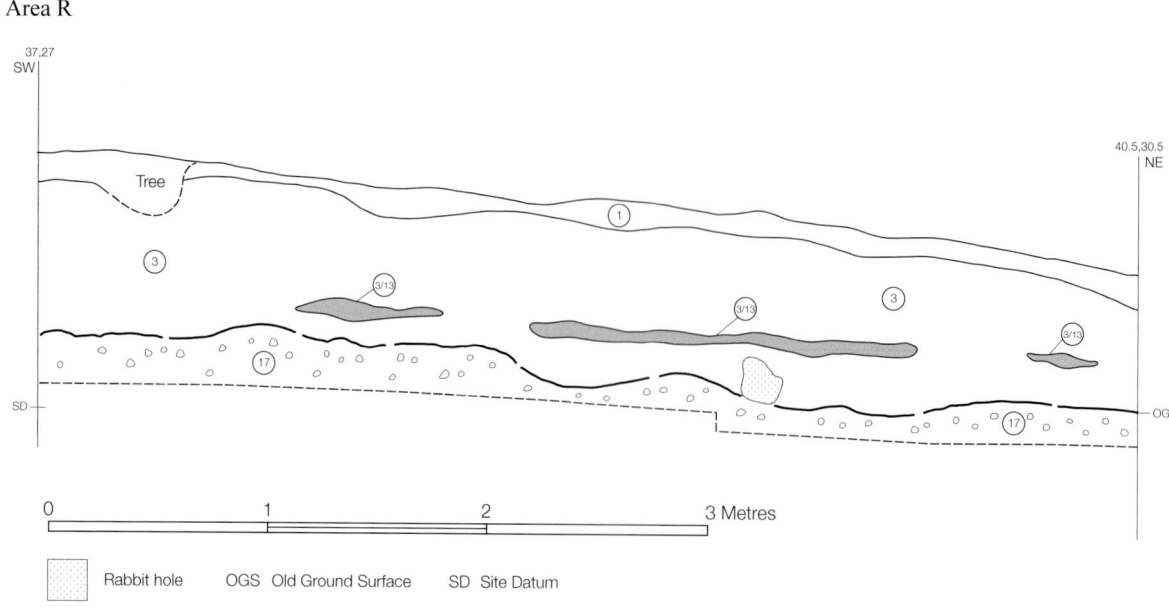

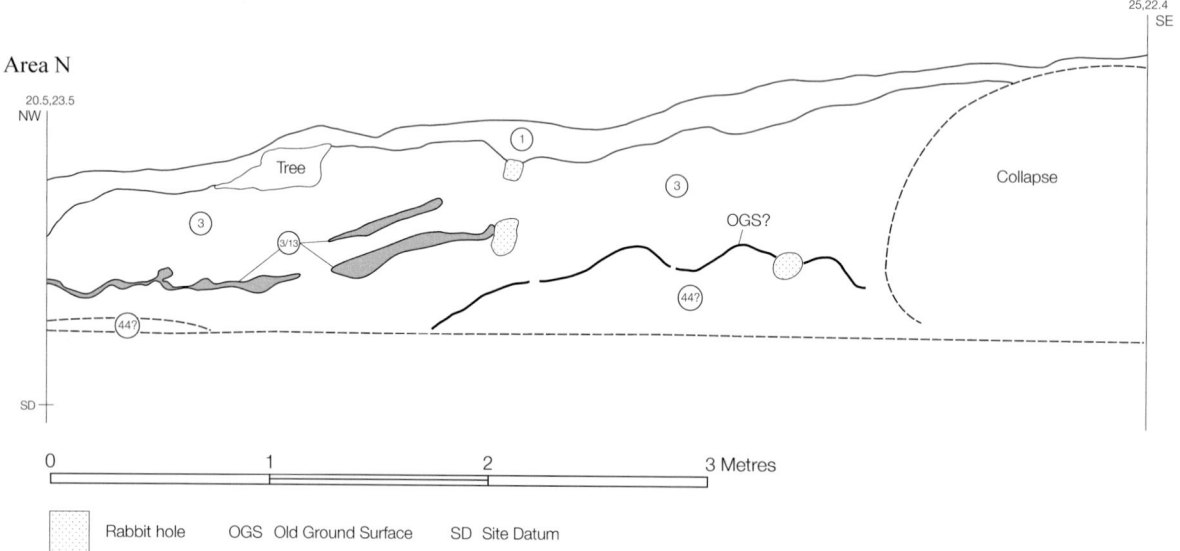

Figure 2.12 King's Low: section drawings for Areas R and N.

Beaker, and several sherds of the scattered Collared Urn KL11 from the Phase 2 mound show the extent of rabbit disturbance.

The next event is the enlargement of the Phase 1 barrow by the addition of a layer of clean orange sand (Context 43), increasing the diameter of the mound to c. 18 m (Fig. 2.5 and Pl. 2.5). This Phase 2 barrow shows no indication of turf and contains few artefacts, 9 sherds of pottery and two flints all un-diagnostic. Context (43) occurs as a 'doughnut' shape in plan around the outside of the Phase 1 mound and whether it originally extended over the top of the turf mound is impossible to establish. Given the current limited distribution of (43) in both horizontal and vertical extent it could have been an addition to the sides of the mound only, the sections in Figures 2.3 and 2.4 show the extent of (43). A possible reason for this could be to accommodate a secondary burial in a Collared Urn (KL11) found as a tight distribution of sherds mainly in Area H which may indicate the position of the burial (Fig. 2.5). If this was another cremation burial then the large number of pieces of cremated bone found scattered throughout the mound may be from this origin. Figure 2.11 shows the distribution of the bone pieces, 1,692 in total, although this primarily reflects the activity of rabbits as they were all found redistributed within filled in runs. Although the actual location of the burial was not established and was likely to have been obliterated by rabbit activity there is a possibility that Context (1064), a shallow pit c. 35 cm in diameter and 5 cm deep cut through natural (17) and (24) could be where it was located as it is beneath the 'doughnut' of (43), shown on Figure 2.5. The fill of (1064) contained charcoal and pieces of cremated human bone but was very badly disturbed by rabbit activity and almost completely destroyed by a filled in rabbit run. Alternatively, (1064) may have contained an un-urned cremation and not be associated with the KL11 sherds.

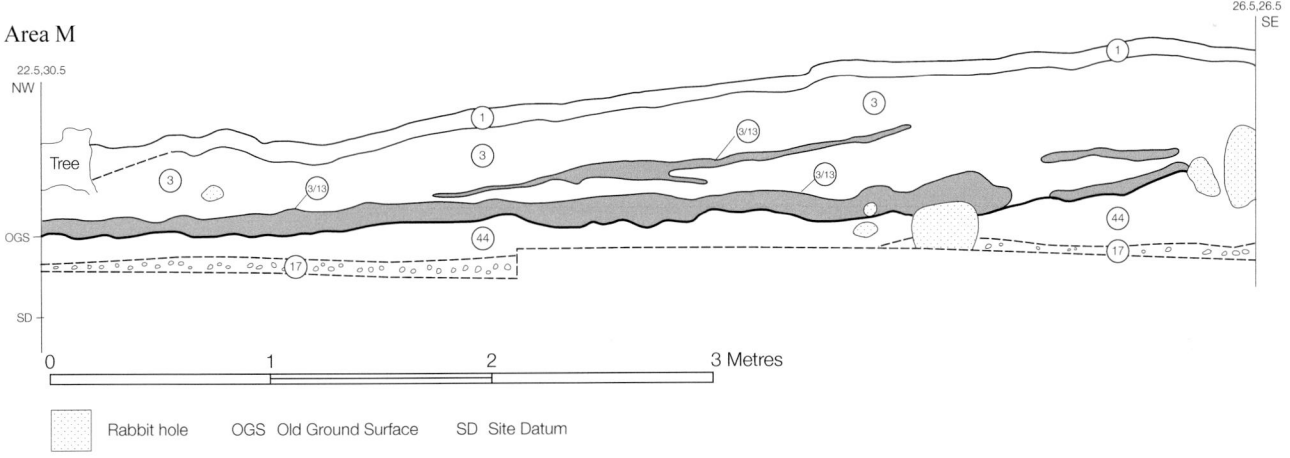

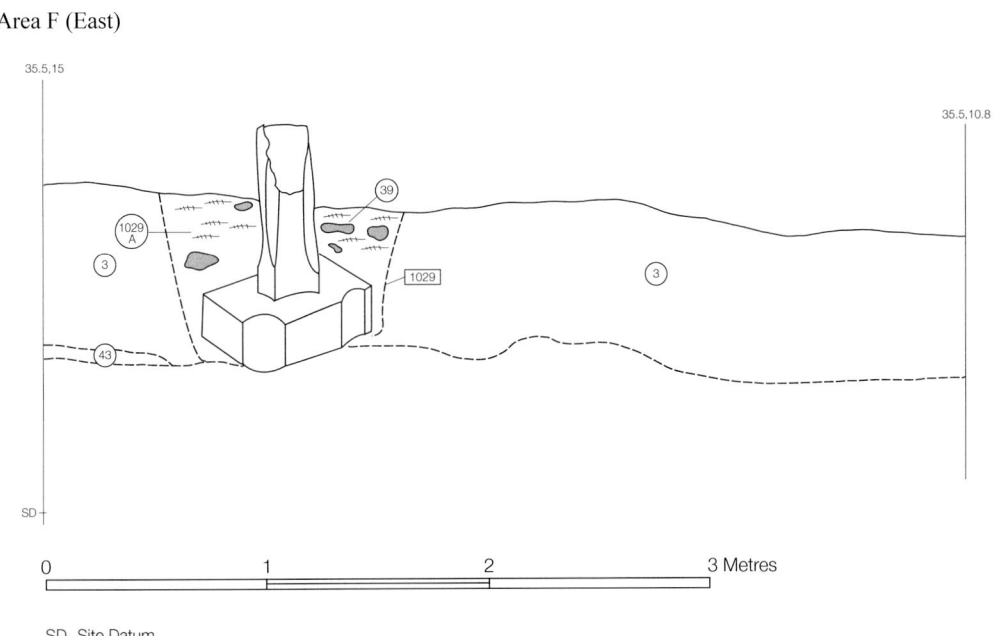

Figure 2.13 King's Low: section drawings for Areas M and F, the latter showing the stone cross and its socket hole.

It is apparent that there is far more material comprising the existing mound of King's Low than can be accounted for by the Phase 1 turf mound and its Phase 2 sand extension. This suggests a later increase in the size of the mound, perhaps a Phase 3 barrow. This material is mainly Context (3) which is directly below the modern topsoil and is a variable brown/red/grey firm sand, very disturbed in places by rabbits and roots, containing a few small pebbles. Patches of colour become gradually more frequent towards the base of the context and it's boundary with (10). The thickness of (3) varies and is thicker on the flanks of the mound. Much of Context (3) is grey in colour and represents the leached zone in the podsolisation process so that minerals, particularly iron, have been removed by water percolation and re-deposited deeper within the mound. Over the central area this redeposition seems to have been concentrated within the turf layers of the Phase 1 mound while around the outside of the mound it takes the form of blackened sand with very hard black patches and layers of hard-panning which occur mostly beyond the limits of (43), as shown in the sections of Areas R, N, M and F at the outer edges of the mound (Figs 2.12 and 2.13).

There is no evidence to comment on any possible structure to this Phase 3 mound nor to offer a date for its construction. Areas C, L, M, K and R were all located partially to check for the existence of a ditch. As for the Phase 1 and 2 barrows, there was no evidence of a ditch. Of potential importance however, are the two early La Tène knobbed and ribbed bracelets found as four individual pieces scattered within Context (3), Bracelet 1 SF664 and SF3269, Bracelet 2 SF1101 and SF1834. Foster suggests that these can be seen as a pair and probably accompanied a burial (Ch. 4.4) although there is no evidence of an actual grave or skeleton. Assuming that any burial would have been an inhumation the lack of bones can be accounted for by the high acidity of the soil and being as the grave is likely to have been in the upper half of the mound the complete lack of evidence for its cut is probably due to rabbit disturbance.

The final event evident at King's Low is the positioning of a stone cross on its south eastern flank, probably medieval in origin and placed there in 1803 (see Andrews and Longdon below). The socket hole for the base of the cross was identified, Context (1029), its size and shape closely

Excavations at King's Low and Queen's Low

Figure 2.14 King's Low: the stone cross during excavation.

matched the base stone of the cross and appeared to be cut to fit it (Fig. 2.14). This was approximately 1.0 m square and 0.7 m deep, filled with pale sand and layering in the upper fill suggesting turves originally, Context (1029A) (Fig. 2.13). Broken pieces of the stone cross were found within the top of the foundation pit and around it, Context (39).

Summary

Pre-barrow activity is suggested by limited pollen evidence and by Mesolithic, Neolithic and Beaker material culture within and beneath the mound. A low sand platform was constructed upon which a series of activities took place concerning the burial of a sub-adult aged 9 to 11 years. Two long stakes were driven approximately 1m into the ground, a pit was dug and the cremated remains of the body buried in a Collared Urn within the pit. The funerary pyre was probably nearby, bone and charcoal were carefully separated with the former placed in the pot and a scatter of the latter spread over the platform surface, dated to 1750–1527 cal BC. Various artefacts including flint tools, a faience bead and possibly a copper-alloy sheet object were burnt with the body. A turf mound was built over the platform and burial. In Phase 2 the mound was extended in size by a layer of clean sand around its outer edge, and possibly over its top, an act that may have been associated with one or more secondary burials, cremations in at least one urn. Two copper-alloy bracelets dated to the early La Tène period, 450–200 BC, suggest the possibility of an Iron Age burial within the mound which may have been associated with a third increase in size. In the early 19th century a stone cross was erected on the south-eastern flank of the mound. Due to extensive rabbit activity and the effects of podsolization the mound was severely disturbed.

2.1.2 The cross
Anne Andrews and Rose Longdon

On the southern slope of King's Low stands the base and fragmented remains of a stone cross (SMR 43500852). According to the HER record (undated):

> remains of the smashed shaft and head of a shaft-on-stops type of medieval cross. The shaft is now in about seven fragments but the largest part still stands to a height of 1m on the southern slopes of King's Low: it is octagonal but has angle stops so that the lowest part is square. The hexagonal head, 0.6 m high, 0.4 m broad and 0.2 m thick, is largely intact and in one piece. The carvings on three faces suggest a 15th century date … it was smashed accidently by a cart during tree felling c. 1918[1]

Erdeswick's survey of 1844 describes the cross as 'of hard moorstone and sculpted with figures of a crucifix and the virgin' (70). By the time of the excavation the head of the cross was missing (Fig. 2.15) although a photograph taken c.1954 shows its form and one decorated face (Fig. 2.16). This appears to show a (male?) figure wearing something on his head, with arms crossed across his chest, sitting up in a box-like structure (a coffin?). Several fragments of the shaft remained above and within the ground, these are made from greywacke, the stone probably originating in the Welsh borders[2]. Excavation showed that the shaft of the cross was fixed into a base in the form of a block of local Tixall Stone, probably added at its time of erection within a foundation hole cut down through the barrow material (Fig. 2.14 and excavation details above).

There is some confusion amongst antiquarians, and possibly continuing, between the King's Low cross and another monument called the Tixall Obelisk. According to Kelly's Directory (1904, 403) 'an ancient hexagonal stone cross 18ft in height was brought from a mansion in South Wales in 1803 to stand in Tixall village'. This probably refers to the the Tixall Obelisk, a milestone, dated to 1776 with the names London, Stafford and Lichfield carved on it (HER PRN154, Listed Building Number LB11). It is described as a hexagonal stone obelisk and still stands on the village green at the main road junction in the village centre. Pevsner describes it and dates it to 1776 (1975, 283). As will be shown below, the confusion with the King's Low cross arises from its possible connection with a mansion in South Wales, e.g. at Hensol or Margham, and the date of 1803, although the date of 1776 on the Tixall Obelisk does argue against it being the King's Low cross. The base of the King's Low cross is now in Tixall church (Cockin 2000, 593).

Figure 2.15 King's Low: the stump of the cross at the start of the excavation, 1986.

Historical references suggest that the most likely origin of the cross and reason for it being on King's Low is as follows:

> About the year 1803, a very antique stone cross, which once stood before the gate of a ruined mansion in South Wales, was transported hither and erected on Tixall Heath. It is of a very hard moor-stone; the shaft, which has eight unequal sides, supports a tablet of an hexagonal form, adorned with very rude carvings; on one side a crucifix, on the other, the virgin with the child in her lap. On the edge of the tablet is also a figure, which has been thought by some experienced antiquaries to represent St John the Evangelist. This cross is now erected on one of the lows, amid the congenial gloom of a clump of widely spreading pines, and may be considered as a memorial of the horrible assassination of William Chetwynd. (Clifford and Clifford 1817, 87)

The suggestion being, therefore, that the stone cross was transported from Wales and erected to commemorate the murder of William Chetwynd, an earlier account of which is given by Thomas Pennant in 1780[3]:

> In 1493, an infamous assassination was committed on this heath; which shews how little the vindictive spirit of the feudal times was subdued. A family emulation had

---

1 Referenced as a personal communication from Mr S. Horne, Secretary of the Old Stafford Society.
2 Personal communication from Bob Roach.
3 http://www.visionofbritain.org.uk/text/contents_page.jsp?t_id=Pennant_C2L [accessed February 12th 2012]

Excavations at King's Low and Queen's Low

Figure 2.16 King's Low: the decorated head of the cross photographed c. 1954 by Mr. D. Mayer.

subsisted between the *Stanleys* of Pipe, in this county, and the *Chetwynds* of Ingestre. Sir *Humphrey Stanley* was one of the knights of the body to *Henry* VII; Sir *William Chetwynd* one of his gentlemen-ushers. The former, as is said, through envy, inveigled Sir *William* out of his house, by means of a counterfeit letter from a neighbor; and while he was passing over this common, caused him to be attacked by twenty armed men, and slain on the spot; Sir *Humphrey* passing with a train at the instant, under the pretence of hunting, but in fact to glut his revenge with the sight. It does not appear that justice overtook the assassin, notwithstanding the widow of Sir *William* invoked it. Probably Sir *Humphrey* had no fortune worthy of confiscation.

An earlier still version appears in Dugdale's *History of Warwickshire*, 1656:

Sir Philip Chetwynd, Knt. departed this life, 24. H.6, leaving William his grandchild his heir. Which William, afterwards one of the gentlemen-ushers of the chamber to King Henry VII, became so much envied by Sir Humphrey Stanley, (then of Pipe, Co. Staff.) one of the knights of the body to the same king, and sheriff of that county 9 H.7, as that by means of a counterfeit letter, in the name of Randolph Brereton, Esq. delivered on Friday night before the feast of st John the Baptist's nativity, requesting his meeting with him at Stafford, the next morning by five of the clock – being lured out of his house at Ingestrie, and passing thitherwards accordingly, with no more attendance than his own son and two servants; he was waylayed on Tixall Heath, by no less than twenty persons, whereof seven were of the said Sir Humphrey's own family, some with bows, and others with spears, all armed with brigantines, and coats of mail; who issuing out of a sheep-cote, and a dry pit, furiously assaulted him, saying that he should die, and accordingly killed him; the said Sir Humphrey at that time passing by, with at least twenty-four persons on horseback, upon pretence of hunting a deer. All which, the petition to the king made by Alice, his widow, wherein she craves that the said Sir Humphrey and his servants might answer for it, doth manifest.

Although according to Clifford and Clifford (1817, 86):

From other accounts it appears, that Sir Humphrey had interest enough at court to silence the matter; and that no redress was ever given to Alice, nor any notice taken of the assassination of her husband!

It is strange that if according to the Cliffords' account the cross was erected in 1803, to commemorate this Chetwynd murder, the land at Tixall Heath belonged at that time to the Clifford family, not the Chetwynds of Ingestre. The lands at Tixall, including Tixall Heath, had passed to the Astons when Joan or Jane Littleton married Sir John Aston of Heywood c. 1488, and their son Edward built the first known house at Tixall in 1555. Tixall then remained in the hands of the Astons until James, 5th Lord Aston died in 1749, leaving two young daughters Mary and Barbara. Barbara married the Hon Thomas Clifford in 1761. Their son inherited estates at Burton Constable in Yorkshire, taking the name Clifford Constable. Their grandson, Thomas Aston Clifford Constable moved to Yorkshire, putting Tixall Estate up for auction in 1833, when it did not meet the reserve price, and then finally selling it to Charles Chetwynd Talbot, 2nd Earl Talbot (1777–1849) in 1845.

There are various possibilities for the original location of the cross and, therefore, where it was moved from to be erected on King's Low. There are connections between South Wales and the Chetwynds of Ingestrie in that John, 2nd Viscount Chetwynd, had a daughter, Catherine, who married the Hon. John Talbot in 1748, and on her father's death in 1767, inherited his estates. This John Talbot was the third son of Charles, first Lord Talbot of Hensol, Glamorgan, and his eldest son, John Chetwynd Talbot succeeded to the barony in 1782 on the death of his uncle. In 1784, John Chetwynd Talbot was created Viscount Ingestrie, and Earl Talbot. This mansion at Hensol, three miles south of Llantrisant, Glamorgan, no longer exists. However, the Talbots also have connections with Margam, four miles south-east of Port Talbot in South Wales where a Cistercian

Figure 2.17 Sepulchral stone showing the figure of St. Saeran, Llanynys church, Denbighshire (photograph by Dave and Maureen Thomas).

Monastery was founded in the 12th century with the Abbey Church being restored in the 19th century (Evans 1960). After the dissolution of the abbey in 1536, Sir Rice Mansel, a local landowner, turned the remainder of the abbey into a fine country house and in 1786, Thomas Mansel Talbot began the glory of Margam – the magnificent 327 ft long Orangery. His son built the castellated Gothic mansion at Hensol known as 'The Castle' around 1835.

The Margam Stone Museum contains a collection of locally found inscribed stones and Christian crosses dating from the 5th to the 11th centuries and many of these were being moved around the country in 1803.[4] Although the geology of many of these stones is similar to the cross shaft from Kings Low, there are not parallels in terms of style so Margam can be ruled out as a source.

Clifford and Clifford (1817, 88, footnote 1) cite a parallel in Britton (1807–26, vol. 1, plate A, figure 3) to suggest that the King's Low cross was a memorial cross 'commonly set up as sepulchral momentos, and as a memorials of battles, murders, and other fatal events'. The style and location of the King's Low cross also suggests that it is a memorial cross according to a more recent classification of crosses (Langdon 1997). A good example of possible similar stones occur at Llanynys Church in Denbighshire (Owen 1886) where a hexagonal stone, similar in size and shape to the King's Low cross head, is a sepulchral stone of the 13th century. On one side it shows Christ on the cross and on the other a bishop in full regalia (Parry Jones 1981, 23) (Fig. 2.17), and it probably was one of two stones, at the head and foot, marking the burial place of a Bishop. The shaft was not intended to be exposed to view and would have originally been embedded in the ground or in masonry.

The possibility of a connection with nearby St Thomas's Priory has also been suggested. The Priory would have had various crosses around the area, two are mentioned in the immediate vicinity[5] although these are roadside crosses rather than sepulchral crosses. Even so, the Priory did have a cemetery, its founder Bishop Peche was buried there as was the last Lord Ferrers, Earl of Derby, located to the 'east of the eastern range' (Greenslade 1970, 266[6]). Following the initial dissolution and dismantling of the Priory in 1538/9, when valuables and lead were stripped from the church, the next major despoliation occurred between 1744 and 1765 when the Honourable John Spencer owned the site and it was used by a company of cotton spinners, during this time the Priory was systematically dismantled and some of its finer features sold off and re-used. At this time William Chetwynd was building himself a hall at nearby Brocton and arches and gargoyles were taken from the priory to be incorporated into it (Pape 1935, 73). However, this William was only a distant relative of the Ingestre Chetwynd's being the great grandson of Thomas, younger son of John Chetwynd of Ingestre. In 1765 Lord Talbot bought St. Thomas's Priory from John Spencer's son (he succeeded to the Chetwynd estates in 1767). This raises the possibility of a head stone being removed from the Priory church yard either by William Chetwynd sometime between 1744 and 1765 or by the new owner, Lord Talbot after 1765. In fact, as late as 1878 there is a report of 'piles of ancient fragments, base, cap, shaft and boss, all of early 13th century work' still lying around where the Priory grounds were located (Lynam 1878). However the boundary of St Thomas's Priory was along the line of Tixall Road, and did not include Tixall Heath where the cross was found. In addition crosses connected with this Priory would probably have been made of

---

4 Personal communication from Richard Avent, Margam Stones Museum (2001).
5 Parker 1887 – Tixall and Hanyards Deeds page 192, Chartulary of St. Thomas
6 Footnote 35 states that 'in 1965 a number of burials were uncovered during the construction of a cesspit, information from Staffordshire County Planning and Development Officer (1968)'.

Figure 2.18 Queen's Low: the view before excavation in 1993.

the local Keuper Sandstone with several quarries nearby, rather than of greywacke which is not found locally.

2.2 Queen's Low
Winston Hollins

Queen's Low is situated in a large field which at the time of the excavations, 1993 and 1994, was used for grazing and had been recently ploughed with grass planted to feed a large herd of milking cattle.

In the early 20th century the barrow is recorded as being 65 ft in diameter, approximately 20 m, and 6 ft high, *c.* 2 m (Page 1908). In the early 1960s Gunstone (1965, 49) records the diameter as being 42 paces and the height as 1.5 ft, *c.* 0.5 m. Upon first inspection in 1992 the mound was not very obvious with only a barely perceivable rise in the ground level (Fig. 2.18).

To try and establish the original size of the mound a detailed topographic survey together with a resistivity survey were carried out (Figs 2.19 and 2.20). The contour survey does confirm the possible diameter as 40 m (Gunstone states 42 paces) but the height difference between this edge and the middle was only 0.28 m. Both surveys indicate considerable disturbance across the centre of the mound and a small hole near the centre, visible in Figure 2.19, had two wooden pegs within it suggesting a possible earlier small excavation although no information on this could be established. The presence of the pegs is curious as it suggests a 'formal' excavation rather than just a hole dug by treasure hunters, and as they still survived in fairly good condition in 1993 the intervention was probably not that long before this. According to local anecdotal evidence the mound was 'dismantled within living memory', and two visitors to the site remembered the destruction, one of them having helped as a boy.

2.2.1 The excavations
The excavation area was laid out on a 5 m north-south grid and sub-areas were designated with letters A to M (plus DX) for reference (Fig. 2.21). Additional areas were added as the excavation progressed and called the western, eastern, northern and southern extensions (WX, EX, NX and SX). In the final season three small test pits were excavated to explore the deposits around the mound.

Beneath the turf layer (Context 1) the plough soil was very compacted and in some places contained a layer of hardcore (Context 2) although the majority had very little. The Context (2) feature is visible in the resistivity survey (Fig. 2.20), as a narrow linear anomaly of variable width, from 3 m to 5 m, running approximately east-west from (30, 57) to (80, 40). This is probably the hard-core for a track, now disappeared, and was found in Areas A, B, C and L. In Area L particularly the layer contained a large amount of limestone chatter and building rubble. An unconnected area of Context (2) was found in Area F and may have been hard-standing for a water trough, here Context (2) contained pottery, SF676, SF677, SF706 and SF684, sherds from four different Collared Urns. There was no obvious boundary between Contexts (2) and (3) because ploughing had blurred the junctions between them. Context (3) represents the layer of modern ploughing, and was present in all the areas excavated. It contained Bronze Age pottery including SF336, SF604, SF7, SF573, SF301 and SF130, representing sherds from both Beaker and at least five Collared Urns together with flints including SF167.

For much of the area assumed to be originally covered by the mound the composition of the bottom of the plough soil changed to include shattered small fragments of yellow sandstone, Context (4). This layer contained Bronze Age pottery including SF773, SF337, SF405, SF49, SF286, SF304, SF459, SF62, SF80, SF449, SF315, SF282, SF350, SF313, SF262, SF656, SF751, and SF7194 representing sherds from at least two Beakers and two Collared Urns, together with the faience bead SF283 and numerous flint waste flakes. Beneath this in places was sandstone bed rock, Context (5), showing many plough marks (Fig. 2.22). Context (5) refers

2 The excavations

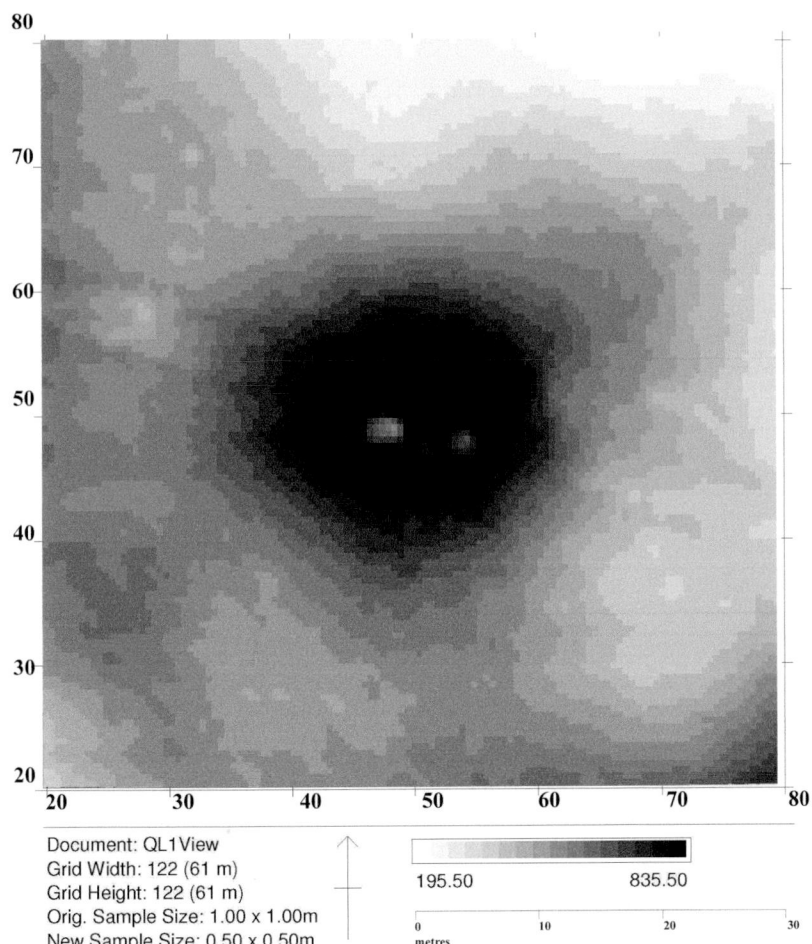

Document: QL1View
Grid Width: 122 (61 m)
Grid Height: 122 (61 m)
Orig. Sample Size: 1.00 x 1.00m
New Sample Size: 0.50 x 0.50m

195.50   835.50

Figure 2.19 Queen's Low: topographic survey.

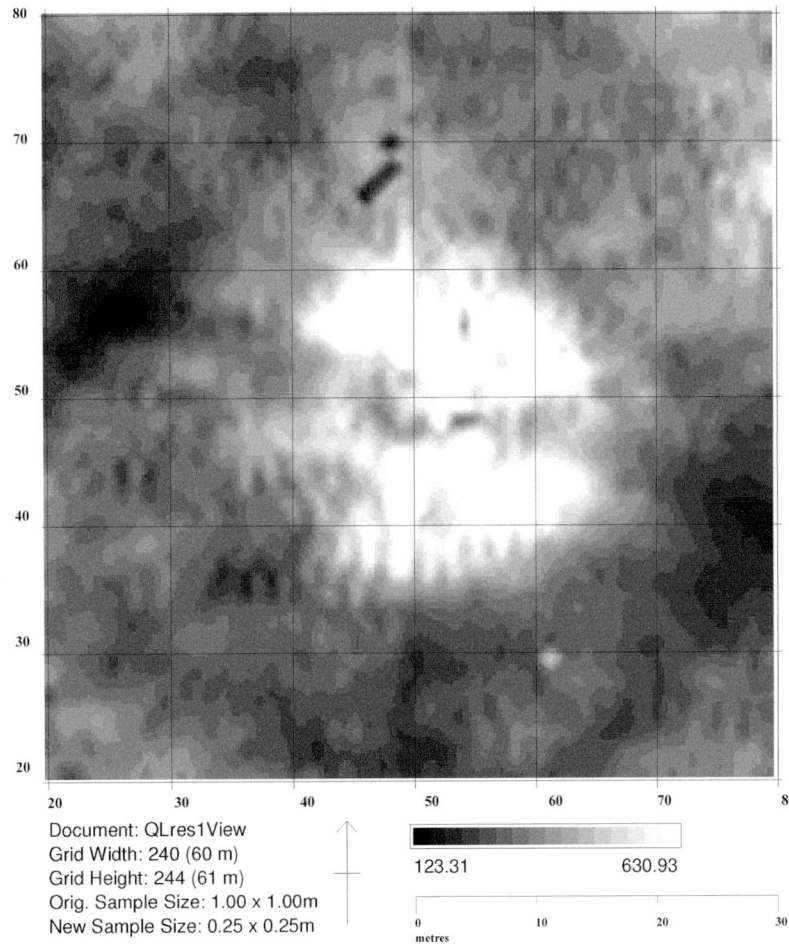

Document: QLres1View
Grid Width: 240 (60 m)
Grid Height: 244 (61 m)
Orig. Sample Size: 1.00 x 1.00m
New Sample Size: 0.25 x 0.25m

123.31   630.93

Figure 2.20 Queen's Low: resistivity survey.

37

Excavations at King's Low and Queen's Low

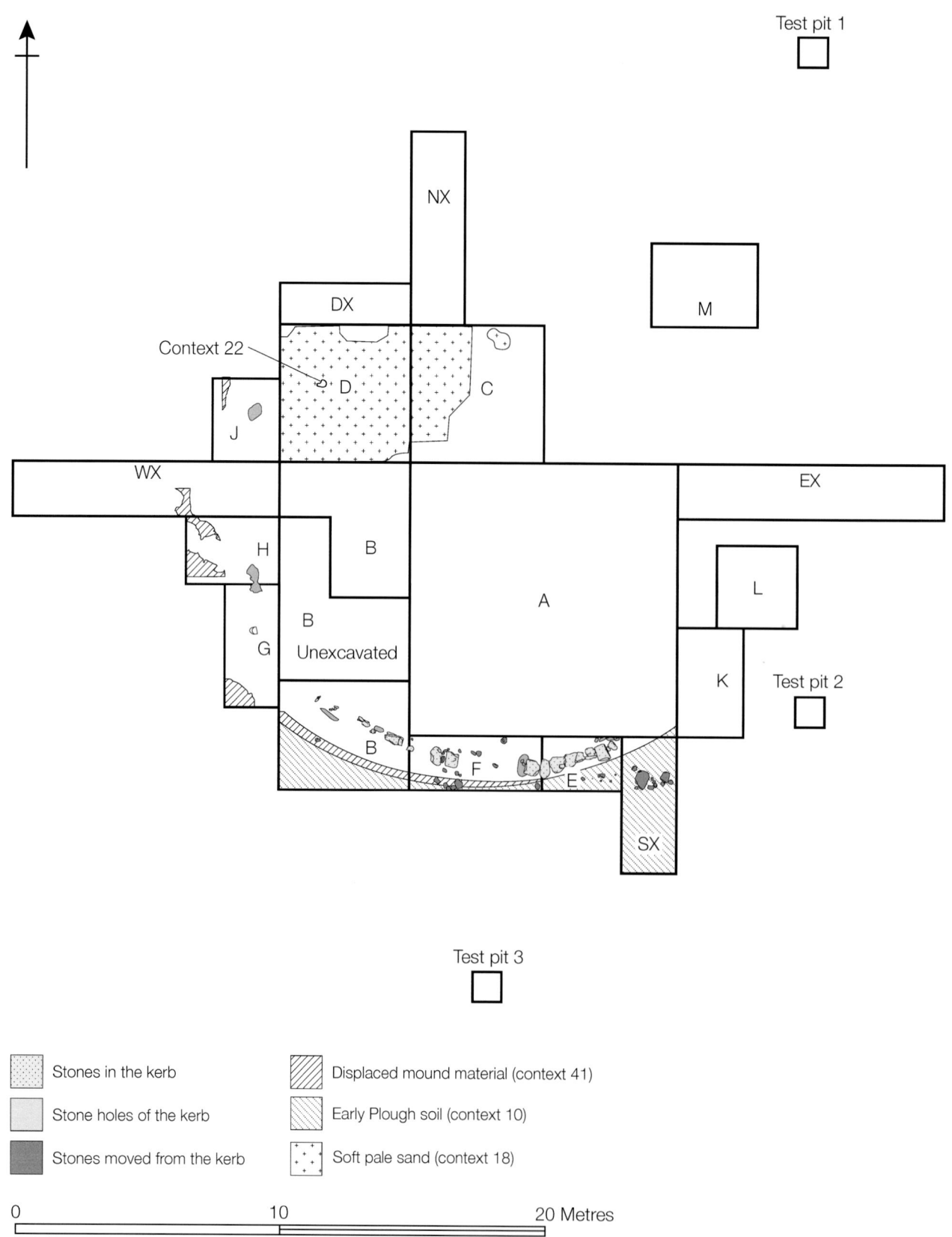

Figure 2.21 Queen's Low: the excavated areas.

to the underlying yellow sandstone throughout even though it varied between a hard compact sandstone to quite loose sand which was disturbed as indicated by the presence of a sherd of Collared Urn within it. In addition a water pipe for a water trough had been inserted into a groove cut into the sandstone, running approximately north-south in Area A.

It soon became clear that the mound had been built on a sandstone outcrop, the top being slightly tilted and higher to the west and north. North to South the outcrop was only just as wide as the mound, and beyond the limit of the mound it falls away in both directions. In contrast, the outcrop extends beyond the mound to the east and west, although for how far wasn't determined. In the

2 The excavations

Figure 2.22 Queen's Low: looking north across the excavated area showing the sandstone natural with incised plough marks.

main area assumed to have been covered by the mound (excavation Areas A, B, C and D), there were few features in the surface of the outcrop (Contexts 7, 8, 11, 12, 14, 15, 16, 17 and 22). Most of these were probably natural faults in the rock or where the plough had pulled out pieces of rock. The exception to this was Context (22) in area D just inside the kerb line (Fig. 2.21). This is a possible secondary cremation, although if this had been placed in a cut feature in the rock, ploughing had removed any evidence for such a cut, alternatively it may represent a partial cremation which had been re-deposited into a hole created by ploughing. Context (22) contained a small amount of cremated human bone, possibly an adult, mixed with charcoal although greatly disturbed by rabbits and ploughing.

In the south and south west (Areas SX, E, F, B and G) the edge of the original mound was clear as the edge of the sandstone outcrop had been cut away to allow the positioning of a kerb of stones made from the same sandstone as the outcrop (Figs 2.23 and 2.24). The cuts for individual stone holes were visible in places, filled with a dark sand and stone fragments. There were some indications of

Excavations at King's Low and Queen's Low

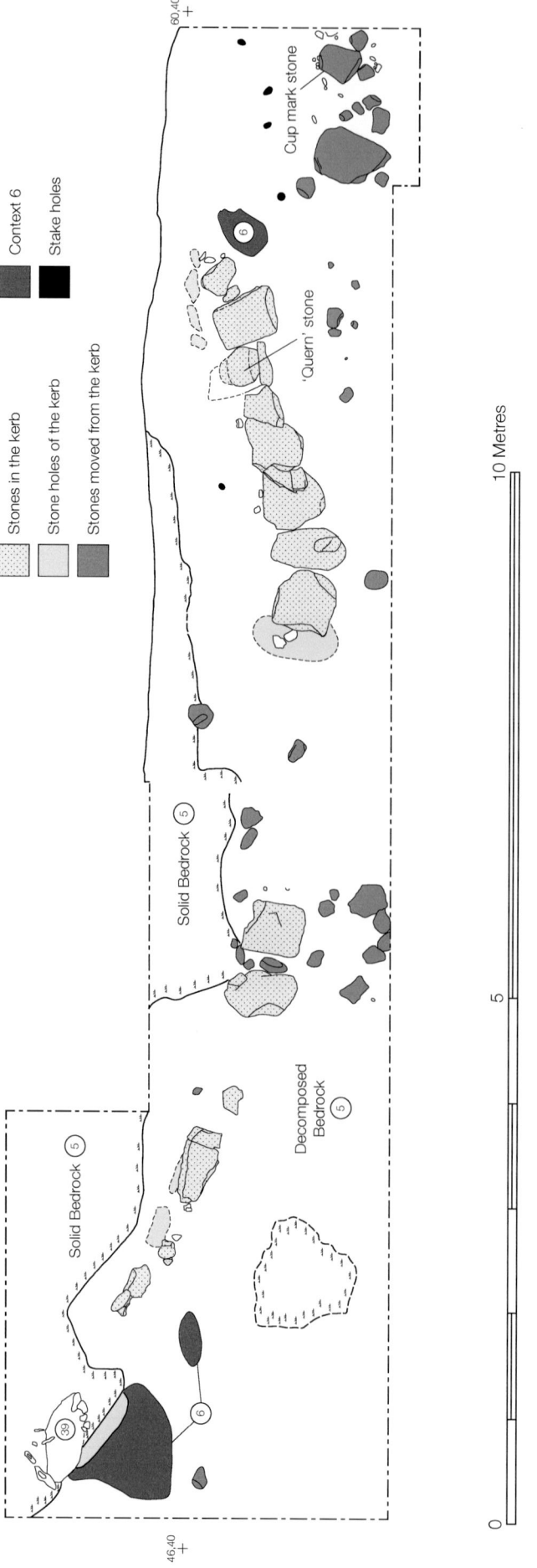

Figure 2.23 Queen's Low: excavation Areas B, F, E and SX showing the main features of the kerb.

40

2 The excavations

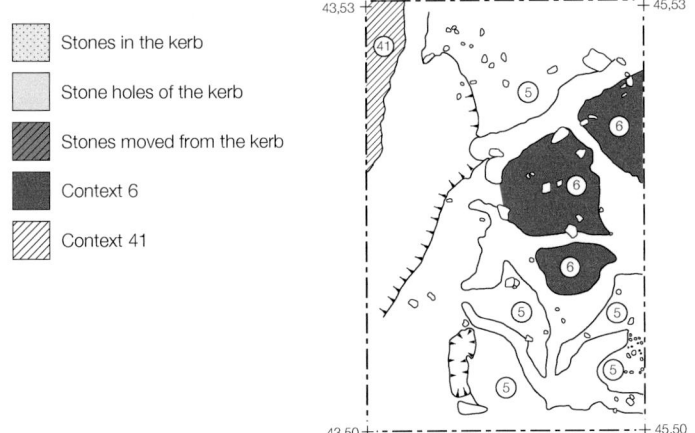
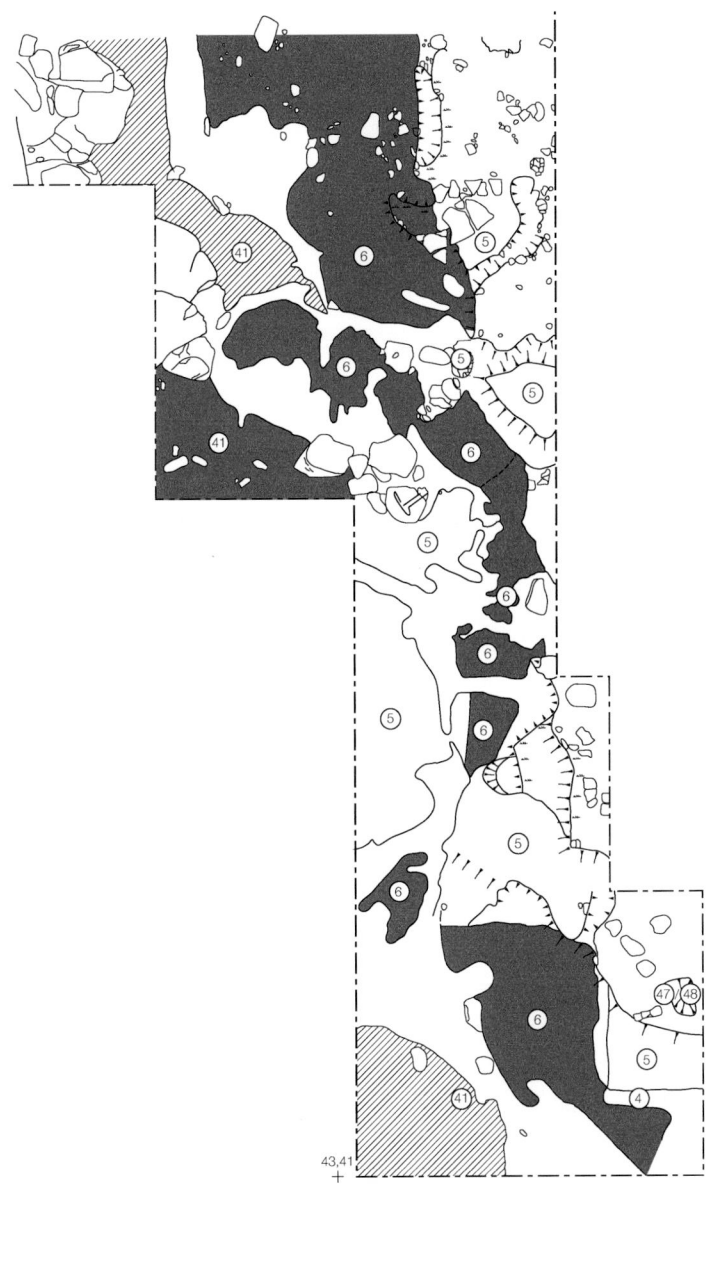
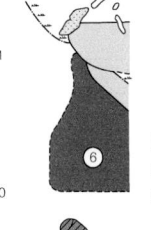

Figure 2.24 Queen's Low: excavation Areas G, H and WX showing the main contexts.

Excavations at King's Low and Queen's Low

Figure 2.25 Queen's Low: the south-eastern kerb stones viewed from above.

Figure 2.26 Queen's Low: the inside face of the kerb.

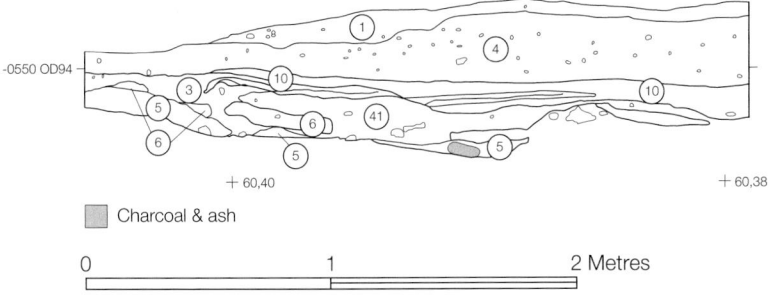

Figure 2.27 Queen's Low: north-south section of the eastern baulk of Area E.

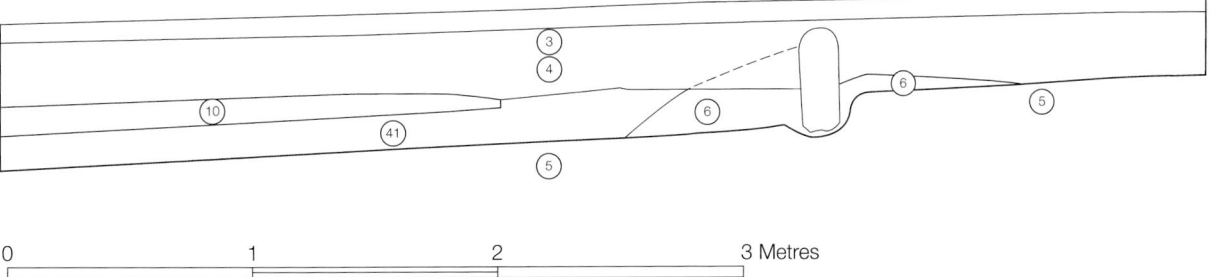

Figure 2.28 Queen's Low: a schematic section showing the main contexts in the area of the kerb stones, not to scale.

marking out the line of the kerb in the form of stake holes (Contexts 29, 30, 34 and 35), curving outside the actual line of the kerb (Fig. 2.23). Twelve stones of the kerb were still in place, several others had been moved slightly from their original position while in other cases just the stone holes remained. Where the stones were still in position they had originally been placed upright, tightly pressing against the next stones edge to edge (Figs 2.25, 2.26 and Pl. 2.9). The standing stones were approximately the same height (70 cm to 75 cm) but one, the possible 'quern' stone described below, is only 40 cm high. They varied in width from 35 cm to 60 cm and are all approximately 20 cm thick. All the stones were scarred by ploughing on their upper surfaces. Three stones showed evidence of human working and they are described below by Derek Outram.

The immediate area round each of the stones showed a consistent pattern. Rabbits had dug around each one but just a little way from the stones was a layer of grey brown sand with mottled patches of yellow orange sand, Context (6). This appears to be material packed in around the stones to support them which extended on the outer side of the kerb perhaps to form a berm. As shown in the section (Fig. 2.27), and summarised in the schematic section (Fig. 2.28), the height of the possible berm is unknown and it may have extended towards the top of the kerb stones. The finds from Context (6) included Bronze Age pottery, SF60 and SF50 being sherds from 2 Collared Urns, and several flint waste flakes. A layer of grey sand with reddish clay (Context 10), a thin layer getting thicker further from the outside of the stones reaching a thickness of 20 cm is probably a product of ploughing associated with the addition of clay to the top soil in an attempt to improve it, pottery from the late 19th and early 20th centuries was found within it. Where the stones were still standing in position this layer started about 1m from the outside of the stones whereas in the areas of missing or displaced stones this spread over the line of the stones. It seems likely that ploughing was carried out right to the edges of the mound before it was deliberately destroyed in the mid-20th century. In most of the places where Context (10) was found, it was immediately beneath modern plough soil, the one exception being in area E, where a layer of dark brown sand (Context 27) was probably material from the mound itself re-deposited when the mound was destroyed. The presence of Context (10) within Test Pit 3 but not the other two suggests that the mound was destroyed by moving material southwards. The layer beneath Context (10) varies. Close to the mound the plough has cut into the yellow sandstone (Context 5) while further away it overlies Context (41) (equivalent to Context 13), a blotchy mixture of yellow brown and grey sand, which is probably original mound material which has been re-deposited when the mound was eroded or demolished.

Just inside the line of the kerb stones two interesting cut features were found: In Area B a small amount of cremated animal (sheep or goat), SF780, together with charcoal and a small amount of human cremated bone including SF657 and SF659, was found in a shallow depression in the bedrock, Context (39) (Fig. 2.23). These are the partial remains of a sub-adult; Contexts (47) and (48) in Area G (Fig. 2.24), refer to a feature cut into the sandstone that contained human cremated bone, probably a secondary burial of an older adult of indeterminate sex, Context (47) was disturbed material (Pl. 2.10).

Located outside the line of stones in Area SX was part of a smashed Collared Urn, the sherds being mainly from the rim and collar of pot QL7, within re-deposited mound material partially beneath a kerb stone moved by ploughing. This was associated with a spread of charcoal although no cremated bone was associated with it. Being as this was located well outside the area of the mound it is likely that

Excavations at King's Low and Queen's Low

Plate 2.9 Queen's Low: the kerb, looking west.

Plate 2.10 Queen's Low: cremation within a hole cut into the bedrock just inside the line of the kerb, Context (48), a) before excavation, b) after excavation.

Figure 2.29 Queen's Low: Context (18), white sand disturbed by ploughing in two directions, where the northern continuation of the kerb would have been.

the pot was smashed when the mound was destroyed and re-deposited in its place of discovery.

It is not known whether the kerb originally defined the whole mound as excavation of the northern and eastern parts of the mound failed to locate any evidence for it. There was, however, an indication of where the edge of the mound might have been by the presence of Context (18). This was found in areas D, DX, in the southern portion of NX, the north-west portion of C and the south-western corner of area M (Fig. 2.21). This consisted of fine light coloured sand and was found nowhere else in the excavation, it curved in the approximate line of the mound's edge and could represent evidence of weathering at the original edge of the mound (Fig. 2.29). Excavation beneath the stones of the kerb revealed smaller pieces of a similar sandstone, either immediately beneath or to one side supporting some of the stones. In at least one instance a kerb stone was supported by a second stone set on its outer side. These additional stones were probably used to level the kerb stones and also, in some cases, to support the kerb stones themselves.

Summary

An elevated outcrop of sandstone was chosen as the site for the mound, its shape being slightly altered, certainly to the south and west, to produce a vaguely circular raised area. In places stakes were inserted to help indicate the required shape of the circumference of the mound to be built. To the south and west a kerb was set into the modified edge of the outcrop (the kerb may have continued all the way around the mound but there is no good evidence for this). The top of the line of kerb stones wasn't exactly level, rising slightly to the west, and the stones of the kerb were positioned correctly by placing smaller pieces of stone beneath them. The kerb stones were then made secure by putting sand, or possibly turves around their outside, possibly producing a berm. A deposit of cremated animal bone was placed behind the kerb, probably at the time when the kerb was built. The central mound would then have been built over an assumed primary burial. Although there is no surviving evidence for this the re-deposited Collared Urn fragments and the faience bead which may have been burnt on a funerary pyre may belong to it. The hole for a probable secondary burial, a cremation, was cut into the mound sometime later. There was no evidence for any phasing or sequence of mound building as practically all the mound material within the line of the curb had been removed, much of it ploughed down to bedrock.

2.2.2 The kerbstones

Derek Outram

As described above, the burial mound was edged with kerbstones which only survive on the southern side, extending some six to seven metres around the circumference. The stones were originally placed upright and edge to edge, with some knocked outwards or displaced away from the mound by subsequent ploughing. Of the dozen or so stones recovered from the site, only three showed signs of possible human working, the locations of numbers 1 and 2 below are shown on Figure 2.23.

2 The excavations

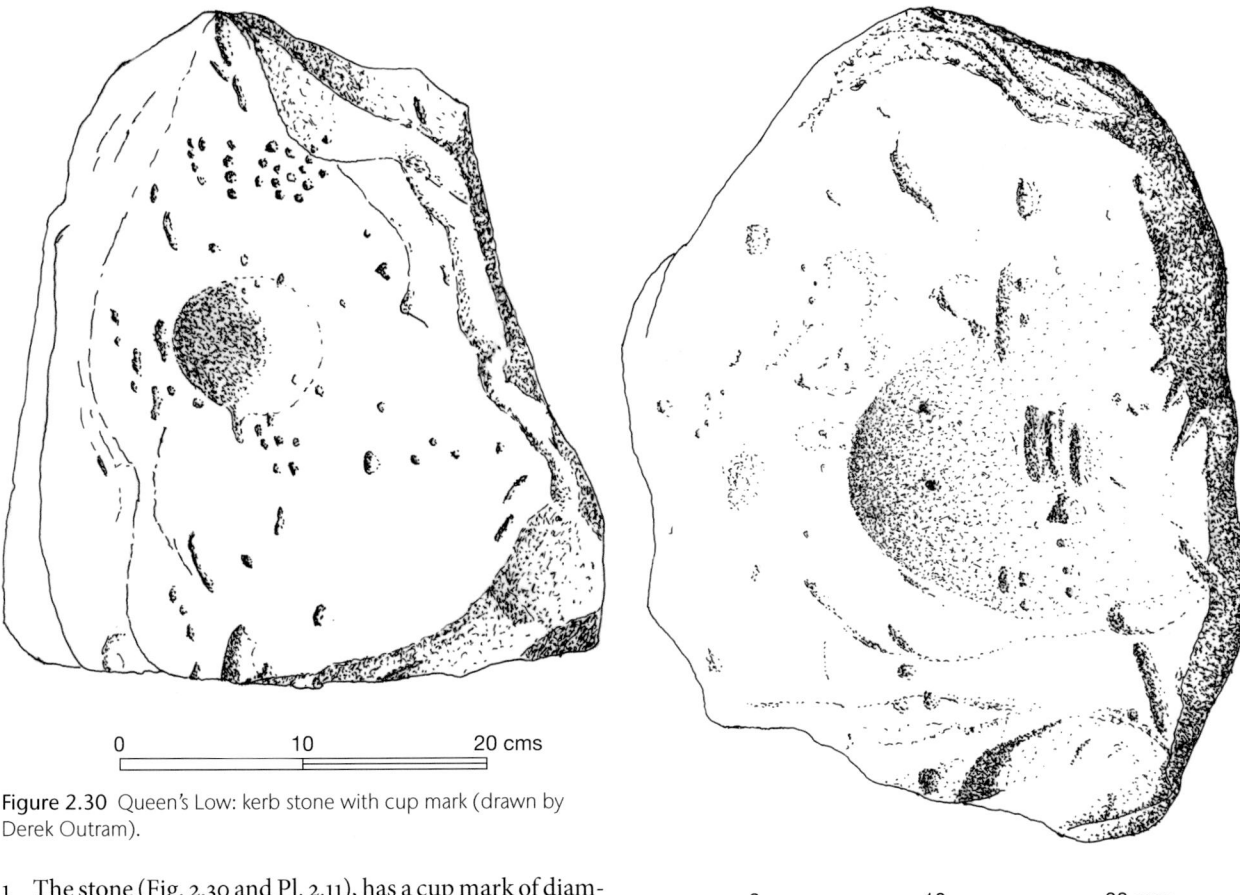

Figure 2.30 Queen's Low: kerb stone with cup mark (drawn by Derek Outram).

1. The stone (Fig. 2.30 and Pl. 2.11), has a cup mark of diameter 70 mm on a flat unworn surface with peck marks within the cup being clearly visible and appearing to be worn smooth on one side. Dr. Linda Hurcombe, University of Exeter, commented that the smoothing effect on just one side of a cup-mark had been noticed on other examples. The worked surface was face down when the stone was excavated, the upper surface being quite worn and rounded, the stone was two metres further out from the ring kerb. To one edge of the surface containing the cup mark, there is a slight depression of several peck marks.

   Cup marks at burial mounds in the region of Queen's Low are relatively rare. A single cup on a rock fragment

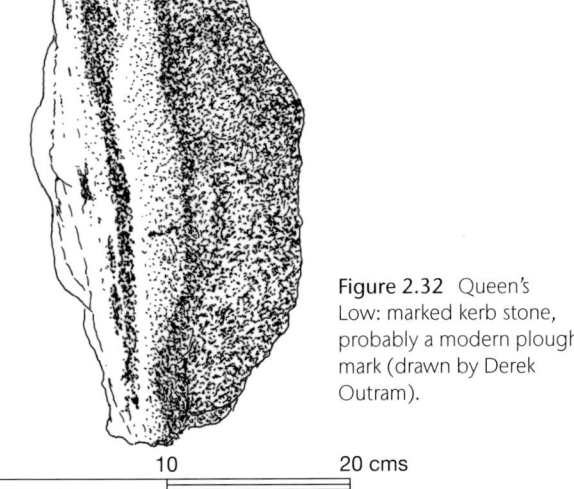

Figure 2.32 Queen's Low: marked kerb stone, probably a modern plough mark (drawn by Derek Outram).

Figure 2.31 Queen's Low: kerb stone, possible saddle quern (drawn by Derek Outram).

from a barrow at Brand, Staffordshire (Beckensall 1999) and again, a single cup at a barrow at Elkstone, Staffordshire (*ibid.*) are the only ones found *in situ*. A survey of finds in the middle and upper Trent basin (Vine 1982) lists cup marks on larger stones, mostly random and undated finds and three stones with multiple cup marks found in a ditch below and in collapsed stone walls of Ball Cross hillfort. At Fulforth Farm cist (Beckensall 1999) decorated stones mainly face the burials and the unworn peck marks indicate specific marking for the burials. At Queen's Low, the surface with the cup mark is un-eroded whilst the opposite surface is quite worn hence it is possible that the stone could have been placed in the kerb with the cup mark facing the mound and could have been knocked away from the kerb in ancient times or by more recent ploughing.

2. An abraided stone (Fig. 2.31 and Pl. 2.12), was found *in situ* in the kerb itself, the rubbed surface facing in towards the centre of the mound. The very smoothly worn bowl shape, between 15 cm and 20 cm in diameter, was very shallow, about 14 mm deep at the centre. There are several scars on this surface with the edges and the back of the stone well worn and rounded. This stone appears to have had a lot of use, possibly as a grinding stone or saddle quern. The deep scars in the middle of the depression may suggest that it was rendered useless before being placed in the kerb.

Excavations at King's Low and Queen's Low

Plate 2.11 Queen's Low: kerb stone with cup mark.

Plate 2.12 Queen's Low: kerb stone, possible saddle quern.

3 A groove lies along the edge of a stone and is Y shaped at one end (Fig. 2.32). It is 24 cm long and quite broad, about 6 mm, with surfaces which are smooth and rounded. The stone was found about one metre away from the mound, its rounded, worn surface uppermost, the other surface was less worn but had a lighter coloured chip on it. This may be due to prehistoric human action but is more likely to be a plough mark as the farmer is known to have ploughed this mound and hit stones.

3 People and the environment

3.1 An environmental history of the River Sow region, Stafford

Heather Sugden and Alan Outram

Introduction

The River Sow has a wide floodplain containing a considerable depth of organic deposits, both floodplain peat and alluvial silts. Such waterlogged acidic deposits preserve pollen well and may, therefore, contain a valuable environmental record. The suitability of the floodplain sediments for pollen coring was confirmed by archaeological test pits sunk for the purpose of an evaluation ahead of a planned road development (Klemperer and Barnett 1993). The river flows through a valley to the south-west of King's Low and Queen's Low barrows, around a kilometre away. Thus the floodplain deposits provide the best opportunity for studying the vegetational history associated with human activity in the area, especially during the period in which the barrows were in use. These floodplain deposits are also of interest in view of their proximity to a core previously analysed, from the King's Pool kettle hole deposits two kilometres to the north-west, nearer to the centre of Stafford (Bartley and Morgan 1990). This has provided the deepest continuous pollen profile in Britain and presents valuable comparative data.

Site location and geomorphological background

The pollen core extraction site lies on the River Sow floodplain, SJ 945 232, 200 m from the north bank of its tributary, Kingston Brook, and close to the Sow's confluence with the River Penk to the south. In view of the low lying topography of the site and its impeded drainage due to the proximity of the above-mentioned watercourses, current land use is restricted to rough grazing. Vegetation comprises mainly grasses and sedges, although occasional oak, alder and willow trees line the course of Kingston Brook which appears to have been diverted in the past to form a millpond. The exact core position was determined by finding the greatest depth of suitable sediments following a number of test cores across the site denoted in Figure 3.1. Sediments closest to Kingston Brook provided a truncated

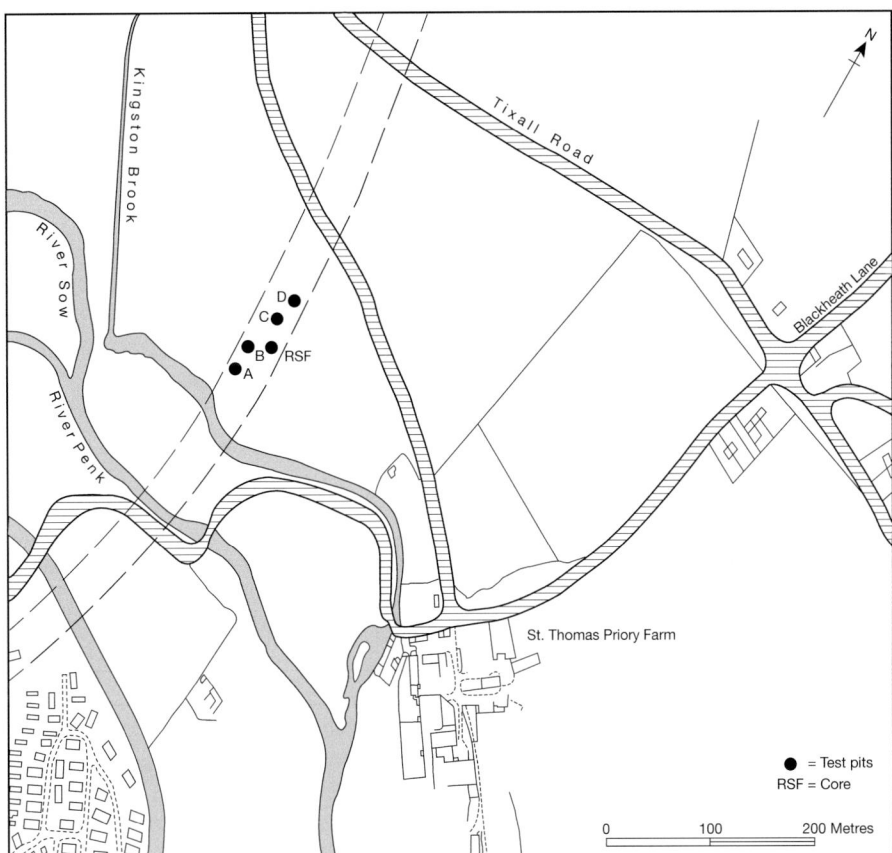

Figure 3.1 The locations of the pollen test pits and the pollen core on the River Sow floodplain (RSF), Stafford.

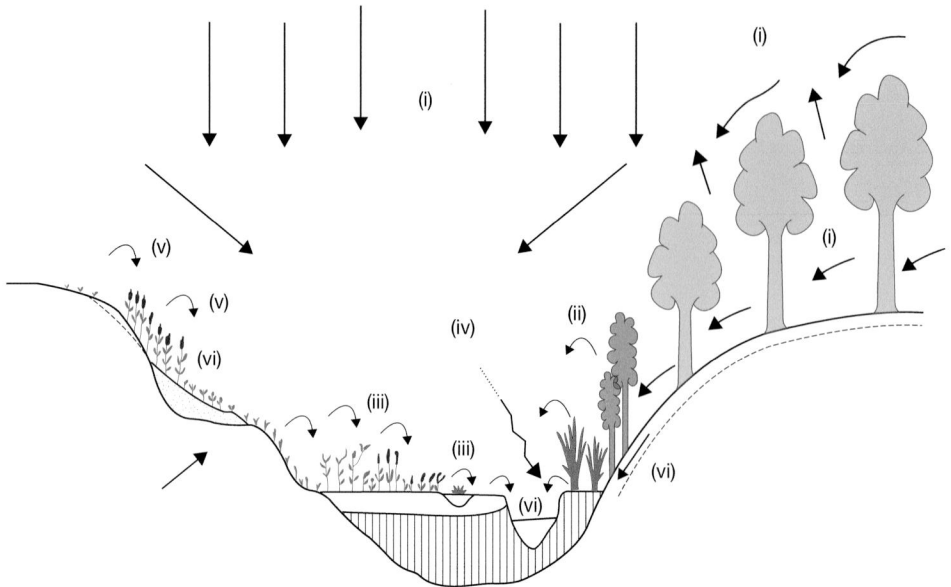

i. Airborne pollen (including rain, canopy and trunk space components)
ii. Pollen derived from fen carr on or adjacent to floodplains
iii. Local component (aquatic, wet meadow, tall herb communities)
iv. Fluvially transported, but contemporary pollen
v. Pastoral and arable environments-aerial transport
vi. Pollen derived from erosion of older alluvial sediments

Figure 3.2 The generalised influx of pollen to floodplain environments (based on Scaife and Burrin 1994).

and indistinct profile, whilst field drains and disturbance by recent manual excavation affected others.

Prior to extraction, 30 cm of topsoil and colluvial deposits (mainly heavy clay) were removed. Approximately 70 cm of organic alluvial muds were extracted using a wide bore (2") gouge, whilst a wide bore Russian corer was used for the underlying peaty deposits. The peat desisted at a depth of three metres and was found to overlay a series of laminated grey/blue silty clays containing layers of well preserved organic remains, resembling sedges and reeds, as well as the shells of molluscs. It was possible to remove superficial amounts of these using a small bore (1") gouge.

Methodology
Molluscs
Although only 0.25 litres of sediment containing molluscan remains was recovered, their abundance and good preservation indicated that a reliable environmental reconstruction could be made. The sample was initially disaggregated by soaking in warm water and flot was collected. This was followed by sieving through a 500 micron mesh and the residue was collected. Both flot and residue were sorted under a low power (×20) stereo microscope, 152 individuals were recovered and identified using the criteria of Macan (1977).

Pollen
The pollen core was sampled at intervals of 8 cm or 4 cm, depending on areas of interest, although this was reduced to 1 cm where lithological changes occurred. Processing involved standard treatment with HCl, KOH, Hydrofluoric acid and acetolysis mixture, and tablets containing known numbers of Lycopodium clavatum (stag's-horn clubmoss) spores were added to allow calculation of pollen concentrations (Moore *et al.* 1991).

Pollen was mounted on slides in silicon oil and identified using a high power binocular microscope (×400). Land pollen was counted to between 300–500 land pollen per level, in addition to aquatic taxa, spores and microscopic charcoal fragments. No quantification of area for charcoal was made. Criteria for pollen and spore identification follow Moore *et al.* (*ibid.*) and those for microscopic charcoal are cited in Patterson *et al.* (1987).

Pollen and charcoal percentages and concentrations were plotted using Tilia and Tiliagraph (Grimm 1991) and preliminary analysis highlighted areas of interest from which bulk samples were removed for radiocarbon dating. These are presented in Figures 3.4 and 3.5.

Loss on ignition
Loss on ignition values were determined using the differences in weight of dry and ignited samples. A quantity of sediment from each sampled level was dried overnight (at least 12 hours) at 105 °C and ignited for 5 hours at 550 °C (Bengtsson and Enell 1986).

Taphonomy and potential problems to interpretation
Prior to discussion of results, reference should be made to certain factors specific to floodplains which bring complications to interpretation. Flood events may complicate the pollen record by re-depositing pollen and charcoal from sources upstream. Berglund (1986) has used ratios of heavily degraded pollen to ascertain such occurrences, and whilst not quantified in this case, the level of pollen preservation was subjectively recorded at each level during identification. Similarly, changes in the sedimentation input

Table 3.1 The numbers of identifiable molluscs recovered, River Sow floodplain, Stafford.

Species	No. in assemblage	percentage of assemblage
Planorbis albus	65	42.76
Planorbis crista	25	16.45
Planorbis planorbis	32	21.05
Zonitoides nitidus	20	13.16
Succinea sp. cf. pfeifferi	4	2.63
Valvata piscinalis	6	3.95

Table 3.2 The lithology of pollen core sediments.

Depth (cm)	Description
0–44.5	orange/brown alluvial silts
44.5–73.0	dark brown peaty silts
73.0–117.0	orange/brown silty peat
117.0–121.0	orange/grey clay
121.0–159.0	dark brown silty peat
159.0–171.0	dark brown clayey peat
171.0–258.0	black wood peat
258.0–300.0	dark brown clayey peat
300.0–317.0	grey/blue silty clay

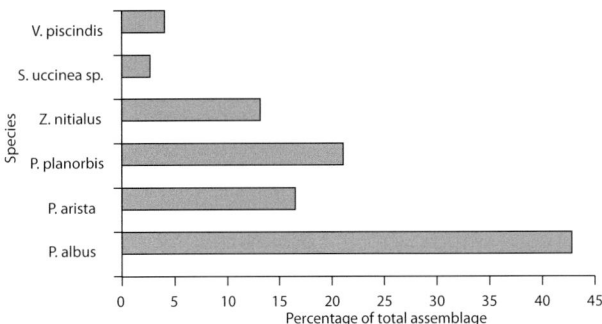

Figure 3.3 The relative percentages of identifiable molluscan species.

to a floodplain catchment may be triggered by climate or land use change. This is particularly problematic as the erosional as well as depositional nature of river systems may cause hiatuses within the pollen profile (Brown 1982; 1988). Whilst sediment deposition may be attributed to clearance by human activity (Robinson and Lambrick 1984), erosional episodes are far more difficult to interpret with certainty (Scaife and Burrin 1992). Indeed, hiatuses are not necessarily obvious within the pollen record, although a combination of anomolous fluxes in the pollen spectra alongside lithological change may indicate such occurrences.

One final consideration regarding floodplain sediments for pollen analysis is the idiosyncratic nature of pollen taphonomy. Compared to upland regions, low-lying floodplains with higher topography at their perimeters tend to accumulate greater proportions of local pollen as well as large amounts of secondary deposits from in-wash and colluviation. This is demonstrated in Figure 3.2 and it is therefore likely that much of the pollen under discussion is of local origin.

Description of Data
The accumulated environmental data is as follows:

Molluscs
The 152 individuals identified were apportionable to six species and these are listed in Table 3.1, together with their relative proportions. Figure 3.3 shows the relative percentages of each species present.

Pollen
Details of the lithology accompanying the pollen profile are provided in Table 3.2, whilst Figures 3.4 and 3.5 respectively show the relative percentages and concentrations of pollen recorded, the following gives a brief description of the characteristics of each zone identified.

RSF1 (264–300 cm) *Betula* (birch), *Pinus* (pine), Poaceae (grasses) are the main taxa, although Cyperaceae (sedges) and some herbs are also present. Loss on ignition values rise from 25% to 85% through the zone.

RSF2 (176–264 cm) *Pinus* (pine), *Corylus* (hazel), *Quercus* (oak), Poaceae (grasses). Expansion of trees dominated by *Pinus*, some of which is likely to be local in view of accompanying macro-fossils. A variety of herbs is introduced and charcoal counts rise sharply to high levels.

RSF3 (114–176 cm) *Alnus* (alder), *Tilia* (lime), Poaceae (grasses). *Alnus* and *Tilia* are established, whilst *Pinus* is substantially reduced. Quantities of *Quercus* pollen persist, as do small amounts of herbs. Charcoal levels are substantially reduced.

RSF4 (66–114 cm) *Alnus* (alder), *Tilia* (lime), Poaceae (grasses), Lactuceae. Reductions in *Alnus* and *Tilia* are accompanied by sudden accumulations of Lactuceae pollen, although the former are re-established in large quantities in the latter part of the zone. Indicators of disturbance are introduced, including Plantago species (plantains) and Chenopodiaceae (goose-foot family). Fluctuations in *Tilia*, *Corylus* and Poaceae are accompanied by similar in the charcoal curve. Loss on ignition values show decreases.

RSF5a and 5b (0–66 cm) *Alnus* (alder), Poaceae (grasses), *Calluna* (heather), Lactuceae, *Plantago* (plantain). This zone shows reductions in tree pollen and the establishment of a series of taxa indicative of clearance. In addition to those above, *Cirsium* (thistles), Chenopodiaceae (goose-foot family) and *Rumex* sp. (dock) occur, and Cannabis type and Cerealia (cereals) type pollen indicate agriculture is locally present. Loss on ignition values steadily decline.

Interpretation
Molluscs
The molluscs retrieved from sediment at a depth of 300–317 cm all currently inhabit freshwater environments in Britain and Europe. *Planorbus albus*, which comprises 43% of the assemblage, is 'common amongst weeds and on the stems of plants in all fresh waters' (Ellis 1969) whilst *Planorbis crista* and *Planorbis planorbis* occupy similar habitats where hydrophytic vegetation is abundant (*ibid.*).

The other species present, although fewer in number, present a similar environmental picture. *Zonitoides*

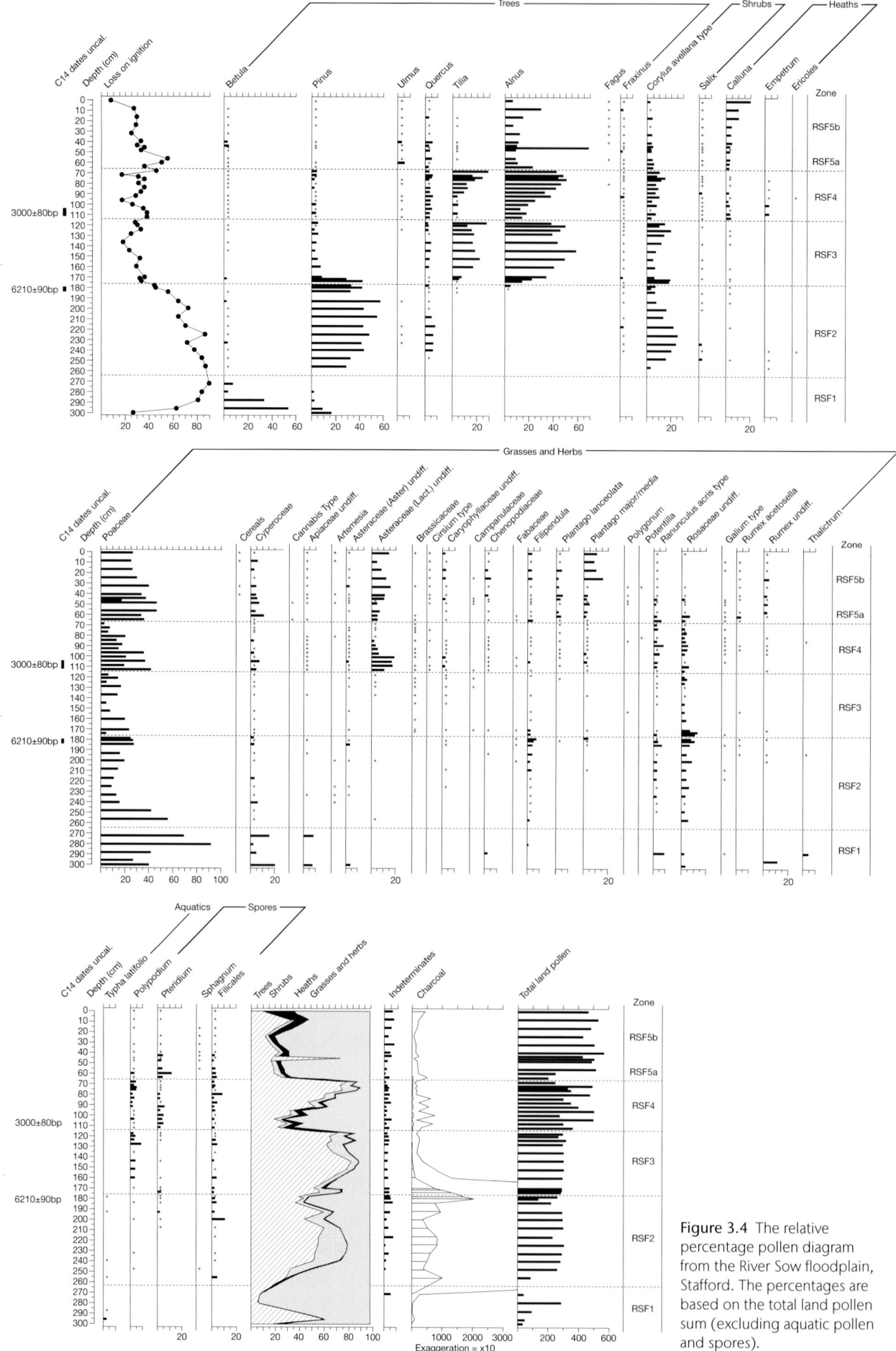

Figure 3.4 The relative percentage pollen diagram from the River Sow floodplain, Stafford. The percentages are based on the total land pollen sum (excluding aquatic pollen and spores).

3 People and the environment

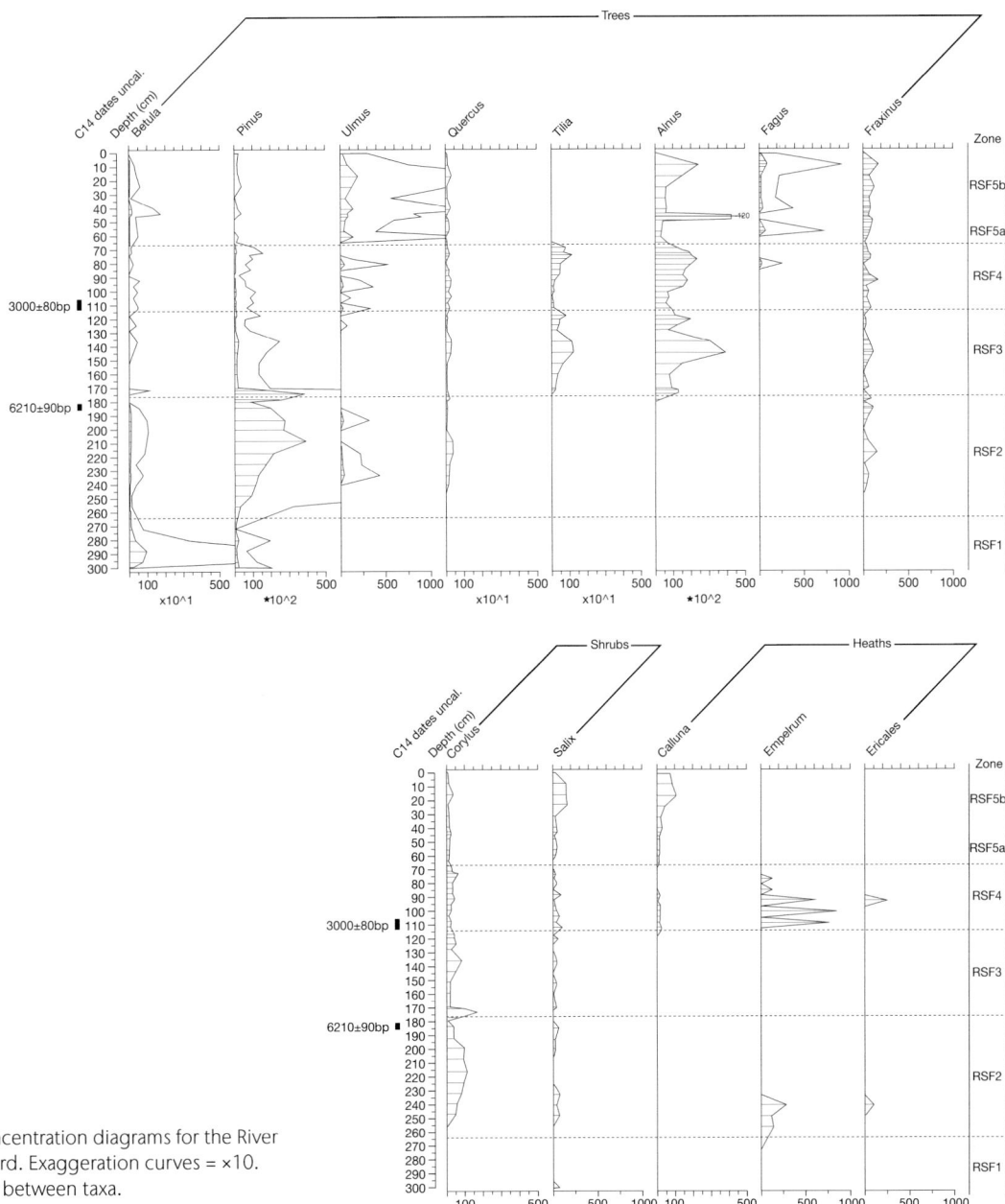

Figure 3.5 Pollen concentration diagrams for the River Sow floodplain, Stafford. Exaggeration curves = ×10. X axis scale may vary between taxa.

nitidus and the *Succinea* sp. inhabit marshy environments although they are also known to occupy riverbanks (Ellis 1969). *Valvata piscinalis* is also characteristic of weed rich environments although it is generally thought to occupy deeper and faster flowing waters than the other components of this assemblage (Boycott 1936).

The ecology of *Valvata piscinalis* raises the possibility that the assemblage is not *in situ* and the abraded nature of the shells recovered does not make this improbable. A coincident hypothesis is that the low resolution of the sampling, which crosses laminations, is unable to detect sudden environmental changes from deep channels to shallow water, typical of late-glacial/early Holocene environments from which these sediments are likely to date. Such dynamics reinforce the supposition that the sediments have been reworked, although there is little doubt that the assemblage is nevertheless of reasonably local origin in view of its components.

Unfortunately there is little information regarding climate which can be gained from this particular assemblage, although the sediment composition and vegetation suggests a colder climate and therefore a late-glacial/early Holocene date. Whilst *Succinea* sp. and *Valvata piscinalis* are currently found in Siberia and Tibet they are also distributed throughout Europe. Conversely, *Zonitoides nitidus* is rare in northern Britain, and all other taxa present are generally distributed throughout Europe, having no particular restrictions with respect to climate (Ellis 1969). However, the fact that some of these species currently occur in cold climates outside Britain is consistent with the assemblage being of late-glacial/early Holocene origin when considered with the above evidence.

Pollen

Zone RSF1 (264–300 cm)

The lithology which accompanies RSF1 consists of a highly compacted layer of dark brown organic clayey silt, and

Excavations at King's Low and Queen's Low

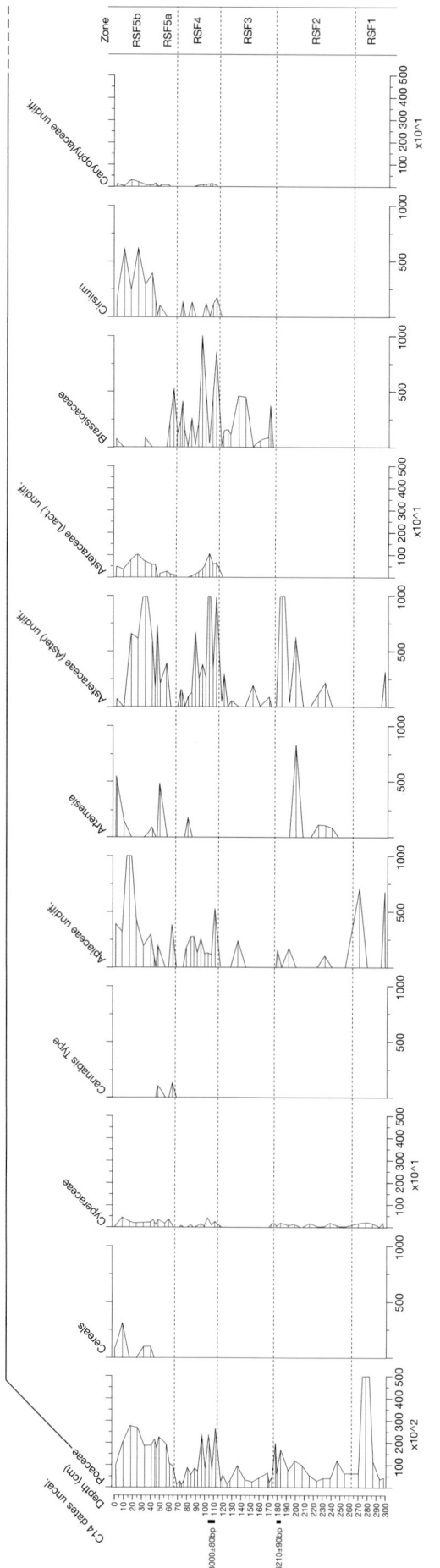
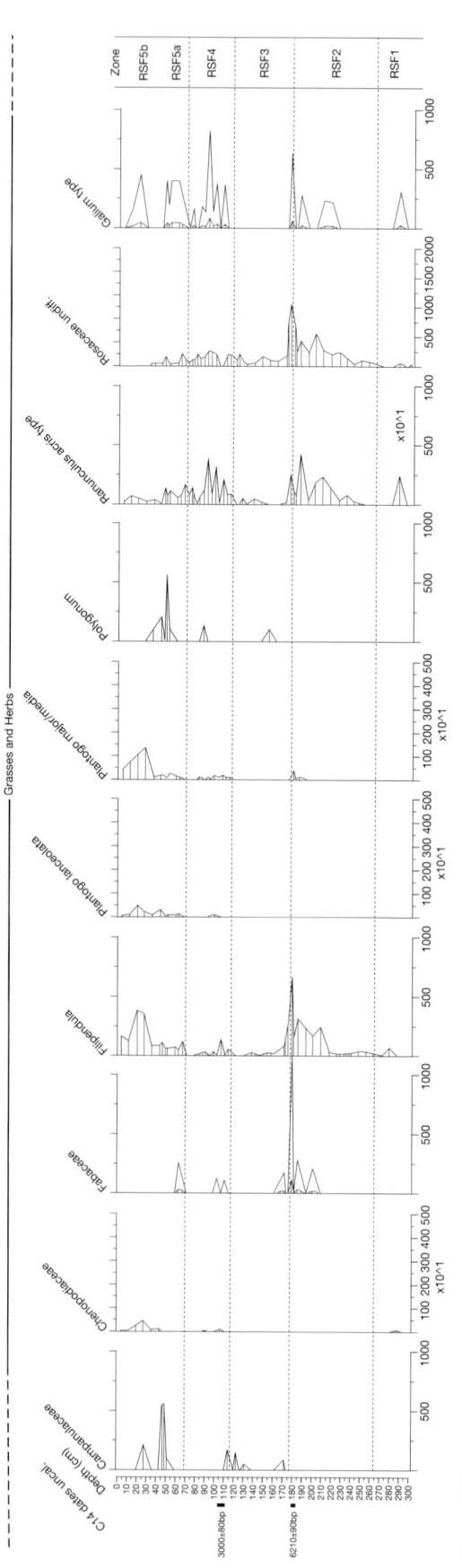

Figure 3.5 cont.

3 People and the environment

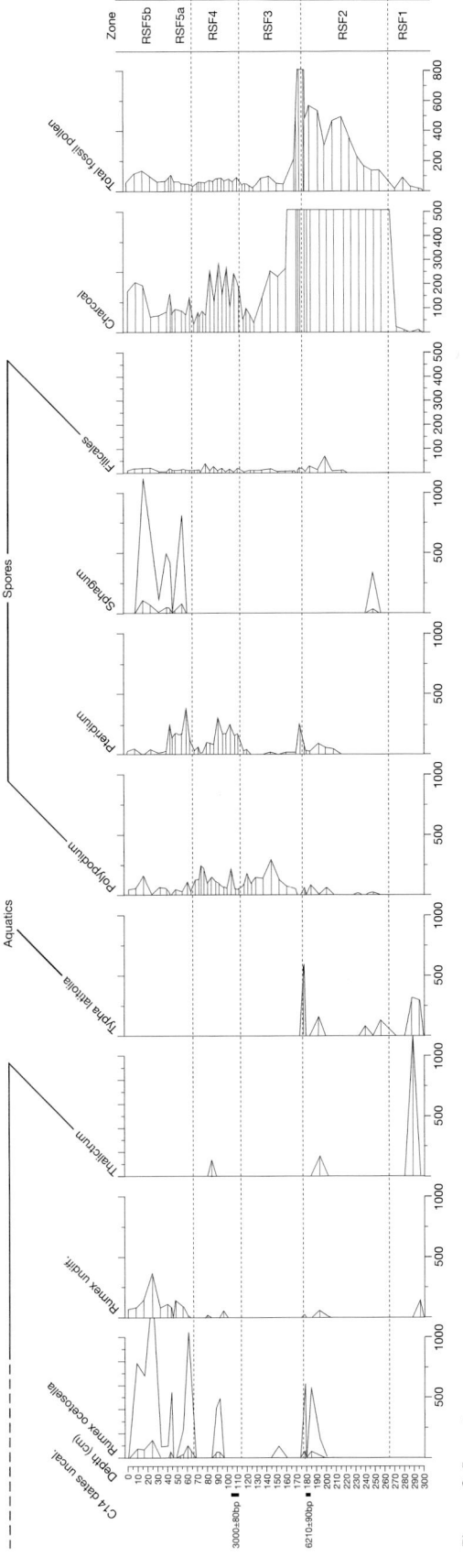

Figure 3.5 cont.

whilst loss-on-ignition tests show the organic content is high, pollen concentrations are low overall. It is possible that rapid sediment accumulation is responsible for this, as pollen preservation is good; grains showing little sign of deterioration. Low pollen concentrations have thus had implications for counting and the assemblage within this zone should be considered as incomplete, for only grains occurring within 100 Lycopodium (club-moss) spores were counted.

RSF1 appears to coincide with zone ST2 of the King's Pool diagram (Bartley and Morgan 1990) which also shows low pollen concentrations at this level. However, they suggest that its rapid sedimentation rates are not responsible for low pollen concentrations, rather the sparse vegetation of early Holocene environments.

Zone RSF2 (176–264 cm)
It is in zone RSF2 that pollen concentrations become of value to interpretation, displaying a greater diversity of taxa. Although grasses are dominant in the lower part of the zone, the predominant taxon is undoubtedly *Pinus* sp. (pine). The pollen of *Pinus* is produced in large amounts and widely dispersed due to the characteristic morphology of its grains (Bennett 1984). However, it may be assumed here that *Pinus* was locally present in view of its pollen values reaching 30–60%. Macrofossils within the peat have also been identified as *Pinus* (Wigfield *pers. comm.*), and these are unlikely to be re-deposited material in view of their abundance and the presence of roots as well as twigs.

Discussing the post-glacial history of *Pinus sylvestris* (Scots pine), Bennett (1984) cites that this was the dominant tree species within the British Isles from 9000–7500 years BP and is particularly significant in valley peats receiving pollen from lowland locations. However, grasses are also present at the base of RSF2 in substantial amounts. Also, notable values of *Salix* (willow), *Filipendula* (meadowsweet) and *Filicales* (ferns) occur, indicating wet conditions, as do other herbs, and the aquatic *Typha latifolia* (Bulrush) is present. This suggests that *Pinus* was dominant on higher, drier ground with probably fewer trees on the floodplain itself, where a wet heathy environment existed.

As the above mentioned taxa decline or become absent, there are increases in *Quercus* (oak), *Corylus* (hazel) and *Fraxinus* (ash). Both *Corylus* and *Fraxinus* are noted as light-demanding pioneer species (Godwin 1975) and *Quercus* is also considered to be an early to mid-successional species unable to tolerate high degrees of shading (Abrams 1992). Although it may be argued that climatic warming may have allowed the expansion of *Quercus* and *Corylus* this will occur only if suitable ecological niches are available for exploitation, in this case unshaded clearing. Thus, the proportional increases of these taxa attest to the infilling of clearances, resulting in the eventual closing of the forest canopy. Abrams (1992) notes that in New Hampshire, USA, 'a change from pine to oak domination (approximately 9000 years BP) coincided with increased charcoal abundance'. It is thus worthy of note that during Zone RSF1 concentrations of microscopic charcoal are extremely high, and indeed the peat itself during this phase is black. Natural fire is not unusual in pine dominated forest and is noted as an important ecological component by Agren and Zackrisson (1990) and Engelmark *et al.* (1994) promoting the regeneration of stands as seedlings and saplings. Although it may be argued that following the invasion of clearings by arboreal species other than *Pinus* subsequent forest fires may destroy these, Lorimer (1985) finds that fire may favour oaks. Fire creates suitable seedbeds, and the trees are resistant to decay after scarring. *Corylus* is also renowned for its tolerance of fire, which aids its production of new shoots (Simmons *et al.* 1981), hence once established it seems unlikely that recurrent forest fires would be significantly detrimental to the increasing diversity of species colonizing the pine forest.

The fact that *Pinus* pollen values show no distinct fluctuations in zone RSF2 may be a function of its extensive pollen distribution, although it is also possible that the sampling resolution of the analysis is too low to provide significant results. Moore (1979) confirms this possibility in research that demonstrates that fires occurring once every eighty years are unlikely to be reflected in pollen and charcoal analyses. The transition to Zone RSF2 shows a decline in arboreal pollen although *Pinus* has only limited fluctuation. This decline is yet accompanied by persistent high levels of microscopic charcoal, whilst *Salix* reappears and there is an expansion in *Filipendula* pollen. Aquatics are also present, which reinforces the overall scheme for an increase in wetness at the site during this period. This may have been due to the climatic shift from a relatively dry, continental climate to a warmer and wetter oceanic climate (the Boreal-Atlantic transition), (Godwin 1975; Pennington 1969; Simmons *et al.* 1981). The introduction of *Tilia* (lime) and *Alnus* (alder) to the pollen spectra in the upper part of RSF2 is conversant with this and the radio-carbon age of 6210 ± 90 BP (uncal), mid 6th millenium BC (cal).

It is interesting to note that charcoal levels persist in high concentrations during this transition (from zone RSF2–RSF3). It is unlikely that natural forest fires would persist to such a degree in a climate of increasing wetness and indeed Smith (1970), Simmons *et al.* (1981) and Edwards (1990) argue that at least some occurrences of microscopic charcoal have resulted from the activity of Mesolithic/Early Neolithic people. Smith (1970) also suggests that such activity assisted in opening up the existing forest cover, thus creating suitable environments for the expansion of *Alnus*. It is therefore a possibility that humans were at least responsible for some production of microscopic charcoal in the Stafford region and Bartley and Morgan (1990) have postulated similar circumstances for the King's Pool diagram.

During the transitional phase there is a notable increase in the diversity of pollen types, particularly herbs, *Galium* type (herbaceous plants), Apiaceae (carrot family), Asteraceae (aster type), Ranunculaceae (buttercup family), Fabaceae (pea family), *Rumex* sp. (sorrel) and *Plantago media/major* (plantains) all being present. Also noted is a single occurrence of *Plantago lanceolata* (ribwort plantain). Smith (cited in Buckland and Edwards 1984) has observed similar occurrences from which he has suggested that pre-Neolithic clearance by humans may be a causative factor, although trampling by animals can also create suitable environments for the growth of *Plantago lanceolata*. Indeed, the overall local herb pollen assemblage is here reminiscent of wet meadows and pasture as defined by Behre (1981). Deforestation within the catchment from forest fires may therefore have increased runoff and associated nutrient supply to the floodplain (Moore 1979) encouraging the growth of a variety of grasses and herbs. Indeed, the potential of fire may have been utilized by humans in order to create areas of open grazing (Mellars 1976).

Zone RSF3 (114–176 cm)
The transition from Zone RSF2 to RSF3 features a wet meadow/pasture assemblage alongside mixed woodland taxa of pine with oak, hazel and ash, and it is noted that during this transition, two key components of Zone RSF3, *Alnus* and *Tilia*, are introduced (although in small amounts) as previously stated. Thus the earlier clearance of *Pinus*, climatic or otherwise, may have allowed for their introduction to the area, particularly as *Alnus glutenosa* (alder) is a pioneer (McVean 1956a and b) and a light demanding species (Chambers and Price 1985).

However, in view of the nature of climatic change mentioned previously, and the sudden increases in *Tilia*, *Alnus* and *Corylus* which coincide with dramatic reductions in Poaceae pollen values, consideration must be given here to the possibility of a hiatus in the palaeo-environmental record, (Brown 1982; 1988). It is noted that a stratigraphic change occurs at 179 cm from a dark brown, clayey peat to a dark brown, fibrous silty peat. However, high resolution sampling across this stratigraphic boundary indicates that a continuous pollen sequence occurs and taxa such as *Filipendula* (meadowsweet family), Ranunculaceae and Rosaceae (rose family) show reasonably fluent curves through this horizon. Indeed, loss on ignition values, determined from contiguous samples through this change in lithology show a stable profile which does not suggest any occurrence of minerogenic inwash. Hence, the change in lithology from black wood peat to a dark brown, fibrous peat is probably a reflection of changing climate and thus changing sediment accumulation rates, the clayey horizon perhaps reflecting the compaction and/or mixing of sediments.

The ecology of *Alnus* is such that it thrives in wet, boggy conditions whilst water is the most effective dispersal mechanism for its fruits (McVean 1956a), hence the sudden rise described above is plausible. Godwin (1975) also notes that *Alnus* flowers at a very early age and 'has an extremely high pollen productivity' so that it tends to be 'over-represented by pollen analysis'.

The relatively sudden increase in *Tilia* pollen is rather more difficult to explain as *Tilia* is an infrequent pollen producer although its pollen does preserve well (Brown 1982; Greig 1982; Kelly and Osborne 1963; Moore *et al.* 1991). However, it may be argued that each of these factors compensates for the other and the substantial presence of relatively fragile pollen types (such as *Quercus*) alongside *Tilia* indicate a low preservation bias (Greig 1982). *Tilia* is not an inhabitant of wet, boggy areas, (Clapham *et al.* 1987), however, it is often associated with *Alnus* and is characteristic of floodplain/fen edge vegetation, particularly of drier slopes and terraces (Godwin 1975; Greig 1982). Thus, with a suitable environment and climate, *Tilia* may reproduce quickly, for although it is insect pollinated (Godwin 1975), it may also reproduce vegetatively (Cliff *pers. comm.*).

With the establishment of *Alnus* and *Tilia* over *Pinus* at the transition to Zone RSF3 the pollen record itself remains relatively stable within this zone, and this is matched by little change in loss on ignition values reflecting a contiguous accumulation of sediment. *Pinus* values fall steadily as *Alnus* rises to become the dominant floodplain taxon, whilst the *Salix* representation becomes continuous. *Tilia* expands steadily with *Quercus* and *Corylus*, and the Rosaceae also show relative stability, whilst *Fraxinus* is better established in this zone. *Polypodium* shows higher frequencies and was probably epiphytic of the woodland taxa present. Poaceae (grass) pollen declines a little as *Tilia* and the other woodland species expand, although it does not fall below 20% TLP, and there are sporadic occurrences of herbs such as Caryophyllaceae (chickweeds), Filipendula (associated with *Alnus*) and Ranunculaceae. Thus zone RSF3 demonstrates the consolidation of *Alnus/Salix* on the floodplain mire and the establishment of mixed woodland on the higher ground of the floodplain edge where *Tilia* and *Quercus* are the dominant taxa and *Corylus*, *Fraxinus* and the Rosaceae form the understory. In view of the herbal components of the pollen diagram, and the persistence of the Poaceae, it seems that certain areas remained open. These are likely to have been local in view of the taxa involved and a wet meadow probably existed on the floodplain itself, interspersing the *Alnus* stands.

Zone RSF4 (66–114 cm)
The transition to zone RSF4 is again marked by a change in the recorded lithology with a shallow clayey horizon marking the boundary. However, loss on ignition values remain stable and indeed show a steady but slow increase in the organic content of the peat which coincides with sharp decreases in arboreal pollen types, as Poaceae, Cyperaceae (sedges), Ericaceae (heaths) and some herbs show dramatic increases in pollen concentrations. The possibility of a hiatus remains, although it is perhaps more likely that, notwithstanding low sampling resolution and possibly inadequate total land pollen counts, other factors may have produced this pattern. Certainly organic content may increase from the inwash of material arising from deforestation within the catchment, thus some pollen must result from this. It is noted that within this phase, herbs not previously present are introduced, some of which are noted to be significant as species of disturbed habitats and/or weeds of arable ground. The Asteraceae (Asteroideae type) show a substantial increase to levels of 15–20% TLP, to being hardly present at the lower zone boundary, and the aryophyllaceae (carnation family) show consolidation at the middle of this zone. *Cirsium* (thistle) is introduced within RSF4 and there are occurrences of *Plantago lanceolata* and *Plantago media/major* type. The latter are significant, particularly *Plantago lanceolata*, as these are generally accepted as indicators of human activity involving woodland clearance and pastoralism/agriculture (Behre 1981; Buckland and Edwards 1984). Similarly, it is in this zone

that *Pteridium* (bracken) spores become positively established, *Pteridium* being an inhabitant of woodland clearings and open disturbed habitats (Clapham *et al.* 1987; Godwin 1975).

It may also be noted that quantities of microscopic charcoal increase during zone RSF4, and these show intermittent peaks. Whilst the King's Pool diagram suggests a single sustained event (Bartley and Morgan 1990), the fluctuating charcoal curve from the River Sow floodplain more likely represents a series of small clearances. Although *Tilia*, *Alnus* and *Corylus* show severe initial declines, their overall curves in this zone resemble a series of peaks and troughs, and the Poaceae and Cyperaceae mirror this. Whilst this pattern may initially be considered a function of relative percentage statistics, it also occurs in the concentration data, most notably for Poaceae and charcoal. In addition, *Quercus*, *Fraxinus* and *Salix* show little change in both relative percentage and concentration terms, and of the other taxa with significant values, Lactuca type and *Pteridium* have similarly undisturbed curves. Thus, the stability of some pollen types over others, in conjunction with the concentration data, signifies that the fluctuations recorded are unlikely to be an artefact of the relative percentage diagram.

A radiocarbon age of 3000±80 BP (uncal), 1430–1010 BC (cal) is ascribed to the commencement of the phase of clearances, which suggests Middle to Late Bronze Age origins. An expansion of the significance of these clearances within a local and regional context is given below.

It is interesting that *Quercus* values remain constant throughout this phase of clearances. A possible explanation is the resistance of *Quercus* to fire as mentioned for Zone RSF1. Alternatively, with the local reduction in the *Tilia* dominated woodland, *Quercus* pollen, which travels further than *Tilia* pollen may have originated from wider ranging sources.

Zone RSF5a (45–66 cm)
The base of the zone is marked by some peculiarities in the pollen curves, especially notable for *Tilia* where pollen reaches 25% TLP and is then depleted to virtual absence. This decline is abrupt, regardless of sampling resolution, and it is likely that an erosional episode has occurred and that part of the pollen profile is absent. Whether or not human activity was at least partially responsible for this is not clear as charcoal levels show no substantial or sustained increase at this point.

The zone itself, in addition to the virtual absence of *Tilia*, and greatly reduced proportions of *Alnus*, is characterized by a contraction of the other arboreal taxa and an expansion in Poaceae and Cyperaceae. The ruderal/arable indicators mentioned previously also reappear or persist in greater percentages, particularly the Lactuceae, *Plantago lanceolata* and *Plantago media/major* and *Rumex* sp. The appearance of *Cannabis* type pollen in this zone is probably indicative of an Anglo-Saxon date (Bartley and Morgan 1990). In view of the likely depositional hiatus at the base of the zone, the extent to which the landscape was cleared during the preceeding Iron Age/Romano-British period cannot be determined, the pollen record being absent.

Turner (1962) notes that a widespread *Tilia* decline occurred during the Early Iron Age and that whilst this may have been partially influenced by climatic deterioration, some enhancement was due to anthropogenic pressures in view of associations with ruderal indicators. Roman activity in the Stafford area was probably considerable in view of the settlements of Penkridge and Wall, hence it is likely that Anglo-Saxon settlers found an already cleared landscape (Limbrey 1987).

Sub-zone RSF5b (0–45 cm)
The base of sub-zone 5a is denoted by a huge spike in the *Alnus* pollen curve when preceding and succeeding values are relatively low, and a fall in loss on ignition values of 20%. It was also noted during identification and recording that many of the grains at this level were severely degraded. It is therefore again probable that a hiatus occurs at this level, and that flooding caused the inwash of large amounts of water-borne pollen.

The pollen record of sub-zone 5a may be of relatively modern origins. *Alnus* persists, probably as part of the river edge flora, whilst other arboreal pollen are extremely scarce. The Poaceae form a large proportion of the vegetation recorded and grasses and herbs are dominant in the profile. Cereals are also noted within this zone, indicating the occurrence of agriculture in proximity to the site. Cereal is probably absent in the lower profile not due to the absence of agriculture in the region, but to the unsuitability of the floodplain environment for the growing of cereals, the low production and short travelling distance of cereal pollen, and the shielding of the pollen core site by other vegetation. Overall, the zone resembles open conditions where agriculture is local and the arboreal landscape has been cleared to virtual absence.

Summary
The River Sow floodplain molluscs and pollen diagram may be summarised thus:

A slow flowing fluvial environment depositing fine sediments and supporting hygrophytic reeds and sedges existed in the late-glacial/early Holocene. A relatively sparse landscape in terms of vegetation existed locally, including birch, grasses and herbs, characteristic of the early Holocene. Peat began to form in situ in parts of the floodplain, and subsequent drying allowed the colonization of these by pine, particularly at the floodplain edges and on higher ground. Pine persisted as the dominant taxon throughout Zone RSF2, although fires, some possibly created by humans, allowed the expansion of oak and hazel within this woodland. Locally, areas of wet heath and reeds were colonized by alder circa 6000 BP and climatic warming and increased wetness reduced local pine populations and promoted the growth of lime on the floodplain margins. A series of small scale, temporary clearances occurred from circa 3000 BP onwards in the Mid–Late Bronze Age and thereafter the local woodland re-colonized. Further clearance may have occurred in the Iron Age and Romano-British period for which there is evidence from the nearby King's Pool pollen core (Bartley and Morgan 1990). However, this is not readily substantiated in the River Sow pollen record. There is a strong possibility that a hiatus covering this period occurs in the pollen profile, due to a change in lithology to clay, and a sharp decrease in arboreal pollen. From the early medieval period (denoted by the presence of *Cannabis* type pollen in sub-zone 5a) clearance is extensive, and evidence of cereal cultivation arises. Such clearance, as expected, continues into the present.

Discussion

The focus of this investigation is to assess the extent of human impact on vegetation within the region, particularly that which is contemporaneous to the King's Low and Queen's Low sites. There is tentative evidence in the River Sow and King's Pool diagrams that initial human interference occurs in the Mesolithic, as mentioned previously. However, the first substantial clearance shows in the King's Pool analysis as reductions in arboreal pollen types and increases in anthropogenic indicators dating from 4170 BP (uncal.) onwards. Pollen has also been extracted from the ground surface immediately under the King's Low barrow from which 'considerable human induced disturbance must be inferred (Chambers and Wilshaw Ch. 3.2). However, the pollen profile from the River Sow floodplain shows nothing so significant as to be interpreted as human disturbance of the landscape until zone RSF4, dated to 3000 BP (uncal.).

The later timing of the clearance in the River Sow diagram does not however contradict the above. The contrast between the three sites in the timing and extent of human impacts is explained by Limbrey's (1983) hypothesis that pollen relating to woodland clearances is often masked by surrounding forest, particularly at the floodplain edge. Hence clearance patterns may be indistinct or absent in pollen diagrams from floodplains as these areas tend to be latterly and inconsistently exploited.

Thus the accumulated evidence seems to suggest that human clearance of the landscape occurred in the region on drier ground from the Early Bronze Age. This clearance continued in a sporadic and intermittent fashion through to the Later Bronze Age. At this time, the pollen evidence from the floodplain suggests that human use of the environment temporarily encroached onto the wetter ground, perhaps indicating the expansion of human activity in the area leading to the use of more marginal land.

Acknowledgements

The authors wish to thank Winston Hollins, Derek Outram, Leslie Sugden and Ted Royle MBE for assistance in the field. Thanks are also due to landowners Mr and Mrs Madders for granting access to the site and to Bill Klemperer and Rob Barnett for providing the initial information. We are also indebted to Pat Wagner and Rob Craigie at the University of Sheffield for their technical support, and to Stoke-on-Trent Museum Archaeological Society for providing funding for the radiocarbon dates. Professor Kevin Edwards provided a useful commentary on the text.

Table 3.3 Pollen taxa in a sample from King's Low, Context (51) (as percentage of total land pollen sum of 250 grains).

Taxon	%
Betula (birch)	1.6
Ulmus (elm)	0.4
Quercus (oak)	2.0
Alnus (alder)	7.2
Tilia (lime)	1.2
Corylus (hazel)	19.9
AP: arboreal pollen	**32.3**
Gramineae (grasses)	40.2
Plantago lanceolata (ribwort plantain)	25.1
Rumex (sorrel)	1.2
Chenopodiaceae (goosefoot)	0.4
Caryophyllaceae (chickweed)	0.4
Succisa (devil's bit scabious)	0.4
NAP: non-arboreal pollen	**67.7**
Typha/Sparganium (reedmace/bur-reed)	2.4
Pteridium (bracken)	0.2
Polypodium (polypody)	2.8
Filicales (ferns)	1.0

3.2 The King's Low pollen
Frank Chambers and Ian Wilshaw

Methods

Samples were prepared after Barber (1976), mounted in silicone fluid and examined for their pollen content. The sample with the best preserved and least sparse pollen was counted at a magnification of ×400, results are shown in Table 3.3. Spores and possible aquatic types were excluded from the pollen sum.

Results

Pollen was very sparse in the prepared samples, and rather eroded but in a recognisable condition. In total 14 samples were tested (7 from Context (32), 2 from Context (42), 3 from Context (51) and 1 each from Contexts (17) and (24)). Only one sample from Context (51) had sufficient pollen for a count to be attempted. Less resistant taxa (e.g. *Quercus* – oak) are probably under-represented in the count (Havinga 1974; Dimbleby 1985). The count was dominated by *Gramineae* (grasses) pollen (40%) with abundant *Plantago lanceolata* (ribwort plantain) (25%) and significant *Corylus* (hazel) representation.

Discussion

The AP/NAP ratios of <1:2 indicate a substantially deforested landscape. The major forest tree taxa are sparsely represented, although the low *Quercus* (oak) representation may partly be a reflection of differential decay. Of arboreal taxa, *Corylus* (hazel) and *Alnus* (alder) have the highest representations, and may reflect vestigial scrub around the site. Spores of *Polypodium* (polypody) (fern), which can be epiphytic on trees, might be taken to imply that trees were growing near the site, but *Polypodium* spores are notoriously resistant to decay, and their relative abundance may merely reflect differential preservation.

One of the most significant aspects of the pollen spectrum is the complete absence of *Ericaceae* (heath) pollen.

In view of the highly podsolised soils and the abundant *Calluna* (ling) growing near the site in the present day, this is a rather unexpected finding. The absence of pollen from heathers cannot be ascribed to differential destruction, as *Ericaceae* pollen is readily preserved and recognisable at an advanced state of decay. Rather, its absence implies a very different vegetational community and soil base status at the time the barrow was constructed.

The sample contains very high representation of *Plantago lanceolata* (ribwort plantain) pollen. Often taken to be an indicator of pastoralism (Behre 1986), this species is also closely associated with other types of human-induced disturbance. Its relative abundance may be due in part to the resistance of its pollen to decay. Nevertheless, to be so well represented, considerable human-induced disturbance may be inferred. Overall, the pollen evidence implies a locally disturbed damp grassland community, but with some hazel and alder in the vicinity.

3.3 The cremated human bone
Angela Boyle

Methodology

A large assemblage of very fragmented cremated bone was recovered from various contexts within both King's and Queen's Low. This entailed assigning a small finds number and noting both the grid reference and the level of the fragment within its appropriate context. In post-excavation each of these fragments was scanned in order to determine if anything of significance could be recorded. A number of samples with individual small finds numbers actually comprised more than one fragment. The following aspects were recorded for each fragment: context, small find number, number of fragments, colour, minimum and maximum fragment size, level of distortion, weight and any identification. It was hoped that discernible groups might be identified and selected contexts were examined specifically with this in mind. The methodology for the recording of the cremated material follows standard recommendations (McKinley 2000; McKinley 2004). The details of all the cremations appear in Tables 3.4 and 3.5.

King's Low

The cremation from King's Low was centrally located and had originally been placed in a Collared Urn within a pit adjacent to a pair of stake holes. Preservation of this cremation was excellent: all parts of the body were represented and only 6.8% of the deposit belonged to the 2 mm fraction. Therefore very little post-burn fragmentation had occurred. It has been suggested (McKinley 1994a, 84) that such a limited level of fragmentation could occur during cremation, collection of bone for burial and post-depositional disturbance including excavation. The remains were those of a sub-adult aged approximately 9–11 years. The age estimate is based on dental development (Van Beek 1983) and epiphyseal fusion (Workshop 1980; Brothwell 1981). In keeping with standard practice no attempt was made to sex

Table 3.4 Summary of cremation data from King's Low and Queen's Low.

Context	Age	Sex	Identifiable bone
Queen's Low 22	?adult	?	skull vault, long bone
Queen's Low 39	?subadult	?	?long bone
Queen's Low 47	?subadult	-	skull vault, long bone shaft, tooth root
Queen's Low 48	?older adult	?	frontal, petrous, mandible, vault, tooth roots, pelvis, sacrum, vertebrae, femur, patella, metapodials, phalanges, tibia, fibula
King's Low	9–11 y	-	All parts of the body are represented

the sub-adult. Preservation was so good that it was possible to lay out the cremation in anatomical position as one would do in the case of an inhumation for photographic recording (Pl. 3.1).

Queen's Low

At Queen's Low a single *in situ* cremation was identified. Context (48) was a cut feature containing cremated bone and charcoal. The bone is in extremely poor condition and moderate distortion has occurred. The largest fragment measured 77 mm in length. The deposit weighs 409 g and appears to represent the incomplete remains of an ?older adult (45+ years) of uncertain sex. The age estimate is based solely on the appearance of the ectocranial and endocranial sutures of the skull which are almost obliterated. Insufficient data was available to determine the sex of the individual. Context (47) was a 'disturbed area' of Context (48) which contained a further 62 g of cremated bone.

Possible schmorl's nodes were present on the body of a single vertebra. Schmorl's nodes are depressions observed in the end plates of vertebrae. The exact cause of the lesions is unclear and there is some debate as to whether they are caused by a herniation of material from the intervertebral disc (Rogers and Waldron 1995, 27) or whether the herniation of material is secondary to necrosis beneath the end-plate (Peng *et al.* 2003, 879). However, whatever the exact pattern of events in disruption of the vertebral end-plates and herniation of disc material, such nodes have been linked to physical activities, such as contact sports (Resnick and Niwayama 1988, 1530) and to acute trauma (Fahey *et al.* 1998). The lower thoracic and upper lumbar vertebrae are most commonly affected in archaeological bone (Rogers and Waldron 1995, 27).

A further two discreet contexts containing cremated bone were identified. Context (22) contained 99 g of cremated human bone which has been identified as a possible adult (18+ years). A single wormian bone was present on a fragment of skull vault. A wormian bone is a small accessory fragment of bone which may be present in the sutures of the skull. It is of no pathological significance although the frequency with which the trait occurs is known to vary among different populations.

A badly disturbed feature, Context (39), contained 12 g of cremated human bone and a small quantity of animal bone.[1] A few long bone fragments were tentatively

---
1 Three fragments from the acetabulum of a sheep or goat plus other indeterminate fragments, identified by Dr Alan Outram, University of Exeter.

3 *People and the environment*

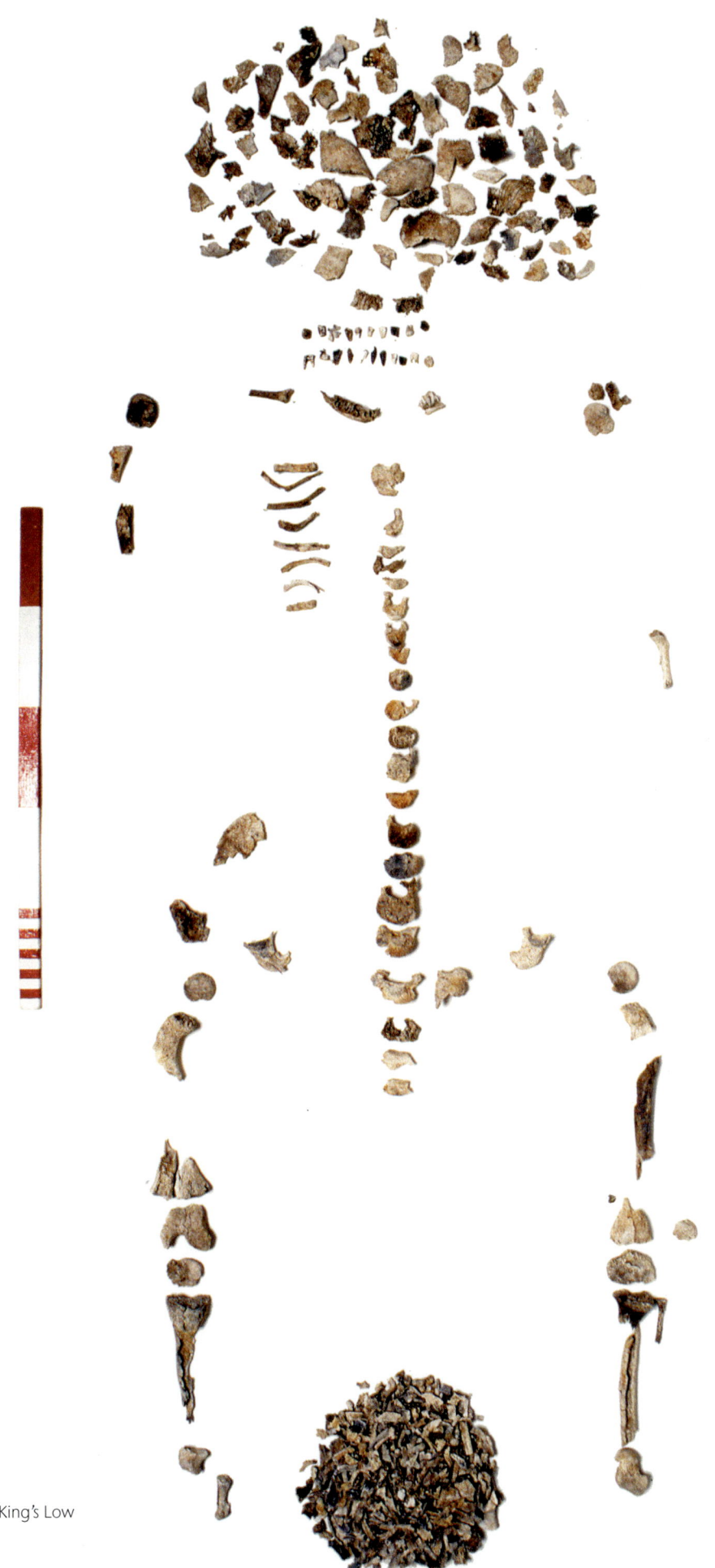

Plate 3.1 The King's Low cremation.

Table 3.5 Weight of cremated bone within anatomical categories and size ranges, King's Low and Queen's Low. * = bone classified as long bones only (i.e. combination of upper and lower limbs).

Context	10 mm					5 mm					2 mm					Total weight
	Skull	Axial	Upper limbs	Lower limbs	Unidentified	Skull	Axial	Upper limbs	Lower limbs	Unidentified	Skull	Axial	Upper limbs	Lower limbs	Unidentified	
Queen's Low 48	57 g	8 g	*62 g	-	85 g	4 g	1 g	-	4 g	98 g	-	-	-	-	90 g	409 g
Queen's Low 22	-	-	-	-	-	-	-	-	-	-	-	-	-	-	-	99 g
Queen's Low 39	-	-	-	-	-	-	-	-	-	-	-	-	-	-	-	12 g
Queen's Low 47	-	-	-	-	-	-	-	-	-	-	-	-	-	-	-	62 g
King's Low	195 g	123 g	23 g *(59 g)	138 g	24 g	-	10 g	73 g*	-	247 g	-	-	-	-	65 g	957 g

identified as sub-adult (*i.e.* less than 18 years). The fragments were white with blackened cortex.

Discussion

The quantity of bone recoverable from a modern adult cremation is 1600–3600 g, with an average of 3000 g, which is roughly the same as a dry bone specimen (McKinley 1989, 66). Clearly, then the cremation from Queen's Low Context (48) is only *representative* of the remains of a complete adult individual. The selection of specific body parts for either burning and/or burial can be paralleled at other sites such as Barrow Hills (Boyle 1999). The weight of the example from King's Low and its identification as a sub-adult suggests that the deposit is substantially complete. This is in contrast to an example from Marsh Lane East, Taplow, Bucks (Boyle in preparation) which was also buried within a complete Collared Urn. It has been identified as an adult, possibly male and weighs c.1459 g. It is therefore likely to be *representative* rather than complete. Cremations associated with Collared Urns from Barrow Hills ranged in weight from 137–1529 g and only one was identified as sub-adult.

The fragmentary bone from both barrows was examined but little of interest was noted. The details of this material can be found in the archive. The material is significant in that it suggests that a number of satellite or secondary cremations were originally deposited in both barrows and were subsequently disturbed by animal burrowing and by tree roots.

3.4 The King's Low wood charcoal
Dana Challinor

Introduction
A number of large concentrations of wood charcoal were encountered during the excavations which were hand-collected and stored in boxes or bags. Several large pieces of charcoal, which appeared to be the remains of charred timbers, were lifted in plaster for laboratory examination. These were mostly concentrations of charcoal within Contexts (51) and especially (53), the sand platform underlying the Phase 1 mound, although samples of charcoal were collected from a range of contexts from within the mound material. Since the central burial of the barrow was a cremation urn, from which charcoal was also retrieved, it was assumed that the provenance of the wood charcoal was the cremation pyre. Two charcoal samples from Contexts (51) and (53) were dated by radiocarbon dating to 1750–1598 and 1751–1527 cal BC, placing them firmly in the Bronze Age. The research aim of the charcoal analysis was to investigate the pyre remains and the use of fuel wood for cremation purposes.

Methodology
Over a hundred samples of wood charcoal of various sizes were collected, of these, eleven were from five concentrations of large pieces of charcoal, some of which appeared to be the remains of charred timbers and one was from the primary cremation burial; the rest were smaller samples of a few fragments. In addition to the 11 large charcoal samples and cremation sample, representative fragments (approximately 50%) from 55 randomly selected samples were chosen for examination.

Charcoal fragments were examined on the basis of their anatomical features, revealed by fracturing to expose fresh transverse, tangential and radial surfaces and observed under a Meiji incident-light microscope at up to ×400 magnification. Identifications were made with reference to Schweingruber (1990) and modern reference material. In order to satisfy the potential of the charred timbers, additional investigations were considered: the growth patterns and the maturity (i.e. sapwood/heartwood) of the wood were recorded and broad surfaces were examined for tool marks and other evidence of woodworking. In practice, the poor preservation and minimal size of many fragments has prevented comment in many instances.

Results
Only one taxon, *Quercus* sp. (oak), was positively identified. This occurred in 59 samples taken from throughout the building sequence, i.e. the pre-mound sub-soil, the sand platform, the fill of the pit and Phase 1 and Phase 2 mound material. It is not possible to distinguish anatomically between the two native species of oak, although it is assumed that a single species is represented here. The charcoal from the remaining examined samples was unidentifiable. In most cases, the preservation of the wood charcoal was too poor to enable identification or the anatomical structure was distorted by the presence of knots or small twiggy wood. In two cases, the samples did not comprise wood charcoal but unidentifiable burnt organic material. There was great variability in the condition of the charcoal, which in some cases was finely comminuted, and yet in other cases, large fragments were preserved. In some instances, the charcoal was extremely friable or had a vitrified appearance. Where it was possible to assess the growth rate, the majority of the wood was slow-grown, with only

Table 3.6 Summary of large charcoal samples, King's Low.

Context no.	Description	Find no.	Weight (g)	Conversion method	Maturity	Growth rate	Notes
51/53 (1015)	Pre-mound platform	3978	24	-	-	Q slow	Highly vitrified
		3979	28	-	-	Q slow	Highly vitrified
51/53 (1016)	Pre-mound platform	4014	34	-	Heartwood	Slow	
		4013	75	-	Heartwood	Slow	
51/53 (1017)	Pre-mound platform	-	179	Radial	Heartwood	Slow	Plank
		3984	2	-	-	Slow	Badly distorted
		4018	2	-	Heartwood	Slow	
		4017	1	-	Heartwood	Slow	
53 (1050)	Pre-mound platform	6057	20	-	-	Variable	Small fragments
		6056	18	-	-	Variable	Small fragments
	Collared Urn	-	8	-	Heartwood	Q slow	
1027	Fill of pit 245	3450	344	-	Heartwood	V slow	No evidence of structure

three samples showing evidence of fast growth. Poorer preservation meant that it was not always possible to identify the maturity of the wood. Fifteen of the samples produced charcoal containing tyloses, indicating that heartwood had been used, and the identification of sapwood (based upon the absence of tyloses) was confirmed in six samples.

A summary of the large charcoal samples is given in Table 3.6. All of these samples were identified as *Quercus* charcoal and all but one (1050) were slow-grown. In some cases, the rate of growth was so slow that annual growth ring was largely occupied by springwood vessels. Sample 1050 was the only one to exhibit variable growth rate with separate fragments showing different growth rates. The presence of tyloses was positively identified in four contexts (1016, 1017, 347 and the fill of the Collared Urn) but no sapwood was positively identified.

Only one sample was recognisably in the form of a fragment of plank (1017; Pl. 3.2); although some of the other samples exhibited some characteristics of structure, the charcoal was less well preserved and fragmented upon examination. The preservation of the plank fragment was not good enough for tool marks to be visible. The curvature of the growth rings indicated that the wood had been radially split, although the thinness of the plank (10 mm depth) suggests that much of the original wood had burnt away and charcoal fragments taken from underneath the plank were badly distorted and highly vitrified.

Discussion

No accurate interpretations of charcoal assemblages may be made without a full understanding of the taphonomy (Boyd 1988, 603). At King's Low, the charcoal derived from several deposit types; within the Collared Urn, from the layers including lenses of large charcoal pieces on the surface of the sand platform, from within the burial pit and generally dispersed throughout the mound. Most of these represent redeposited pyre debris, some of which could, potentially, have come from multiple events of burning. However, the fact that the burial comprised the remains of a single individual (Boyle, above) implies a single burning event. The paucity of charcoal within the urn itself indicates careful separation of the bone from the pyre. The large pieces of charcoal, and particularly Context (53), the surface of the sand platform, probably represent the remains of the pyre structure or bier of the individual buried in the Collared Urn.

Species selection

Since trees have different physical and chemical properties which determine their usefulness for different purposes, the selection of a suitable wood can be important (Coles *et al.* 1978, 25). Although the casual gathering of fuel wood from locally available trees was appropriate for certain tasks, such as collecting wood for domestic hearths, there were also tasks requiring more careful selection of species (Brunning and O'Sullivan 1997, 163). The predominance of *Quercus* in the King's Low samples is not surprising, as it makes a high energy wood fuel (Edlin 1949) suitable for cremation purposes, particularly when the dense heartwood is used. Certainly, the preference for *Quercus* as a fuel wood in cremations was common during the Bronze Age (e.g. Challinor 2010; Boyer 1992; Cartwright 1985; Cutler 1978; Dimbleby 1965; Dimbleby 1981; Keepax 1976). Indeed, the predominance of a single taxon in Bronze Age cremation assemblages has been noted at a number of sites; such as Radley Barrow Hills (Thompson 1999, 352), Lechlade, Gloucestershire (Robinson 1998, 25) and the Rollright Stones (Straker 1988). It is assumed from this fact that one type of wood, perhaps even a single tree, was deliberately chosen for the funeral pyre (Thompson 1999, 352). The large pieces of charcoal from Context (53) at King's Low all exhibited similar growth rates, which could indicate that a single tree had been used.

A possible correlation between the age/sex of the deceased and the fuel-wood used has also been suggested by research on Early Bronze Age cremation burials from Raunds, Northamptonshire (Campbell 2007, 31). Campbell suggests that infants and male adults tend to be associated with a single species and children with mixed assemblages. Assuming that the sub-adult at King's Low who was aged at 9–11 years fits with the adults rather than the children, the choice of oak as dominant fuel wood is appropriate.

Pyre construction

It has been suggested that the abundance of oak in cremation deposits, compared to other species, is a result of

Plate 3.2 The charred plank fragment, Context (51/53) (1017).

the pyre structure; the timber from these trees providing the supports in a central position, less likely to have been totally reduced to ash (Gale 1997, 82). Experimental evidence for pyre construction indicates that an effective pyre structure would be of large logs in-filled with brushwood to aid ignition and allow the circulation of air (McKinley 1997). Certainly, ethnographic and historical sources indicate that a similar structure is used, regardless of geographical and temporal differences (McKinley 1997, 132). In contrast, the evidence from the King's Low charcoal shows that the wood was radially split into planks. Most oak planking was cut in this way from the Neolithic to the medieval period, as oak splits naturally along the rays providing a less wasteful method of conversion (Morgan 1975, 225). Indeed, the planks may not have been cut specifically for the purposes of pyre construction but could have been a construction timber re-used on the cremation pyre. While it is not possible to determine from charcoal whether the wood came from re-used timbers, it does seem unlikely in a ritual context, especially a barrow burial, which represents an investment in the funerary rites of this individual.

It is interesting that there was no evidence for branch wood nor smaller shrubby species in the King's Low assemblage. Scrub/hedgerow species such as members of the *Maloideae* family (hawthorn, apple, pear etc.) are ideal for kindling fires. Indeed, many cremation deposits, in which *Quercus* was predominant, also contained branch wood fragments or other more shrubby species, such as *Maloideae* (e.g. Cartwright 1982; Gale 1998; Keepax 1985). However, the lack of branch wood may be due to differential deposition, indicating that the charcoal assemblage may not reflect the exact composition of the original pyre construction.

Woodland management

Woodland management practices, in the form of coppicing and pollarding, were commonly used to increase woodland yield, ensure a constant supply and produce long, straight poles for construction (Taylor 1981, 9) and evidence for coppicing is certainly known from the Early Neolithic period (Rackham 1990, 38). Such evidence comes from waterlogged timbers, as it is very difficult to prove directly the practice of woodland management from charcoal. The evidence from King's Low, where the wood was slow grown, is not particularly indicative of coppiced wood which tends to exhibit very rapid growth.

Conclusion

The charcoal evidence from King's Low indicates that oak formed the main wood used in the burial, both for the pyre fuel and the bier or pyre structure. A radially converted plank was recovered from a platform constructed below the mound, suggesting the remains of a bier or coffin. The widespread presence of slow grown oak, including heartwood, supports the suggestion that part of the Bronze Age funerary rite may have been to fell a single, whole tree for the cremation of significant individuals.

Acknowledgements

The kind assistance of Professor Mark Robinson, both for helpful discussions and reading an earlier draft of this report, is gratefully acknowledged. Thanks are also due to Dr. Dominique de Moulins for her valuable comments.

4 The material culture

4.1 The pottery
*Alex Gibson**

The pottery from King's Low and Queen's Low barrows represents an assemblage of Later Neolithic to Early Bronze Age date from a variety of contexts within and below the disturbed mounds. The earliest ceramic identifiable with certainty in the assemblages is the Grooved Ware from King's Low (Catalogue KL1–3). KL3 appears to be from a small fine tub-shaped vessel with a slightly in-turned rim similar, perhaps, to the vessel P5 from Redgate Hill, Hunstanton (Bradley *et al.* 1993, 46), P452 from Durrington Walls (Wainwright and Longworth 1971, 138) or P6 from Trelystan, Powys (Britnell 1982). Grooved Ware is generally rare in the West Midlands though this important find as well as recent find spots in Warwickshire (Palmer *pers comm*) and the Welsh Marches (Britnell 1982) are gradually filling the gap in distribution. This phase at King's Low may date to *c.* 3000–2400 cal BC. on typological grounds.

The Beaker pottery from King's Low and Queen's Low is generally unremarkable due to its fragmentary nature. Five vessels (minimum) seem to be represented at King's Low with both comb and incised decoration visible. It is difficult to date these vessels typologically due to the lack of re-constructable profiles or decorative schemes but the incised crosshatching on KL7, possibly representing a chevron or lozenge motif, might suggest that this vessel at least is late in the sequence probably belonging to Clarke's (1970) Southern Series or to steps 4–7 of Lanting and van der Waals's (1972) scheme. It is almost certainly after Needham's stage 2 (Needham 2005). There is a minimum of six Beakers represented at Queen's Low but they are again fragmentary. Once more a filled lozenge or chevron motif seems to be represented on QL1 with similar implications for dating as described above.

While a new corpus of Beaker pottery is long overdue, Clarke (1970) lists only 17 beakers from Staffordshire, 12 of which are capable of being assigned to a specific group. Of these 12, ten belong to the Southern Series and are typologically late as was suggested for the King's Low and Queen's Low assemblage. In view of the fragmentary nature of the assemblage and our present inability to assign rigorous chronologies to available typologies (Kinnes *et al.* 1991), a date range of *c.* 2200–1900 cal BC for this material may be estimated.

Collared Urn is by far the largest represented ceramic group from both sites. There is a minimum of ten vessels represented at King's Low (KL10–20) and seven vessels at Queen's Low (QL7–13). QL14 may possibly raise this figure to eight. Once more and with notable exceptions, the vessels are fragmentary and rarely are decorative schemes or profiles re-constructable. KL10 is by far the best-preserved of these vessels and is unusual in the dimpled decoration in the neck and shoulder of the vessel (Fig. 4.1a and b and Pl. 4.1). Usually these dimples are restricted to shoulder or collar bases as defined on Pennine Urns by Varley (1938) though having a distribution extending to well beyond the Pennine massif (Longworth 1984). Random fingertip dimples in the neck area such as here on KL10, is an unusual mode of decoration but presumably is closely linked to the stabbed and jabbed decoration found in a similar position on urns from elsewhere such as Stanton Moor, Derbyshire (Longworth 1984, No. 291d) or Wykeham, North Yorkshire (Longworth 1984, No. 1318). The Urn may be placed in Longworth's (1984) Secondary Series and late in Burgess's (1986) sequence, as supported by the ^{14}C dates associated with this vessel.

KL11 is much more fragmentary than KL10 but the fabric is equally fine and well-made with smooth burnished surfaces. This too has been a tripartite urn, smaller than KL10 and with slight evidence for twisted cord decoration in the neck below the collar which in turn has been decorated with fine twisted cord herring bone motif. It probably also belongs to Longworth's Secondary Series and is late in Burgess's scheme. For a possible reconstruction see Outram, below.

QL7 is the best preserved of the Collared Urns from Queen's Low. It is well-fired but in a much coarser fabric than the King's Low vessels with, in this case, inclusions up to 5 mm across. It would also appear to be rather squat and similar to a bipartite vase Food Vessel in shape, though the well defined collar base and thickness of the fabric suggests that the Collared Urn identification is more accurate. Traces of a triangular motif decorate the collar. This may also belong to Longworth's Secondary Series and is almost certainly late in Burgess's scheme. A Primary Series Urn, however, is probably represented by QL8 where the rim formation and use of whipped cord decoration would be seen as early traits by both Longworth (1984) and Burgess (1986). It is dangerous to read too much into this early/late distinction, however, in view of the considerable chronological overlap between the two series and further in view of the fragmentary nature of the present assemblage. It is possible that this vessel actually represents a bowl Food

---
* Report revised by AG March 2011.

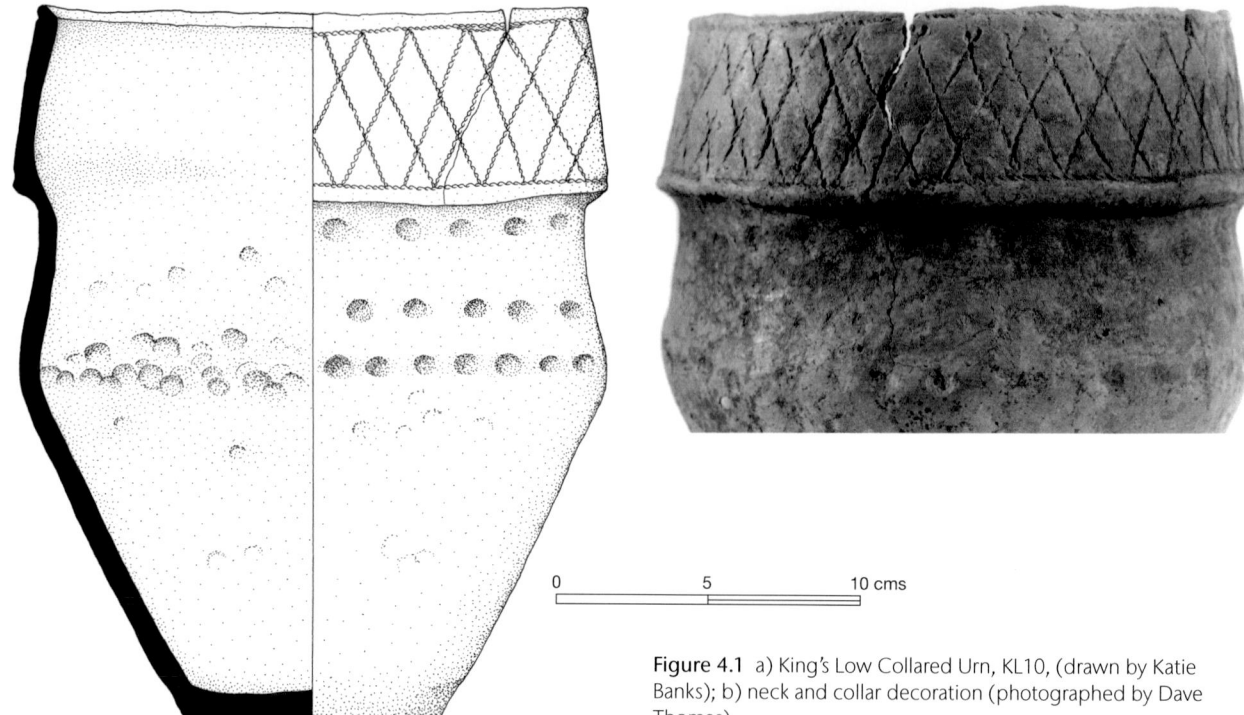

Figure 4.1 a) King's Low Collared Urn, KL10, (drawn by Katie Banks); b) neck and collar decoration (photographed by Dave Thomas).

Vessel but the sherd evidence makes reconstruction difficult (see Outram below). Consequently it would be dangerous to assign a date narrower than c. 2000–1600 cal BC for this material.

Longworth (1984) lists 11 Collared Urns from Staffordshire, a total virtually doubled with the publication of the present assemblage. Of these 11, four are assigned to his Primary Series and three to the Secondary. Those from Swinscoe (No. 1414) and Farley 5 (No. 1415) exhibit a triangular motif on the collars paralleled in the present assemblage (QL7 and 8). Herring-bone motif on the vessels from Stoke-on-Trent (No. 1418) and Trentham (No. 1420), both Primary Series Urns, is paralleled here on KL11. The lattice arrangement on KL10 and KL20 is paralleled in the neck of the Swinscoe vessel (No. 1414) but is otherwise un-paralleled in the county. Both the Farley vessel and the unusual vessel from Wetton (No. 1421) have oval impressions in the neck and on the shoulder though they do not exactly parallel the unusual decoration on KL10.

The assemblages from King's and Queen's Low, therefore, add an important body of albeit fragmentary data to the county ceramic corpora. The Grooved Ware from King's Low is an important addition to the national database and, at c. 3000–2400 cal BC, is the earliest ceramic type represented. Beakers, at least 11 vessels, extend the chronological span of the assemblage into the second millennium while the Collared Urns, representing the latest and most numerous ceramic element theoretically extend the chronology further towards the middle of the second millennium BC as supported by the radiocarbon dates of 1750–1598 and 1751–1527 cal BC.

King's Low catalogue

Grooved Ware

KL1. SF5514, Context (3), Area E. (Fig. 4.2a). Single rim sherd in a soft, gritty and crumbly fabric. It is grey throughout and abundant sandy inclusions break the surface but lie flush with it. The inner surface is largely missing. The rim is simple and rounded. Externally traces of a horizontal groove c. 5 mm broad lies 11 mm from the rim.

KL2. SF7108, Context (3), Area A. Single sherd in a hard, well-fired fabric, brown externally and grey-brown internally. The surfaces are smooth and well-finished and the fabric is c. 10 mm thick. Decoration on the outer surface comprises two? horizontal grooves, each 6 mm wide.

KL3. SF6381, Context (3), Area E; SF6383, Context (51), Area E. (Fig. 4.2b and c). Single vessel in a fine, grey and well-fired though slightly pitted fabric. It is decorated with well-spaced rows of shallow incised grooves. The rim (SF6381) is simple and rounded and has a diameter of c. 120 mm. The grooves average 2 mm wide. The angle of a flat base is represented by SF6141, Context (51), Area E (not drawn), but too little survives to allow an estimate of diameter.

  SF6203 Context (53), Area E
  SF6237, Context (3), Area E
  SF6235, Context (53), Area E
  SF6042, Context (3), Area E
  SF6228, Context (3), Area E
  SF6444, Context (3), Area H
  SF6186, Context (53), Area E
  SF6189 (2 sherds), Context (51), Area E
  SF6187, Context (53), Area E
  SF6236, Context (3), Area E
  SF6200, Context (53), Area E
  SF6232, Context (53), Area E.

KL4. SF5081, Context (3), Area B. Single rim sherd in a grey porous fabric with black interior. The rim is simple and rounded with an estimated diameter of 100 mm. Undecorated.

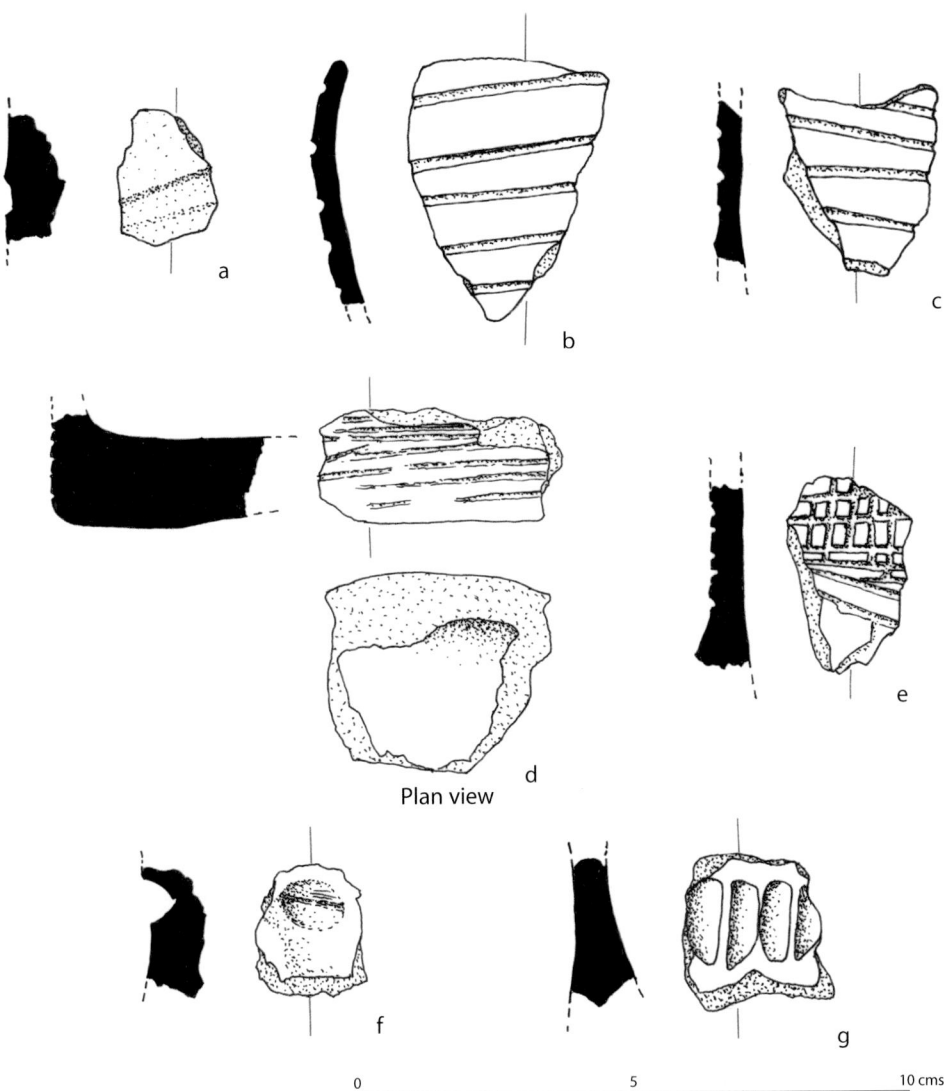

Figure 4.2 King's Low pottery:
a) KL1, SF5514; b) KL3, SF6381;
c) KL3, SF6383; d) KL5, SF5049;
e) KL7, SF7160; f) KL15, SF7025;
g) KL19, SF3016
(drawn by Derek Outram).

Beaker

KL5. SF5049, Context (3), Area B. (Fig. 4.2d). Four sherds plus crumbs from the base and lower wall of a Beaker. The base is up to 15 mm thick and has had a diameter of c. 140 mm. The fabric is orange-brown with a dark grey interior. The outer surface has been decorated with multiple horizontal lines incised in short lengths with overlaps clearly visible. Six lines are visible on the largest sherd.

SF5081, Context (3), Area B.

KL6. SF6523, Context (10), area H. Single sherd in a fine orange-brown fabric with smooth well-finished surfaces. The fabric is 6 mm thick. The decoration appears to comprise two horizontal lines of comb impressions above which are traces of a possible chevron-type motif.

SF653, Context (10), area H.

KL7. SF7160, Context (3), Area N. (Fig. 4.2e). Single sherd from near the base of a late incised Beaker. The fabric has an orange-brown outer surface, dark brown inner surface and black core. It is decorated externally with incised lines forming a zone of cross-hatching, probably filled chevron or lozenge, above a double horizontal line.

KL8. SF7148, Context (3), Area J. Single sherd in a hard, well-fired fabric with a light brown exterior and dark grey-brown interior. There are traces of possible cross-hatching on the outer surface.

KL9. SF5470, Context (3), Area D. Single soft and abraded sherd in a light brown sandy fabric. There are traces of a cross-hatched motif on the outer surface. Not certainly Beaker.

Sherds too small for discussion

SF444 (1 sherd Beaker?), Context (1), Area D
SF359 (2 sherds Beaker?), Context (1), Area C
SF6424 (1 sherd Beaker?), Context (3), Area H
SF6308 (1 sherd Beaker?), Context (3), Area H
SF7017 (1 sherd Beaker?), Context (3), Area H

Collared Urn

KL10. SF5113, Context (1027), Area B. (Fig. 4.1, Pl. 4.1). A near complete Collared Urn in a well-fired fabric of a uniform brown colour with grey-brown interior and dark grey/black core. The portion missing from the collar does not appear to be a new break and it may be that the urn was incomplete when deposited.

The vessel is 230 mm high, has a rim diameter of 178 mm, a base diameter of 85 mm and the fabric varies between 6 and 8 mm thick. The rim has an internal undecorated bevel 8–10 mm deep and with a slight

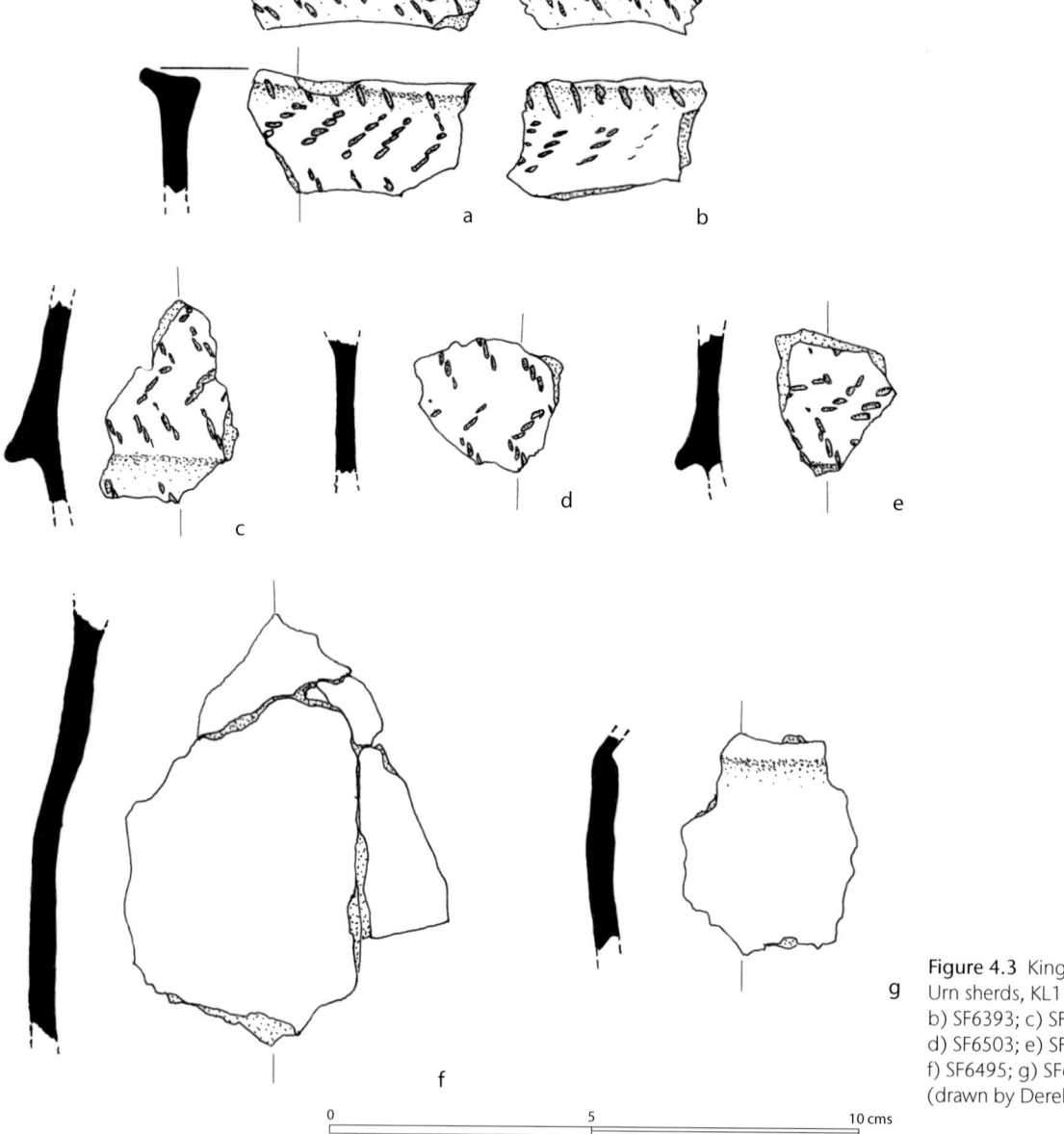

Figure 4.3 King's Low Collared Urn sherds, KL11: a) SF6541; b) SF6393; c) SF6330; d) SF6503; e) SF6025; f) SF6495; g) SF6339 (drawn by Derek Outram).

internal lipping. Externally, the collar is 55 mm deep and decorated with an encircling twisted cord line below which is twisted cord open cross-hatching which is bordered below by another encircling line in the same technique.

The neck is 55 mm deep with two encircling lines of dimples, each dimple being c. 8 mm in diameter. A further line of similar dimples occurs on the shoulder. The belly of the vessel is undecorated.

KL11. Multiple SFs and Contexts. (Fig. 4.3). Fine Collared Urn represented by sherds from the upper portion. The fabric is c. 5 mm thick, fine, hard and well-fired with good smooth surfaces. The colour is reddish-brown with a grey core. The rim has had a diameter of c. 150 mm and has an internal bevel decorated with diagonal lines of fine twisted cord impressions. Externally, the rim is slightly everted and the collar is decorated with fine twisted cord herring bone. There is slight evidence to suggest that the vessel may have been decorated with twisted cord below the collar. SF6339, Context (10), Area H, (Fig. 4.3.g) has traces of a slight carination suggesting that the vessel has been tripartite.

SF6330, Context (10), Area H (Fig. 4.3.c)
SF6342, Context (3), Area H
SF6495, 7 sherds, Context (3), Area H (Fig. 4.3.f)
SF5409, Context (3), Area G
SF6541, Context (3), Area H (Fig. 4.3.a)
SF6396, Context (3), Area H
SF6509, Context (3), Area H
SF6533, Context (3), Area H
SF6458, Context (3), Area H
SF6393, Context (10), Area H (Fig. 4.3.b)
SF5368, Context (3), Area F
SF6336, Context (3), Area H
SF6024, Context (3), Area C
SF6346, Context (3), Area H
SF6503, Context (3), Area H (Fig. 4.3.d)
SF6344, Context (3), Area H
SF6246, Context (3), Area H

SF6459, Context (3), Area H
SF6488, Context (3), Area H
SF6394, Context (3), Area H
SF6286, Context (3), Area H
SF6337, Context (3), Area H
SF6321, Context (3), Area H
SF6303, Context (3), Area H
SF3559, Context (3), Area C
SF7105, Context (3), Area J
SF7045, Context (3), Area H
SF3684, unstratified, Area C.

See section 4.1.1 below for a possible reconstruction of KL11.

KL12. SF3781 Context (32), Area A; SF3619, Context (3), Area A. Pink-brown fabric, c. 8 mm thick and with smooth well-finished surfaces. One incised line on the outer surface of SF3781 may be accidental in which case the sherds are undecorated. Sherd SF3619 is a rim sherd from a flat-topped square-sectioned rim.

SF3787, Context (3), Area A; SF3314, Context (3), Area C.

KL13. SF7162, Context (3), Area N. Small rim sherd in a soft red-brown fabric. The rim is rounded and everted and below the rim on the outside are what appear to be fingernail impressions. The inside of the rim is undecorated.

KL14. SF6233, Context (53), Area E. Large body sherd in a soft crumbly light grey-brown fabric. The sherd is c. 14 mm thick and undecorated.

KL15. SF7025, Context (3), Area J. (Fig. 4.2f). Single sherd in a red-brown fabric with a smooth well-finished outer surface. The inner surface is missing. The sherd is decorated with a deep oval dimple or fingertip impression with traces of a second on the break. Possibly rusticated Beaker.

KL16. SF5409, Context (3), Area G. Soft abraded body sherd in a light brown fabric. Undecorated.

KL17. SF6498, Context (10), Area H. Body sherd in a red-brown fabric with fine sand inclusions and an internally striated surface. There are traces of paired fingernail impressions on the outer surface. Possibly rusticated Beaker.

KL18. SF3674, Context (3), Area A. Three sherds plus crumbs in a soft light brown fabric and with a dark grey core. Undecorated.

KL19. SF3016, Context (3), Area D. (Fig. 4.2g). Rim and collar in a dark grey-brown fabric with smooth, hard and well-finished surfaces. The rim is internally bevelled and the collar is decorated externally with close-set near-vertical grooves.

KL20. SF6053, Context (3), Area D. Rim and collar in a fairly hard fabric, 7 mm thick and with brown outer surface, grey inner surface and dark grey core. The rim has a slight internal bevel and a diameter of c. 140 mm. Externally, there is a horizontal line of fine twisted cord impression and below this an open lattice motif in the same technique.

SF5343, Context (3), Area D.
SF5583, Context (3), Area D.
SF6154, 1 sherd + crumbs, Collared Urn?, Context (3), Area H.
SF3157, 1 sherd, Collared Urn?, Context (3), Area D.

Unidentifiable sherds

SF6077, 1 sherd, Context (53), Area D
SF6441, 1 sherd, Context (3), Area H
SF6445, 1 crumb, Context (3), Area H
SF6195, 1 sherd, Context (3), Area H
SF6473, 1 sherd, Context (3), Area E
SF7163, 1 sherd, Context (3), Area N
SF6438, 1 sherd, Context (3), Area H
SF6305, 1 sherd, Context (3), Area H
SF6282, 4 crumbs, Context (3), Area H
SF6115, 1 crumb, Context (3), Area H
SF6255, 1 crumb, Context (3), Area H
SF6177, 1 sherd, Context (3), Area H
SF6258, 1 crumb, Context (3), Area H
SF3512, 1 sherd, Context (43), Area C
SF7125, 1 sherd, unstratified, Area C
SF7143, 1 sherd, Context (3), Area J
SF3981, 1 sherd, Context (32), Area A
SF7030, 1 sherd, Context (3), Area H
SF7038, 1 sherd, Context (3), Area H
SF7015, 1 sherd, Context (3), Area J
SF5437, crumbs, Context (3), Area D
SF5428, 2 crumbs, Context (3), Area D
SF5511, 1 sherd + crumbs, Context (53), Area E
SF5218, 2 crumbs, Context (3), Area F
SF5400, crumbs, Context (3), Area F
SF5432, 1 sherd, Context (3), Area F
SF3930, 1 sherd, Context (3), Area F
SF7158, 1 sherd, Context (4)
SF5077, 1 sherd, Context (3), Area A
SF6197, crumbs, Context (3), Area H
SF3003, crumbs, Context (3), Area E
SF3158, crumbs, unstratified, Area C
SF6230, crumbs, Context (53), Area E

Queen's Low catalogue
Beaker

QL1. SF823, Context (41), Area H; SF7253, Context (41), Area B. (Fig. 4.4.a and b). Two sherds possibly from the same vessel. Both sherds are in a hard and well-fired fabric, dark brown throughout and with well-finished surfaces. Sherd SF823 is decorated with traces of what is possibly a filled lozenge/chevron motif. The decoration is deep, broad incision. Sherd SF7253 is decorated above a moulded cordon with horizontal filled chevrons in the same technique as SF823 with traces above of a motif such as filled lozenge, hexagon, or chevron. The decoration might suggest that this vessel is of Lanting and van der Waals's (1972) step 5 or later.

QL2. SF7175, Context (41), Area J. Single sherd in a dark reddish-brown fabric with crazed outer surface. Decorated with a single incised line.

QL3. SF791, Context (41), Area B. Single fine sherd in an orange-brown fabric. Decorated with three lightly incised lines.

QL4. SF773, Context (4), Area NX. Single sherd in a fine orange-brown fabric. Undecorated.

QL5. SF336, Context (3), Area D. Single sherd in a fine orange-brown fabric. Decorated with an incised line? below which are traces of a zone of incised herringbone motif.

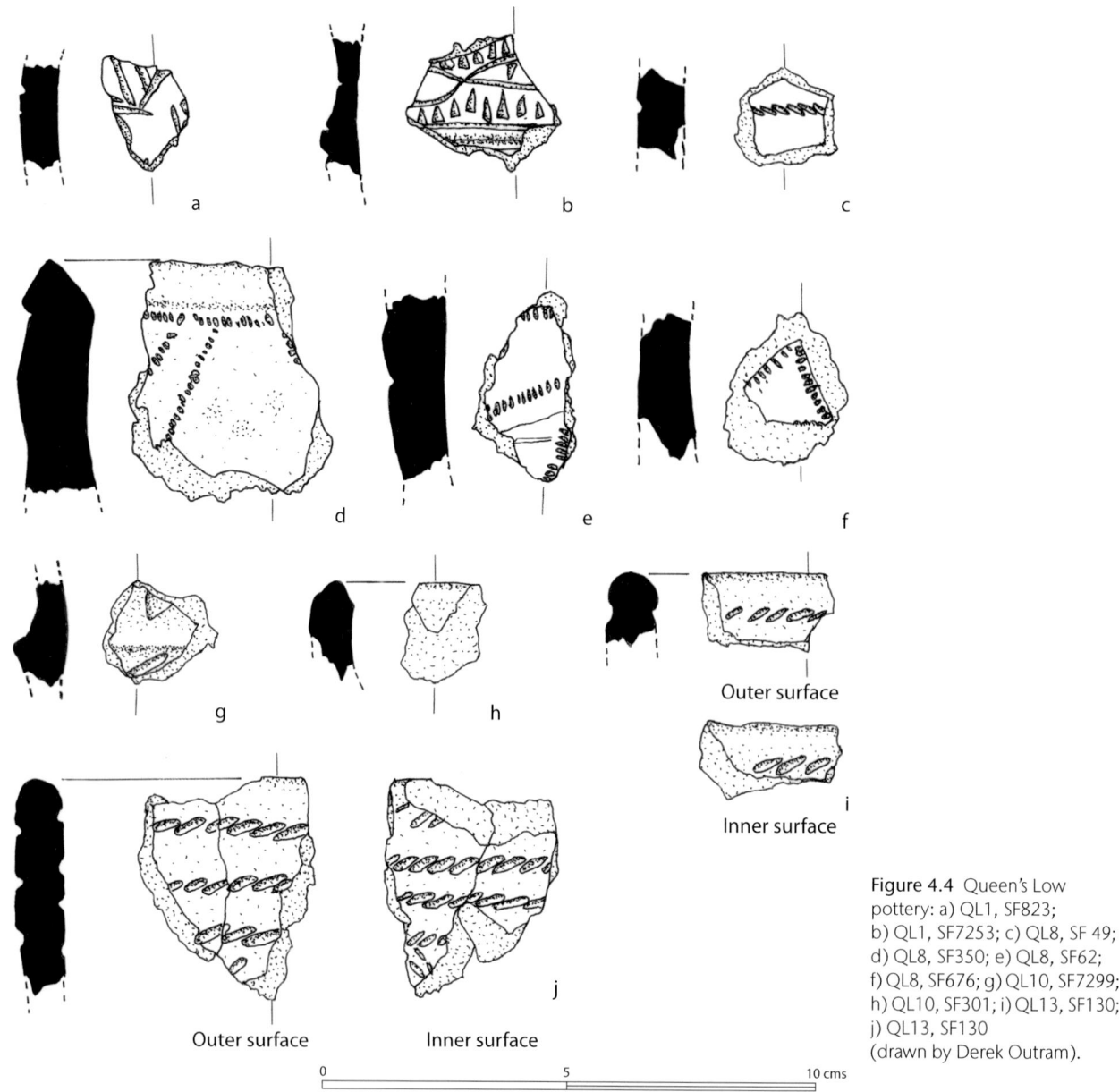

Figure 4.4 Queen's Low pottery: a) QL1, SF823; b) QL1, SF7253; c) QL8, SF 49; d) QL8, SF350; e) QL8, SF62; f) QL8, SF676; g) QL10, SF7299; h) QL10, SF301; i) QL13, SF130; j) QL13, SF130 (drawn by Derek Outram).

QL6. SF337, Context (4), Area D. Single sherd in an orange-brown fabric with a black core. The sherd has traces of a lightly incised zone of cross-hatching.

Sherds too small for discussion
SF331, 3 sherds, Beaker?, Context (3), Area D
SF264, 1 sherd, Beaker, Context (3), Area D
SF408, 2 sherds, Beaker, Context (4), Area E
SF756, 1 sherd, Beaker?, Context (41), Area B

Collared Urn
QL7. SF160, Context (6), Area A; SF604, Context (3), Area A; SF7312, Context (41), Area SX, a total of 41 bagged sherds plus numerous loose undecorated sherds from the upper portion of a Collared Urn. The fabric is light brown with a grey core, has well-finished surfaces and abundant stone inclusions up to 5 mm across. The rim has had an estimated diameter of about 160 mm. It has a rounded external lip, and slightly concave internal bevel decorated with crescentic fingernail impressions arranged radially. Some rim sherds have a slight internal lip below which are traces of accidental fingernail impressions formed during the formation of the rim. Externally, the collar has deeply incised diagonal lines apparently representing some filled triangular motif such as opposed filled triangles.

See section 4.1.1 below for a possible reconstruction of QL7.

QL8. (Fig. 4.4.c, d, e and f). Collared Urn fragments (18) in a hard, well-fired fabric with smooth dark brown surfaces and a black core. Both surfaces are uneven as large stone inclusions up to 6 mm across erupt at intervals. The fabric of the main collar sherd is 12 mm thick. The rim is upright and pointed with an internal bevel 13 mm deep. Decoration comprises externally below the rim a single horizontal line of fine whipped cord impressions. From this a line of similar impressions runs diagonally. SF676, Context (2), Area F, (Fig. 4.4f) has a triangular arrangement of the same technique.

SF405, Context (4), Area E
SF49, Context (4), Area A
SF286, Context (4), Area E

sf304, Context (4), Area E
sf459, Context (4), Area E
sf62, Context (4), Area E
sf11, Context (3), Area A
sf80, Context (4), Area A
sf7, Context (3), Area A
sf449, Context (4), Area E
sf677, Context (2), Area F
sf315, Context (4), Area E
sf282, Context (4), Area E
sf350, Context (4), Area E
sf313, Context (4), Area E
sf262, Context (4), Area E
sf656, Context (4), Area B

QL9. sf573, Context (3), Area F; sf706, Context (2), Area F. Two sherds, probably from a Collared Urn, in a red/brown fabric with abundant finely crushed quartz inclusions giving the fabric a speckled appearance. sf573 is a rounded rim sherd, much abraded, with traces of a single vertical external groove. sf706 appears to be from the base of a collar and is undecorated.

QL10. sf7299, Context (41), Area K; sf751, Context (4), Area B; sf7194, Context (4), Area K; sf301, Context (3), Area E. Four sherds probably from a small Collared Urn in a hard dark grey-brown fabric with smooth well-finished and slightly burnished surfaces. sf301 is a rounded simple rim sherd, 8 mm thick, while sf7299 is from the base of a collar and appears to be decorated above and below with broad diagonal incisions, (Fig. 4.4.h and g).

QL11. sf752, Context (41), Area B; sf7274, Context 5, Area F; sf7288 (crumbs), Context (41), Area SX. Collared urn fragments in a medium hard, brown fabric. The sherds have a slightly laminated texture and are about 10 mm thick. sf752 has two broad vertical grooves similar to sf301 above.

QL12. sf184, Context (41), Area A; sf684, Context (2), Area F; sf50, Context (6), Area A. Sherds in a dark grey-brown fabric with abundant quartz inclusions up to 3 mm across. The abundance of the inclusions gives the fabric breaks a slightly speckled appearance. The inner surface of sf50 has parallel wipe-marks from finishing. Undecorated.

QL13. sf130, Context (3), Area A. (Fig. 4.4.i and j). Three rim sherds in a dark brown fabric with abundant finely crushed quartz inclusions. The fabric is hard and well-fired with well-finished surfaces. The rim is simple and rounded. External decoration comprises three well-spaced horizontal lines of coarse twisted cord impressions. Internal decoration comprises four horizontal lines in the same technique.

> sf117, Context (6), Area A, 1 sherd, Collared Urn?
> sf7307, Context (41), Area SX, 6 sherds, Collared Urn?
> sf792, Context (41), Area B, 1 sherd, Collared Urn?
> sf7280, Context (4), Area E, 1 sherd, Collared urn

Other Sherds

QL14. sf7242, Context (4), Area B. Single sherd with slight carination suggesting that it is from the shoulder of a tripartite Collared Urn. The fabric is brown in colour, fairly hard and well-fired. The inner surface is less intact than the outer. The identification as Collared Urn is not certain.

QL15. sf138, Context (6), Area A; sf71, Context (4), Area A. Two sherds plus crumbs in a soft quartz-filled fabric, dark grey-brown with a black core. sf71 comprises a simple rounded rim and the fabric is only 7 mm thick. sf138 is thicker at 9 mm. Undecorated, possibly from a small cup or bowl.

Sherds too small to be diagnostic

sf320, Context (3), Area D, 1 sherd
sf233, Context (3), Area D, 1 sherd
sf63, Context (4), Area A, 1 sherd
sf54, Context (6), Area A, 1 sherd
sf110, Context (6), Area A, 1 sherd
sf131, Context (6), Area A, 1 sherd
sf165, Context (3), Area A, 3 sherds
sf72, Context (4), Area A, 1 sherd
sf281, Context (4), Area E, 1 sherd plus calcined bone
sf340, Context (4), Area E, 1 sherd
sf103, Context (6), Area A, 1 sherd
sf456, Context (4), Area E, 1 sherd
sf473, Context (4), Area E, 1 sherd
sf469, Context (4), Area E, 1 sherd
sf447, Context (4), Area E, 1 sherd
sf465, Context (4), Area E, 2 sherds
sf500, Context (4), Area E, 1 sherd
sf159, Context (6), Area A, 1 sherd
sf99, Context (6), Area A, 1 sherd
sf91, Context (4), Area A, 1 sherd
sf78, Context (6), Area A, 1 sherd
sf7306, Context (41), Area SX, 1 sherd
sf666, Context (4), Area B, 1 sherd
sf661, Context (4), Area B, 1 sherd
sf7269, Context (41), Area SX, 2 sherds
sf713, Context (4), Area B, 1 sherd
sf660, Context (4), Area B, 1 sherd
sf819, Context (41), Area G, 2 sherds
sf7271, 2 Context (4), Area E, sherds
sf7283, Context (4), Area K, 1 sherd
sf7261, Context (41), Area E, 2 sherds
sf7264, Context (66), Area E, 5 sherds
sf7263, Context (41), Area E, 1 sherd
sf814, Context (47), Area G, 1 sherd
sf813, Context (48), Area G, 1 sherd

4.1.1 Pottery reconstructions
Derek Outram

Collared Urn KL11

Attempts to reconstruct KL11 have suggested that the vessel could have been decorated below the collar. The sherd sf6330 (Fig. 4.3c) shows four small indentations below the collar which match the decoration above. The sherds sf6541 (Fig. 4.3a) and sf6330 (Fig. 4.3c) cover the whole width of the collar. Their cross-sections show that the collar width varies, being thick at the rim and the base and tapering towards the middle. The decorated sherd sf6503 (Fig. 4.3d) has a uniform thickness and, therefore, would not fit within the rim but further

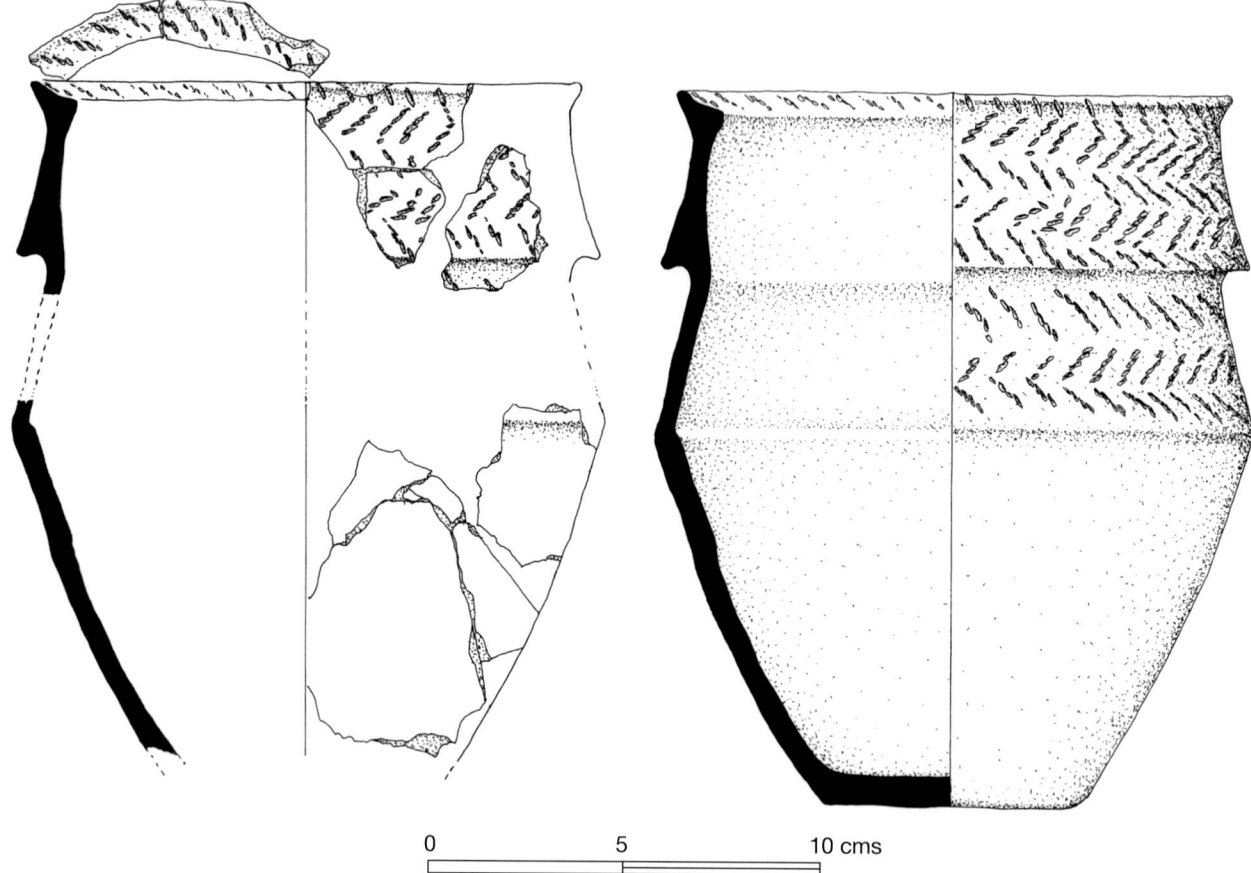

Figure 4.5 A possible reconstruction of the Collared Urn KL11 from King's Low: a) the conjoining sherds; b) the reconstruction (drawn by Derek Outram).

down. Figure 4.5a and b shows a possible reconstruction drawing of KL11 and Plate 4.2 a possible reconstruction of the pot. These are partly based on parallels from Barrow 2 at Cossington, Leicestershire (Thomas 2008, 32, figure 3 (8) and plate 13).

Collared Urn QL7

The sherds from the vessel were extremely fragmented and abraded. Those from the rim were quite thick, varying from 12 mm to 14 mm in cross-section, and consequently had survived in a less damaged state and were the easiest to apply reconstruction methods to. By a very detailed study of the sherds, taking into consideration shapes, thickness of cross-section, colour and texture of the body material and markings, the probable sequence of the sherds of the rim was determined (Fig. 4.6a and b). Useful markings were both the deliberate patterns on some pieces and the scratch marks on the inside of the vessel where it had been smoothed. It was apparent that the rim had cracked along the decorative incisions in several places. The inside diameter of the rim was between 130 mm and 140 mm and the outside diameter was between 164 mm and 174 mm. The colour of the body and surfaces varied significantly from light brown to black/brown.

Decoration

Along the top of the rim, which curved gently upwards towards the outer edge, a regular pattern of curved marks had been made, almost certainly with a thumb nail and by the left hand. On the outside surface, the pattern consists of unevenly-spaced chevrons and slanting incised lines under a horizontal incision running immediately below the proud edge of the top of the rim (Fig. 4.6b). The pattern, probably made with a sharply pointed implement, has the appearance of being rather haphazard in places.

The shape of the pot

The approximate weight of the sherds from the top rim was 170 g, representing nearly all of the rim. The decorated sherds from between the rim and carination weighed only approximately 97 g and their thickness was at least as much as the sherds of the top rim, therefore less than 50% of this region was found. The total weight of the remaining sherds (below the carination) was 335 g, approximately equivalent to the total of the sherds from above the carination, thus a large percentage of the lower part of the pot was missing.

There were several pieces which showed evidence of carination just below the decorated area. By matching the outer curvature to concentric circles, the radius was estimated to be between 90 mm and 100 mm. By comparing the cross-sections of the upper part of the pot (above the carination), the inner wall lined up when the lower piece was at a radius of 95 mm. Only two very small sherds (together 32 mm in length) were found showing the inside curve at the junction of the side and the base of the pot. The radius of this curve was estimated to be 45 mm. The position of the above sherds was estimated from this radius and the line of the inside surface from the carination as shown in Figure 4.7a. A possible reconstruction of QL7 is shown in Figure 4.7b and Plate.4.3.

4 The material culture

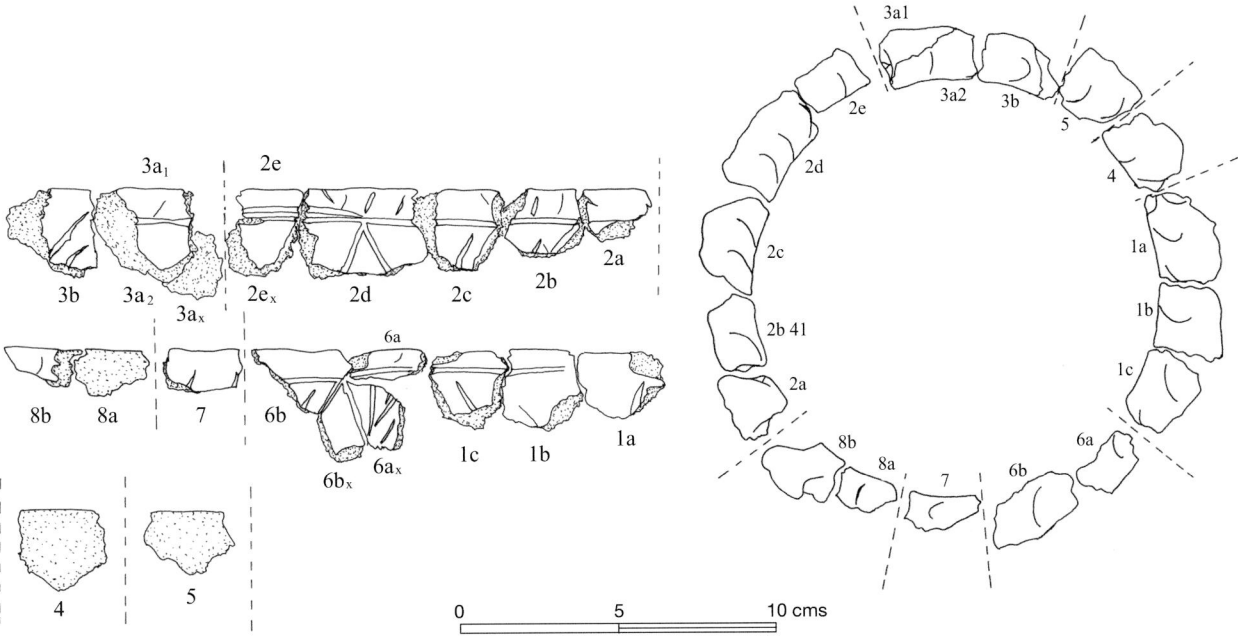

Figure 4.6 a and b. A possible reconstruction of the position of rim sherds of Collared Urn QL7 from Queen's Low (drawn by Derek Outram).

4.2 The worked flint
Philippa Bradley

Introduction
A total of 400 pieces of worked flint, 10 pieces of burnt unworked flint and a single piece of worked stone was recovered from the excavations at both barrows. The material was recovered from various contexts, but the mounds themselves and associated layers were most productive. The barrows had suffered much plough damage and disturbance through rabbit burrowing. As such the collection is discussed as a whole, but specific contexts or noteworthy artefacts are dealt with in more detail. Diagnostic retouched artefacts of Mesolithic to Early Bronze Age date were recovered. The material is summarised in Table 4.1, selected pieces are illustrated in Figure 4.8 and described in the catalogue. Further details of the flint may be found in the project archive.

Raw materials
The flint is mostly very poor quality and occurred in a variety of colours, including brown, grey, orange, white and yellow. Its flaking quality is varied, but is generally very poor, the material is very cherty and cortex, where present, is thin and worn. Cortication is light to medium. This material is likely to be from a derived source. Some better quality flint was used, for example for the two barbed and tanged arrowheads (Fig. 4.8f, g), and also for some of the other retouched forms.

Technology and Dating
Mesolithic activity is represented by three microliths from King's Low: two obliquely blunted points and a possible rod (Fig. 4.8a, b, and c). They are all small examples, but this is unsurprising given the poor quality of the flint available. Obliquely blunted points occur throughout the Mesolithic period (Pitts and Jacobi 1979, 164–5); although there are some differences in the size of the artefacts between the earlier and later Mesolithic (*ibid.*, 169, fig. 5). The rod microlith (Fig. 4.8c), however, indicates later Mesolithic activity (*ibid.*, 164–5). A small minimally retouched piercer with a worn point may be of Mesolithic date (Fig. 4.8d), as may a number of blades and blade-like flakes (Table 4.1), but the quantity of material is not large and they might equally belong with the Neolithic activity that was occurring on site. The presence of the microliths does indicate some fairly sporadic Mesolithic activity in the area.

A leaf-shaped arrowhead from King's Low and a chisel arrowhead from Queen's Low indicate Earlier and Later Neolithic activity respectively (Fig. 4.8e and t). No Early Neolithic ceramics were recovered so it would appear that this phase of activity was relatively limited. Later Neolithic activity, as indicated by the chisel arrowhead (Fig. 4.8t), was perhaps more widespread given the occurrence of

Table 4.1 The worked flint assemblage composition.

	Flakes	Blades, blade-like flakes	Chips	Irregular waste	Cores, core fragments	Retouched forms	Total	Burnt unworked flint	Worked stone
Queen's Low, Staffordshire	56	1	1	12	8	15	93	1	-
King's Low, Staffordshire	197*	5	44	15	6	40	307	9	1
Totals	253	6	45	27	14	55	400	10	1

* including two core rejuvenation flakes (face/edge types)

Excavations at King's Low and Queen's Low

Plate 4.1 King's Low Collared Urn, KL10, (photographed by Dave Thomas).

Plate 4.2 A possible reconstruction of the Collared Urn KL11 from King's Low (made by Les Higgins).

Plate 4.3 A possible reconstruction of the Collared Urn QL7 from Queen's Low (made by Les Higgins).

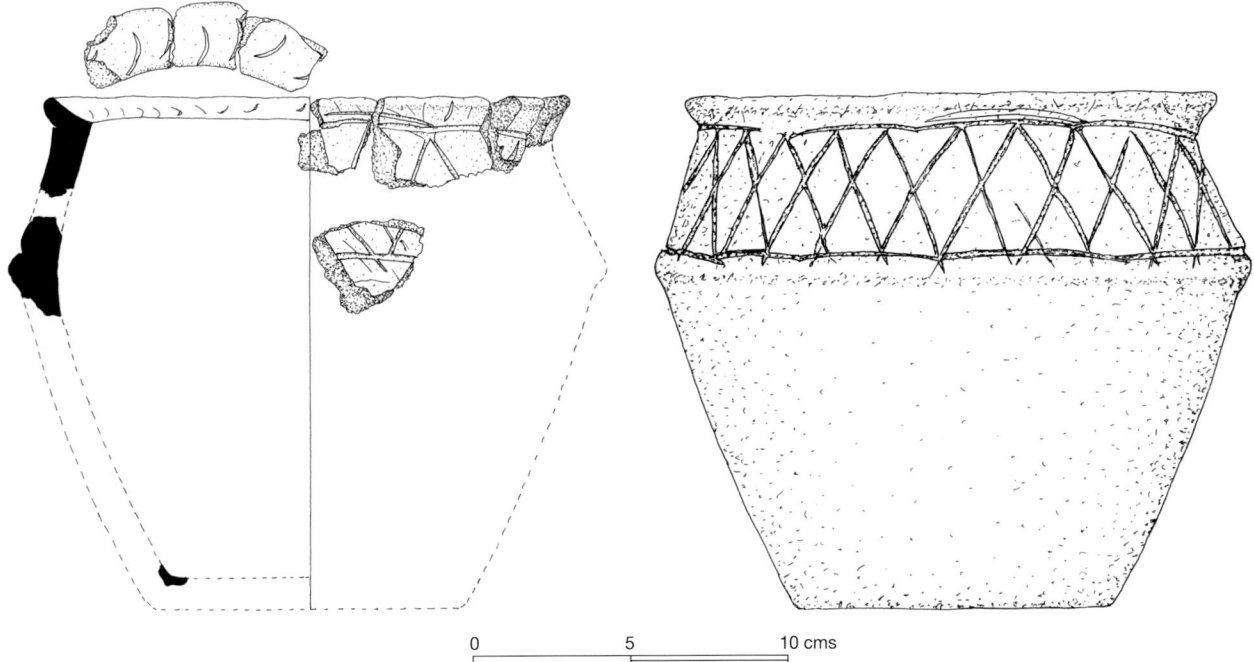

Figure 4.7 A possible reconstruction of the Collared Urn QL7 from Queen's Low: a) the conjoining sherds; b) the reconstruction (drawn by Derek Outram)

Grooved Ware pottery (Gibson, above). Two barbed and tanged arrowheads and four 'thumbnail' scrapers from King's Low indicate Beaker activity (Fig. 4.8f, g, h and i). Another two 'thumbnail' scrapers were recovered from Queen's Low (Table 4.2). These 'thumbnail' scrapers are quite varied in form, but all are relatively finely retouched. The blanks vary from thin and non-cortical with retouch confined to the edges to thick and cortical with inverse retouch, scraping angles range between 35–70°.

The barbed and tanged arrowheads have been extensively and carefully worked over much of both faces (Fig. 4.8f and g). Better quality flint was used for these implements, SF3550 is a yellow, slightly cherty flint and a dark brown to black flint was used for SF7109. The latter example has slightly drooping barbs and an asymmetrical outline, it is in pristine condition and is unlikely that it was ever fired. The other example (SF3550) has some damage, but this is likely to be post-depositional as its edges are sharp and its tip intact; it also seems to have been unused. This arrowhead has slight serrations down its edges, a decorative feature that can be paralleled only rarely in Britain, for example, Breach Farm, Glamorgan and Culduthel, Inverneshire (Clarke et al. 1985, 161, figure 4.98, 171, figure 5.8; 297, 94, figure 4.16, 267) and has more in common with Continental examples (e.g. the exquisitely worked arrowheads from La Motta, Saint-Adrien and Saint-Thégonnec (Clarke et al. 1985, 133, figure 4.66, 136, figure 4.70, 138, figures 4.72–3, 4.76). Stephen Green's study demonstrated that serration was much more commonly applied to 'fancy' types and he concluded that it was a decorative rather than a functional feature (1980, 53). An undated bone serrated barbed and tanged point found on the Thames foreshore at Bermondsey may be a rare skeuomorph (Cotton and Green 2004, 138–9, figure 13). It seems likely that the arrowheads from King's Low may have originally accompanied a burial as they are of such high quality.

Many of the other retouched forms would also be consistent with a Neolithic to Early Bronze Age date, and they include cutting, scraping and piercing tools (Table 4.2, Fig. 4.8h, i, j, k, l, m, n, o, p and q). Scrapers and retouched flakes dominate the retouched component of the assemblage (Table 4.2). Scrapers are difficult to date with certainty (cf. Riley 1990), but the six 'thumbnail' scrapers are classically associated with Beaker activity (e.g. Fig. 4.8h and i), the remaining examples are all end and side types (Fig. 4.8j and k). The majority of these are well made on thin blanks and are likely to be of Neolithic or Early Bronze Age date (cf. Riley 1990). Knives are another well represented category, all of the examples recovered are backed knives (Table 4.2), with varying degrees of secondary working (Fig. 4.8m, n, o and p). At least one of these knives seems to have been a pyre good

Table 4.2 The worked flint: retouched forms.

	Scrapers	Backed knives	Retouched flakes	Arrowheads	Microliths	Piercers	?Fabricator or rod	Misc. retouch	Total
Queen's Low, Staffordshire	2 (thumbnail)	1	4	1 chisel	-	1	-	6	15
King's Low, Staffordshire	8 (3 thumbnail, 5 end and side)	4	5	3 (1 leaf-shaped, 2 barbed and tanged)	3	2	1	14	40
Totals	10	5	9	4	3	3	1	20	55

Excavations at King's Low and Queen's Low

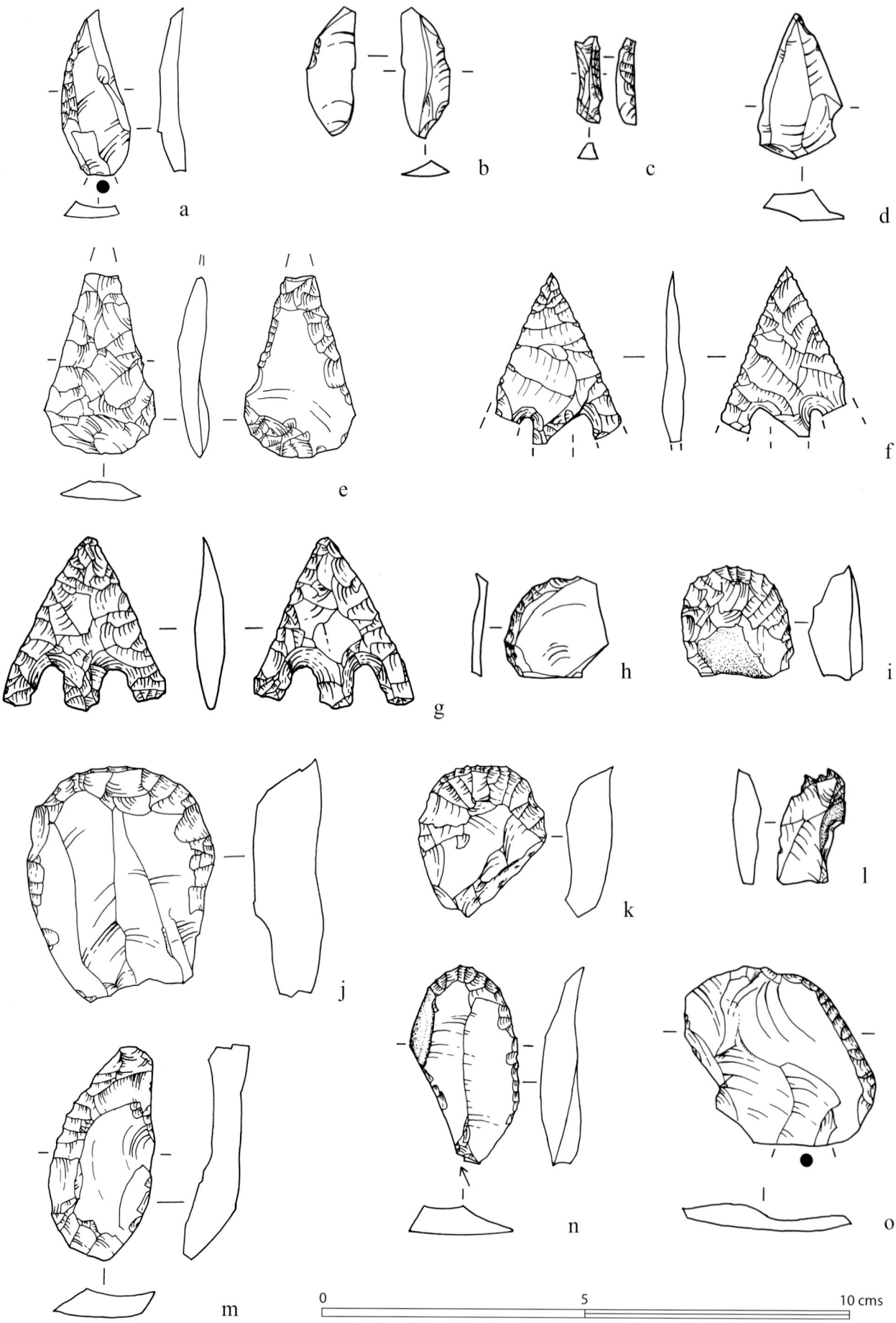

Figure 4.8 The worked flint, a) to s) from King's Low, t) from Queen's Low; a) SF653; b) SF6470; c) SF3632; d) SF228; e) SF2144; f) SF3550; g) SF7109; h) SF6334; i) SF3353; j) SF14; k) SF6218; l) SF328; m) SF317; n) SF1600; o) SF5043; p) SF3970; q) SF1442; r) SF83; s) SF3572; t) SF167 (drawn by Noel Boothroyd).

4 *The material culture*

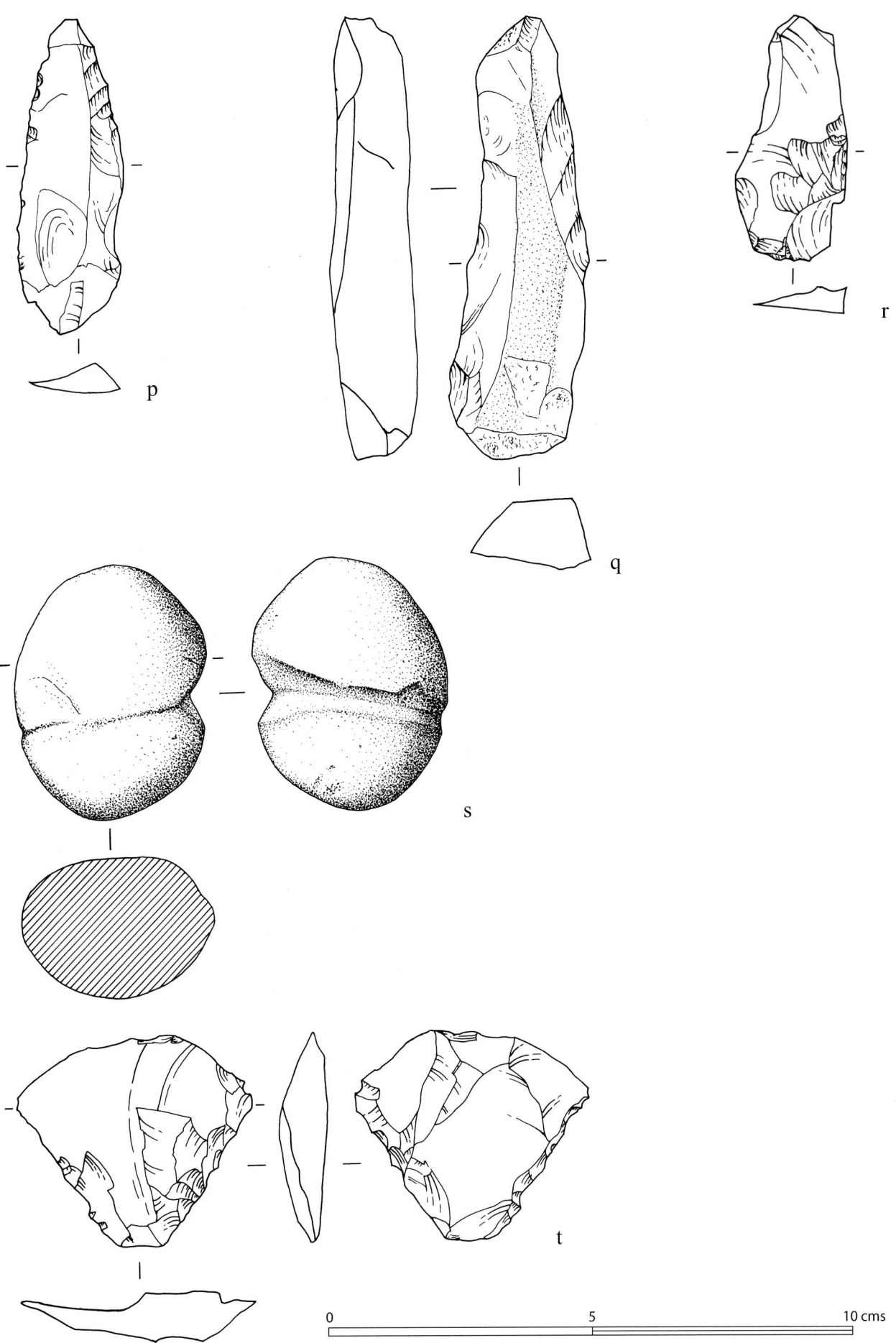

Figure 4.8 cont.

(SF3970, see below; Fig. 4.8p). This example and others, including SF5043 also from King's Low, are likely to be of Early Bronze Age date.

Two apparent pyre goods were recovered from the heavily disturbed mound and at King's Low (SF3970 and SF1442; Fig. 4.8p and q). The first object (SF3970) is a heavily burnt backed knife, which has been steeply retouched along its right-hand side and more minimal retouch occurs along its left side. An Early Bronze Age date would be entirely consistent with these objects. The other object is a large (c. 80 mm in length), rod-like implement with apparently worn edges. It has been extremely heavily burnt and therefore much of the detail of the retouching has been lost, however it seems likely that this was a fabricator or rod-type implement originally. Longworth (1984, 68) lists two probable and one possible fabricators associated with Collared Urns (Handley, Dorset; Staintonvale, Yorkshire and Risby, Suffolk). The examples from Handley and Staintonvale were also burnt, and are likely to have been pyre goods. The possible fabricator from Risby as illustrated by Longworth (1984, 272) does not appear to be a fabricator, although it is possible that it is an atypical example. Longworth also lists associations of Collared Urns and knives (1984, 67–8), many of which have been burnt. Compared with plano-convex knives the other forms listed by Longworth, and that are comparable to the King's Low examples, were more commonly placed on the pyre (Longworth 1984, 67–8). The transformation by fire of artefacts together with the body may have been an important part of the funerary rite (cf. Barclay 2002)

Fabricators and flake knives also have Beaker associations (Clarke 1970, 448). Interestingly both artefact types are more strongly associated with male burials (*ibid.* 448). Gibbs also found strong evidence for male association with fabricators in her study (Gibbs 1989, 116), but uni-facially worked knives were more commonly associated with female burials (*ibid.* 113).

Diagnostic debitage is limited, but two discoidal cores, of probable Later Neolithic date, were recovered from King's Low (Table 4.3). Few complete cores were found, but they tend to be very small and well reduced. Other than the discoidal cores, a single platform flake core, also from King's Low and two multi-platform flake cores were recovered from Queen's Low. The core fragments are relatively un-diagnostic, but all come from non-specific flake cores. Two core rejuvenation flakes (face/edge types) were recovered from King's Low indicating that some core maintenance was being practised (Fig. 4.8r).

No technological analysis was undertaken given the mixed nature of the assemblages, but from a scan of attributes it can be seen that hard hammer-struck flakes dominate, and there was no strong evidence for careful preparation of the material before or during knapping. Butt types are mostly plain or cortical and there was little evidence for abrasion, and only two core rejuvenation flakes were recovered (see above). More effort seems to have been directed into the secondary retouching of some of the artefacts, for example the arrowheads, knives and some of the scrapers. Given these general characteristics the debitage is entirely consistent with an Early Bronze Age date, as indicated by the majority of the retouched forms, together with a little Mesolithic and Neolithic activity. No distinctive debitage could be associated definitely with the microliths; the small quantity of blades and blade-like flakes may be contemporary, but may equally be later.

Worked stone
A single piece of worked stone was recovered from King's Low (SF3572; Fig. 4.8s). It is a small oval pebble, probably of local origin, with an irregular groove around its circumference. It may have been used as a small weight.

Context
The majority of the flint from both sites came from the barrow mounds and associated plough-damaged layers, but noteworthy Contexts are discussed in more detail below.

King's Low
As with Queen's Low, the vast majority of the assemblage came from disturbed mound material. A single broken flake came from Phase 2 mound material (Context 43) and a possible Early Bronze Age subsoil (Context 44) produced a chip and a flake. The fill (Context 1027) of a the burial pit (Context 245) produced a single flake. None of the this material is particularly diagnostic.

Queen's Low
The majority of the flint came from Contexts (1–4), ploughsoils, turf and hard core for a track. Context (6), related to the kerb stones and possible berm, produced three broken flakes and a single retouched flake, none of which is particularly diagnostic. Other contexts which produced flint include (10), two broken flakes, and (41), five flakes, one blade-like flake and a small multi-platform core. Two of the flakes from Context (41) are broken and a two are burnt. Both Contexts (10) and (41) are recent disturbance and none of the flint from these Contexts is particularly datable.

Discussion
Archaeological investigations within the county of Staffordshire had very early beginnings, Dr Plot produced his *History of Staffordshire* in 1686. Mesolithic, Neolithic and Bronze Age artefactual remains and, for the later periods, monuments are relatively widespread within the county.

Table 4.3 The worked flint: core typology.

	Single platform	Multi-platform	Discoidal	Core fragments	Total
Queen's Low, Staffordshire	-	2	-	6	8
King's Low, Staffordshire	1	-	2	3	6
Totals	1	2	2	9	14

Wymer (1977, 251–2) lists several sites that have produced Mesolithic flintwork from Staffordshire, and other finds have come to light, for example Later Mesolithic flint from Rugeley (Hilton 1979). A surface scatter of Mesolithic flint was recovered from Cannock Wood (Wymer 1977, 251; Cantrill 1911). The slight traces of Mesolithic activity from King's Low fit in well with the known evidence from the county.

Neolithic and Bronze Age finds are quite widely distributed within the area, and have been summarised by various authors (e.g. Page 1908; Gunstone 1964; Hodder 1980–1). Numerous stone and flint axes have also been recovered from the county, mainly from surface collections, and are summarised by Clough and Cummins (1988, 203–5). Two probable causewayed enclosures are also known from the county (Alrewas and Mavesyn Ridware; Palmer 1976, 184). Bronze Age barrows from the county have been summarised by Gunstone (1965), who lists three from the parish of Tixall – King's Low, Queen's Low and a destroyed example (1965, 49). Extensive evidence for early Bronze Age mortuary activity is also known from the adjoining counties, particularly Derbyshire. The assemblages from both Queen's Low and King's Low are typical of those recovered from barrows in the locality (Gunstone 1964).

The recovery of 'fancy' arrowheads is however, of particular interest and these objects must originally have been grave goods. Whilst both Mesolithic and Neolithic activity is clearly represented, the bulk of the assemblage is of Beaker to Early Bronze Age date.

Catalogue

The catalogue is ordered as follows: Figure number (Fig. 4.8), small find number, context, brief description of the object including condition, and date (where possible).

King's Low

a   SF653, Context (1), Area E. Obliquely blunted point on distal end of flake, butt intact; finely worked. Medium-heavy cortication. Mesolithic.

b   SF6470, Context (44), Area E. Obliquely blunted point, minimally retouched example on proximal truncation. Tip broken. Cherty flint. Mesolithic.

c   SF3632, Context (32), Area A. ?Rod microlith on thick blank, broken. RHS steeply retouched, butt intact. Lightly corticated. Later Mesolithic.

d   SF228, Context (10), Area A. Piercer with worn point, minimally retouched. ?Mesolithic. Cherty flint.

e   SF2144, Context (3), Area D. Leaf-shaped arrowhead, tip broken, possibly unfinished. Marked plano-convex outline, extensively worked over all of dorsal and part of bulbar faces. Lightly corticated. Earlier Neolithic.

f   SF3550, unstratified. Barbed and tanged arrowhead. Extremely finely retouched, both barbs and tang broken (probably post-depositional damage), tip intact and sharp. Edges are serrated, both faces have been extensively retouched. Comparable to Breton examples. Yellow slightly cherty flint. Beaker.

g   SF7109, Context (3), Area A. Barbed and tanged arrowhead. Large arrowhead with slightly drooping barbs and asymmetrical outline, good quality dark brown/black flint. Extensively retouched over both faces. Mint condition. Beaker.

h   SF6334, Context (3), Area H. 'Thumbnail' scraper on a thin neatly worked blank. RHS broken. Retouch confined to edges. Scraping angle 55–70°. Lightly corticated. Beaker.

i   SF3353, unstratified. 'Thumbnail' scraper on a thick, partly cortical blank, but it has been neatly and invasively retouched. Scraping angle 35–70°. Beaker.

j   SF14, Context (3), Area A. End and side scraper, damaged at distal end. Neatly worked on a non-cortical blank. Scraping edges lightly worn. Scraping angle 55–70°. ?Neolithic/early Bronze Age.

k   SF6218, Context (3), Area E. End and side scraper on thick oval blank. Neat invasive retouch. Scraping angle 55–65°. ?Early Bronze Age.

l   SF328, Context (1), Area C. Piercer on a broken blade-like flake. The object has one worn point and several other denticulated ones.

m   SF317, Context (1), Area C. Backed knife with cortical edge providing backing. Shallow invasive retouch. ?Early Bronze Age.

n   SF1600, Context (3), Area E. Scraper/knife on a long flake, distal end slightly invasively retouched, RHS more steeply retouched. Combination scraper/knife. ?Early Bronze Age.

o   SF5043, Context (3), Area B. Backed knife on an oval blank with steep retouch RHS and invasive retouch LHS to provide backing. ?Early Bronze Age.

p   SF3970, Context (51), Area D. Probable pyre good. Backed knife, steep retouch RHS, minimal retouch LHS. Very heavily calcined. Bulbar face obscured by adhering burnt soil. Early Bronze Age.

q   SF1442, Context (3), Area D. Probable pyre good, ?fabricator or rod. Rod-like object with retouched and worn edges, made on a thick partly cortical blank. Very heavily calcined. Early Bronze Age.

r   SF83, Context (17), Area A. Core rejuvenation flake – face/edge type.

s   SF3572, Context (3), Area F. Worked stone object. Small oval pebble with groove, possibly used as a weight.

Queen's Low

t   SF167, Context (3), Area B. Chisel arrowhead, large extensively worked example, marked curvature to the flake. Lightly corticated. Later Neolithic.

4.3 The faience beads

4.3.1 Description and discussion
Alison Sheridan

Introduction
This report offers a physical description of the two faience beads from these barrows, together with an assessment of their archaeological significance based on the author's current research into British and Irish Bronze Age faience beads (Sheridan and Warren in preparation) and takes into account Tite and Shortland's analyses which are presented below. Note also the comments of Higgins, below.

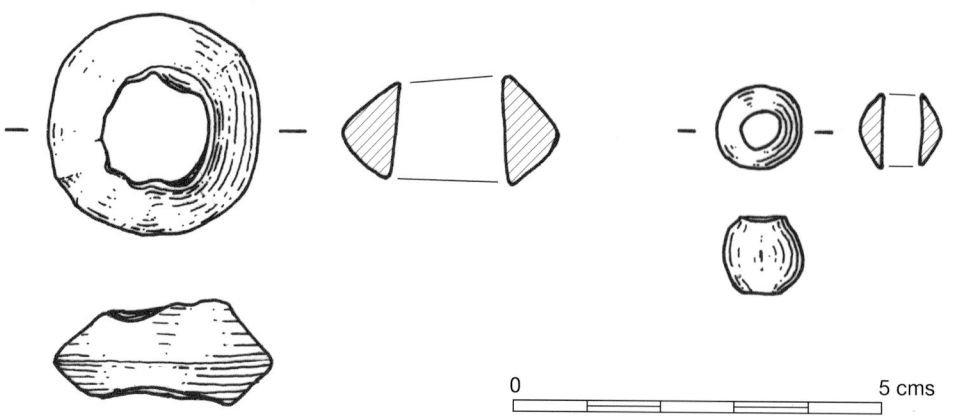

Figure 4.9 The faience beads: left, the Queen's Low quoit-shaped bead (SF283); right, the King's Low spherical bead (SF479) (drawn by members of SOTMAS).

Description

King's Low spherical bead (SF479)

This bead, although found in disturbed topsoil (Context (1), Area D), might nevertheless originally have been associated with the primary Collared Urn burial under the primary turf mound. It is intact but for the tiny fragment taken for analysis (Tite and Shortland below), and measures 5.5 mm across and 5.9 mm high, with an almost circular, centrally positioned hole 3.2 to 3.4 mm across, (Fig. 4.9 and Pl. 4.4. The edge of the hole at either end is slightly lipped. On one side of the bead and inside the hole, its surface is generally fairly smooth and glassy-looking; on the other side, much of the original surface is missing and the exposed sub-surface is vesicular, with a network of deep cracks. The bead's colour also varies. Where the original surface survives, it ranges from a pale grey-green-blue to a dark turquoise, with some sub-surface coppery-red speckles visible. Where the original surface is missing, the coppery red colour is more dominant. In the freshly-exposed cross-section where the analytical sample had been taken, the bead is mostly pale turquoise with a sub-surface patch of coppery red. The factors responsible for the bead's colour are explored below and in the Tite and Shortland analytical report; the paleness in some areas is a function of surface weathering.

Although the interior of the hole is mainly smooth, with only minor vesicular pitting, it has an elongated blob close to one end of the hole. This blob closely resembles the glaze drips that have been observed by the author in several other British faience beads, and may indicate that the bead had been glazed using the 'application' method (see Tite and Shortland below).

It is unclear precisely how the bead's spherical shape and lipped hole had been achieved, although a piece of straw or similarly narrow organic material must have been involved in the creation of the hole. There is no internal rilling in the hole – a feature noted on several segmented beads, where a straw former had been used (e.g. Findhorn, Moray: Sheridan and McDonald 2002, illustration 10).

What was responsible for the cracking and surface loss over part of the bead? Post-depositional leaching (as noted below, concerning the bead's composition) might have led to surface loss, but whether it also caused the cracking is a moot point. Contact with heat is another possible reason: given the bead's likely funerary associations, it is possible that it had been on the body during cremation, or that it had been placed in the urn with the cremated remains while they were still hot. Indeed, heat alteration could account for the coppery red colour, with reducing conditions within the pyre changing the oxidation state of the copper colourant, turning it from blue-green to red (cf. a quoit bead from Cefn Cwmwd, Anglesey: Bowman et al. 2012). However, unlike the Cefn Cwmwd bead and some others that had clearly been through the pyre (e.g. Findhorn: Sheridan and McDonald 2002, 117), there were no unequivocal indications that this had been the case, such as microscopic fragments of cremated bone embedded in the surface.

Queen's Low quoit-shaped bead (SF283)

Although this bead was found in a heavily disturbed Context (Context 4, Area E), it too is highly likely to derive from a burial. It is intact but for the tiny fragment taken for analysis (see Tite and Shortland below). In outline, profile and hole shape it is slightly irregular, reflecting the fact that it has been shaped by hand, rather than in a mould (see Tite and Shortland below). Its external diameter varies from 14.7 to 15.1 mm, hole diameter from 7.3 to 7.8 mm, and thickness from 5.6 mm on one side of the hole, to 7.0 mm on the other (Fig. 4.9 and Pl. 4.4). Its walls are unevenly triangular in cross-section, thinning considerably towards the edges of the hole. Much of the bead's surface is obscured by a tenacious coating of fine-grained, dull brown, matte sediment. Exactly what this sediment is, and how it came to adhere to the surface, is unclear; however, as with the King's Low spherical bead, one cannot rule out the possibility that the bead had been through the pyre, and that this material has been fused to the surface (see below). The original surface is missing at several points, and the sub-surface is obscured by the sediment.

Where the bead's original surface survives intact and is clearly visible, it is fairly smooth, shiny and glassy. The colour is variegated, with some areas that are blackish-blue, others dark turquoise, and others pale and whitish-blue (the last resulting from post-depositional weathering). As with the King's Low bead, there are sub-surface patches of a coppery red colour. Where the surface has been cut to provide an analytical sample (see Tite and Shortland below), the bead is a medium turquoise colour with a patch of coppery red in the centre. The inside of the hole is uneven and slightly knobbly, with a few large open vesicles. It is unclear whether one particular bulge represents a glaze drip, but this is a possibility.

This bead would have been made by wrapping a 'sausage' of faience paste around a twig or similar organic item. It is possible that a linear crease-like feature on one side of the bead is the last surviving trace of the junction.

In addition to the presence of the firmly-adhering sediment, several features suggest that the bead may have been through the pyre (although, once more, no incontrovertible evidence was found, despite examination with a scanning electron microscope). The generally dark colour of the non-obscured areas, together with the presence of coppery-red subsurface patches and the breaks in the original surface could all be the result of heat damage.

Discussion

These two faience beads are a welcome addition to the otherwise rather sparse distribution of faience beads in the north Midlands. They are important in several respects, namely: i) the likely association of the King's Low bead with a burial which has been radiocarbon dated, thereby adding to our understanding of faience chronology in Britain; ii) the fact that the King's Low bead is of a relatively rare and regionally-distinctive type; and iii) the evidence both beads provide regarding the mode of production of Bronze Age faience beads in Britain. In discussing these points, the author draws on the results of a current collaborative project, co-ordinated from the National Museums of Scotland, to document all finds of Bronze Age faience from Britain, Ireland and the adjacent parts of north-west Europe. The results will eventually be published as a *corpus* (Sheridan and Warren in preparation).

Dating

Although the association between the King's Low bead and the primary Collared Urn burial cannot be guaranteed, it is highly likely given the bead's general spatial proximity to the urn. Two samples of charcoal probably deriving from the cremation pyre, produced dates of 1750–1520 and 1740–1520 cal BC. These are well in line with the other radiocarbon dates that have been obtained, not only from pyre charcoal but also from cremated bone, from British and Irish faience-associated graves (Sheridan 2001). Some 16 dates have been obtained to date, and these suggest that faience had already appeared in Britain and Ireland by the 19th (if not 20th) century BC, and that it continued to be used until the 16th century. Such dates convincingly disprove the hypothesis, popular with some archaeologists in the past (e.g. Stone and Thomas 1956), that faience beads arrived here as a result of contacts with Egypt or elsewhere in the eastern Mediterranean during the 14th century BC (see also Tite and Shortland below on the compositional evidence).

One other point to note about the King's Low dates is that they are closely comparable with that of 1880–1450 cal BC, relating to two spherical beads from a cordoned urn from Eagleston Flat, Derbyshire (Barnatt 1996b).

Spherical beads

The bead from King's Low is one of only around 20 beads of globular and similar shape to have been found in Britain (the category encompasses oblate (squashed spherical) and thick annular forms.) It has not hitherto been noticed that these beads have a distinctive and relatively restricted distribution, unlike that of some other faience bead types such as segmented beads. Most spherical, oblate and thick annular beads have been found in central and eastern England, with a few outliers in southern England. Interestingly, the King's Low bead is one of four spherical beads to have been found within the relatively recent past, the others being a malformed sphere from a composite faience-amber-jet and cannel coal necklace from Cossington, Leicestershire (Thomas 2008, Plate 6), and one from another composite piece of jewellery, also featuring amber, cannel coal and (probably) shale components, from Amesbury, Wiltshire (excavated by AC Archaeology, unpublished). No beads of this shape have been found in Ireland, and the spherical and oblate shape is not found in central Europe (the most likely proximate source of technological know-how for faience manufacture), but there is a record from Brittany of a lost bead, possibly of faience, described as being 'globuleuse' (Briard 1984, 147). As will be argued below, the relatively restricted distribution of this bead form supports the idea of small-scale, localised manufacture.

Mode of production

In their report on the analyses of the King's Low and Queen's Low beads, Tite and Shortland suggest that, unlike in Egypt and Mesopotamia where faience production was large-scale and workshop-based, in Britain the mode of production was very different. Their compositional evidence which contrasts these beads with those from Scottish find spots suggests that production was small-scale and locally-based. Other features bear this out. The distributional evidence relating to spherical and similar beads, cited above, suggests that there had probably been some regional preferences in bead shape (and indeed that this particular shape of bead was an English invention). That we are observing the sharing of a design idea, rather than the centralised, production in bulk of individual bead shapes is reflected in the variability within individual bead types. The Queen's Low quoit bead is a relatively small example of this kind of bead; some other British and Irish examples range in size up to *c.* 30 mm in diameter (at Southfield, Fife: Coutts 1971, no. 112f). Although the segmented form is not represented at King's or Queen's Low, there are clearly variations in the shape, size and method of manufacture of this type of bead, with many Wessex examples having been formed with the aid of a 'butter pat' type device, while some Scottish examples were formed by being jabbed at irregular intervals (e.g. at Findhorn, Moray: Sheridan and McDonald 2002). Similarly, some faience beads have evidently been glazed using the 'application' method (as shown, for instance, by glaze drip lines), while others have been glazed by efflorescence, or by a combination of techniques (e.g. at Varley Halls, Sussex: Bowman and Stapleton 1997; Rohl and Needham 1998). Having examined a large number of British faience beads, the current author is of the opinion that they were manufactured 'to order', perhaps by metalworkers who had learned the secrets of faience manufacture. The fact that the two beads presented here are similar in composition does not prove that they had been made in the same place; but it does suggest the localised sharing of a specific 'recipe' for their manufacture.

4.3.2 Technical analyses
Mike Tite and Andrew Shortland

Introduction
Two faience beads were submitted to the Research Laboratory for Archaeology and the History of Art (RLAHA), University of Oxford, for analysis, the aim of which was twofold. Firstly, it was desired to determine the production technology of the faience, including raw materials, shaping and glazing methods. This information would then be used to accomplish the second aim of the analysis, which is saying how these two pieces of faience are related to each other, and to other faience found locally and throughout the UK.

Faience is a ceramic consisting of a crushed quartz or sand core which is held together by variable quantities of interstitial glass and covered by a thin glaze. The method of production was relatively simple. The body of the bead was formed into the correct shape from damp faience paste using a mould or modeling by hand. It was then left to dry. The glaze was created using a glazing powder consisting of an alkali, usually some form of plant ash, and a colorant. The glazing powder was either mixed into the body whereupon it effloresces to the surface during drying (the efflorescence technique), or was applied as a slurry to the surface of the bead (application technique). A third technique, cementation, is possible, but not thought to have been used in Europe during this period. The bead was then fired to give a hard body and turn the glazing powder into a glassy glaze. While faience was fairly common in Egypt and the Near East from the 4th millennium BC onwards, it does not occur in the archaeological record of Britain or Northwest Europe until the early 2nd millennium and then only rarely and in small quantities.

Methodology
The requirement for the analysis was to cause as little damage to the beads as possible. With this in mind, the controlled pressure scanning electron microscope (SEM-CP) at the Department of Earth Sciences, University of Edinburgh was used to examine them. The advantages of this technique are that the surface of the whole beads could be analysed without having to take a sample from it, and that, unlike a conventional high vacuum SEM, the beads did not have to be coated in carbon or gold. Therefore, the technique can be considered to be completely non-destructive. The disadvantages of the SEM-CP are that the precision and accuracy of the analyses is low due to poor peak resolution in energy dispersive analyser attached to the SEM-CP, a disadvantage in these compositionally complex glazes. It should also be noted that only the surface of the beads could be analysed, which again causes problems with highly weathered samples. To counter these two disadvantages of the SEM-CP, the beads were also examined in a second conventional high vacuum SEM (the Cameca SU20 SEM-EDS at the RLAHA). A very small sample was taken from each of the beads from areas of existing damage, mounted on carbon covered stubs and carbon coated. Using these samples, the SEM-EDS gave better quality compositional data and it is these data that are used in this report.

Results
The King's Low bead is small and globular, well shaped with a smooth glazed finish and is mostly light green in colour, with areas of darker green (but see Higgins below). Parts of the glaze have a thin brown accretion stuck it, and a number of cracks are visible under the binocular microscope. Under the SEM-CP cracks can be seen in the glaze and areas where the parts of the glaze have lifted off completely, exposing the core beneath. This type of damage typically results from the extensive weathering that the faience has suffered in the wet soil (Fig. 4.10). Analysis by SEM-CP of large areas of the glaze surface showed that it was mostly silica (often 90–95% SiO_2) with traces of lime and alumina. The surface of the glaze also has 1–3% CuO, which gives the overall green colour. Other components that might be expected in the glaze (for example potash, soda, magnesia, and so on) are usually absent, which again is typical of severe weathering.

The Queen's Low bead is a quoit shape, roughly shaped and irregular, and has a similar preservation to the KL bead, but with a higher proportion of the brown accretions which cover perhaps 80–90% of the bead surface. The small patches of glaze that are visible are a patchy blue colour (but see Higgins below). Analysis by SEM-CP of the little glaze that was preserved showed that, in common with the King's Low bead, it was mostly silica with traces of copper, again indicative of heavy weathering.

The high vacuum SEM-EDS examination of the micro-samples taken from the beads was more revealing, since it showed that under a thin outer layer of heavy weathering, there was a relatively fresh un-weathered subsurface to the glaze, where the inter-stitial glass was well preserved (Fig. 4.11). Analyses taken from the inter-stitial glass and bulk composition of these un-weathered areas of the King's and Queen's Low beads are given in Table 4.4, along with other analyses taken from Scottish faience beads for comparison. These analyses show that both beads have an alkali glaze, with the King's Low bead containing about equal amounts of potash and soda at 8.6% and the Queen's Low bead slightly richer in potash (7.4%) than soda (6.5%). Both are low in lime (1–2% CaO) and magnesia (0.2–0.4% MgO), are coloured with copper and may show a trace of lead, but little or no tin.

Discussion
Macroscopically the rough shape of the beads, particularly of the Queen's Low quoit bead, strongly suggests that the beads were shaped by hand modeling, rather than using a mould. Glazing techniques can in principle be differentiated using either information on the micro-structure of the core (greater or lesser amounts of inter-stitial glass), or macroscopic indicators in the glaze (runs and drips, etc., see Tite *et al.* 1983; Vandiver 1998 and many others). Since the beads were not sectioned, the structure of the cores

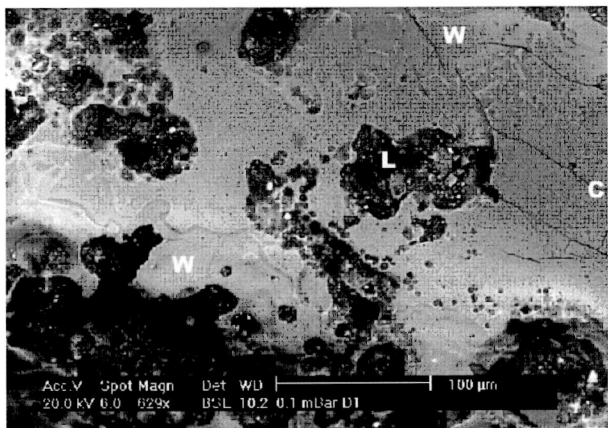

Figure 4.10 SEM-CP image of the highly weathered surface of the QL bead, showing the characteristic structures derived from the weathering due to water, including: watermarks in the glaze, where mobile elements have been leached out (W), cracking (C) and exfoliation and loss of the glaze (L).

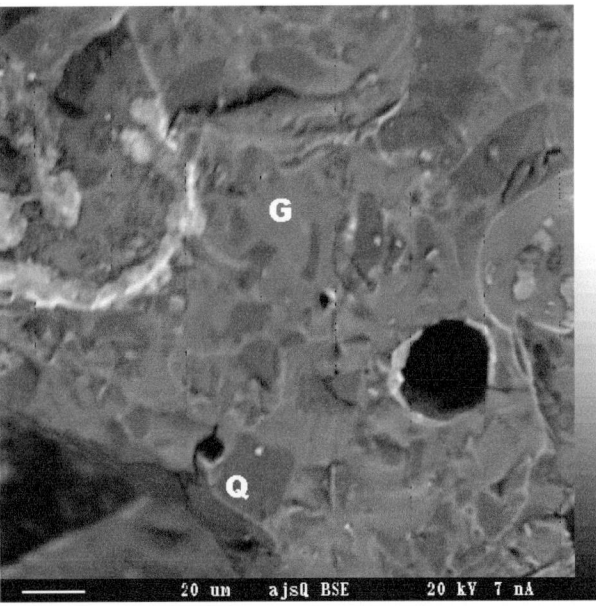

Figure 4.11 High vacuum SEM image of the un-weathered under-surface of a small stub mounted sample of the QL bead, showing well preserved inter-stitial glass (G) and distinct quartz grains (Q).

could not be examined, and the glazes of the beads were insufficiently well preserved to reveal any macroscopic indicators. The technique used for glazing the beads could therefore not be determined.

The heavily weathered nature of the surface of the glazes of both beads, as revealed by the micro-structure and composition of the glaze is not surprising. Most European faience beads are weathered in this way and this has led in the past to difficulties in analysis. However, the un-weathered areas give good analyses, and reveal that the alkali used in these beads was high in both potash and soda, meaning that the glazes of the beads fall into the group known as 'mixed alkali' glazes. The raw materials of mixed alkali glazes are thought to be plant ash and a copper source, but the exact plant and copper compounds that were used has not yet been identified. The King's Low and Queen's Low beads also have low magnesia values, and this combination of high potash and soda and low magnesia has similarities to the low magnesia, high potash (LMHK) glass of the late 2nd millennium BC that is found in Europe, particularly in Italy, Switzerland and Ireland (Henderson 1989, 42).

Very few reliable analyses for British faience are available, but the few that are, all on Scottish beads, are also given in Table 4.4 for comparison. The inter-stitial glass of the Scottish beads is quite consistent and averages 10.7% Na_2O, 3.1% MgO and 7.7% K_2O – a Na_2O/K_2O ratio of 1.4 and a MgO/K_2O ratio of 0.4. This is quite different to the King's Low and Queen's Low beads, which average slightly higher in potash (8.0% K_2O) and lower in soda (7.5% Na_2O), giving a Na_2O/K_2O ratio of 0.9 and much lower in magnesia (0.3% MgO) a MgO/K_2O ratio of 0.04. Since soda is the first element to be weathered from a glaze, the Na_2O/K_2O ratio is not a reliable indicator of compositional variation in the original raw materials since any variation could be caused by different amounts of low level weathering. However, the MgO/K_2O ratio is much less vulnerable to alteration by low levels of weathering, and is different by a factor of ten between the Scottish beads and the King's Low/Queen's Low beads. This suggests that the Scottish faience and King's Low/Queen's Low faience used significantly different plant ashes, one high in magnesia and one low. While it should be emphasised that there are very few analyses of British faience to compare with these results, they might have two interesting implications.

Table 4.4 SEM-EDS analysis of the King's Low and Queen's Low beads, with some Scottish beads for comparison.

		Na_2O	MgO	Al_2O_3	SiO_2	K_2O	CaO	TiO_3	MnO	FeO	CuO	PbO	Cl	SnO_2
King's Low	ig	8.6	0.2	1.0	74.3	8.6	1.1	0.0	0.0	0.3	5.0	0.5	0.3	0.0
Queen's Low	ig	6.5	0.4	2.5	77.5	7.4	2.0	0.0	0.0	0.3	2.7	0.3	0.5	0.0
King's Low	bulk	0.9	0.1	1.4	93.3	0.4	0.3	0.0	0.0	0.3	2.9	0.0	0.3	0.0
Scottish Beads														
Findhorn 4	glaze	1.2	2.1	0.4	91.3	0.0	0.6	0.0	0.0	0.0	3.8	0.0	0.3	0.2
Findhorn 11	glaze	0.6	2.5	1.0	90.4	0.0	0.9	0.0	0.0	0.0	3.2	0.1	0.3	1.0
Culbin 1a	ig	9.2	3.3	1.6	73.1	8.0	1.9	0.0	0.0	0.1	2.2	0.0	0.6	0.0
Culbin 1b	ig	12.7	3.3	0.5	72.6	6.6	1.8	0.0	0.0	0.0	2.0	0.1	0.4	0.0
Culbin 2a	ig	10.9	2.8	1.1	70.7	8.0	1.8	0.0	0.0	0.1	3.8	0.1	0.6	0.0
Culbin 2b	ig	10.0	3.1	1.1	72.1	8.1	2.1	0.0	0.0	0.1	2.7	0.1	0.6	0.0
Culbin 1a	bulk	4.8	1.9	1.1	84.8	4.7	1.0	0.0	0.0	0.1	1.3	0.0	0.3	low
Culbin 1b	bulk	6.5	1.5	0.6	85.1	3.4	1.3	0.0	0.0	0.0	1.3	0.0	0.3	low
Culbin 2a	bulk	5.7	1.9	1.4	82.4	4.9	1.4	0.0	0.0	0.1	1.8	0.0	0.4	low
Culbin 2b	bulk	3.7	2.0	1.6	86.5	3.8	1.1	0.0	0.0	0.2	1.0	0.0	0.1	0.0

Firstly, the King's Low and Queen's Low beads are compositionally very similar, and are distinct from the Scottish beads. This implies that these two beads are closely related, but just how closely related is difficult to say. The fact that the Queen's Low bead (found in a disturbed context) is so similar to the more contextually secure King's Low bead, strongly suggests that the former bead is associated with the King's Low and Queen's Low monuments and is not just a random find.

Secondly, the similarity of the two beads tentatively suggests that both are the product of one 'workshop', whereas the Scottish beads are the product of another or several others. Once again, the analysis of more faience beads is necessary to determine how much variation there is within each of these tentatively proposed workshops. However, the compositions of the beads analysed so far, in particular the wide variation in magnesia values, suggests that it may be possible to define workshops on the basis of compositionally distinct plant ashes.

Conclusions

The King's Low and Queen's Low beads are morphologically similar to many others found in sites of similar age throughout the United Kingdom and Ireland. Compositionally, they are very close and stand apart from the Scottish beads that have been analysed, particularly in their magnesia contents. This suggests that the two beads are connected with the use of the monuments and it is possible that they are the product of a single workshop, but only further analysis will be able to determine whether this is the case.

As noted in the discussion, the mixed alkali compositions seen in the faience is also common in slightly later (11th–7th centuries BC) glass beads in Switzerland, Northern Italy and Ireland. Both faience and glass in these areas are very different from their Near Eastern equivalents. This point is fundamental in the debate concerning the origin of the British beads. Early studies with only semi-quantitative or incomplete analyses (Stone and Thomas 1956; Newton and Renfrew 1970; Aspinall *et al.* 1972) were unable to conclusively distinguish between Near Eastern and Western European faience compositions. However, SEM analysis such as this and the major studies currently being conducted in the British Museum and the National Museum of Scotland (Alison Sheridan above) have shown that faience from Europe and faience from the Near East is compositionally very different. This means that local production of British faience is by far the most likely and lays to rest ideas of Egyptian/Mycenaean links with Britain in the Bronze Age.

4.3.3 Comments based on experimental faience
Les Higgins

The comments below are meant to supplement the two reports above and are based on inspecting the beads immediately after their excavation and on the experimental production of faience.

The glaze colour of the beads as seen by the authors above bears little resemblance to the observed colour of the beads at the time of their excavation. There are two possible reasons for their loss of colour in the post-excavation period, although there may well be other reasons of course. Firstly, de-vitrification of the glaze surface due to chemical attack which is likely to accelerate post-excavation. Secondly, and allied to the first, the oxidation of the glaze surface post-excavation due to atmospheric exposure.

The act of staining an alkali composition such as that of the paste of the King's Low and Queen's Low beads with oxide of copper would under all firing conditions produce a turquoise (Persian Blue) colour. This has been the colour response of all alkali compositions since their first use millennia ago. When first excavated both beads displayed the characteristic turquoise colour which subsequently faded and changed into the colours described in the reports above. Based on this the observed colours in the reports above, *i.e.* that the King's Low bead is 'mostly light green with areas of darker green' containing '1–3% CuO which gives the overall green colour', and that the Queen's Low bead has a 'patchy blue colour', are observations at the time of analysis and not the original colours.

Further to this change in colour, the King's Low bead when first excavated had a reduced copper red core, which covered approximately one half of the area of the threading eye of the bead. No mention is made of this in the reports above as this has also faded with time. I conducted a number of experiments in the early post-excavation period, *c*. 1990, with beads produced using a paste consisting primarily of a Nepheline Syenite base, fluxed with alkali compounds and stained by copper oxide. Successful replication of the reduced copper red core observed on the King's Low bead was eventually achieved, after a large number of experiments, by threading and firing the beads on copper rods. The area of the melted glass matrix that came into direct contact with the copper rod was consequently starved of oxygen this in turn produced the reduced red effect in the threading eye.

The low levels of aluminia in the King's Low and Queen's Low bead samples would seem to preclude the use of local clays as a binding agent/medium to hold the granular silica together during the bead manufacture (Table 4.5).

As a point of interest, the bronze products produced at Acton Park, near Wrexham and only some 40 miles from King's Low and Queen's Low, contain 'moderate amounts of lead (2 to 7%) which will improve casting behaviour and further lower the melting point but not at the expense of mechanical properties' (Savory 1980). The use by bead makers or metal workers (I suspect they are one of the same) of copper ores which contained lead as a

Table 4.5 Typical values obtained from the analysis of bricks made from clays of various geological deposits.

	Na_2O	MgO	Al_2O_3	SiO_2	K_2O	CaO	TiO_3	MnO	FeO	CuO	PbO	Cl	SnO_2	P_2O_5
Glacial clays including Staffordshire Boulder Clay	0.5	3.4	18.6	62.5	2.9	4.1	0	0	6.6	0	0	0	0	0
Etruria Clay (erroneously known locally in North Staffordshire as Etruria Marl)	0.4	1.2	23.1	62.7	2.6	0.9	0	0	8.4	0	0	0	0	0
Coal Measure Clays (Median %)	1.2	1.0	21.6	61.7	3.1	0.6	0	0	8.0	0	0	0	0	0

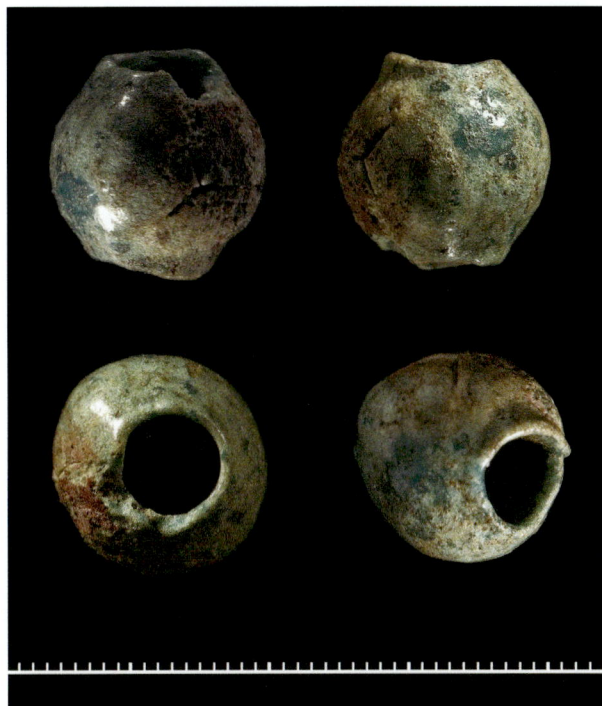

Plate 4.4 The faience beads: left, the Queen's Low quoit-shaped bead (SF283); right, the King's Low spherical bead (SF479) (photographed by Ian Cartwright).

Plate 4.5 Bracelet 1 from King's Low, (photographed by Dave Thomas).

gangue mineral similar to that which in all probability was employed in the Acton Park bronze products are one of many means to supply the lead which is in the King's Low and Queen's Low beads.

4.4 Copper alloy artefacts
4.4.1 The King's Low bracelets
Jenny Foster

Bracelet 1. SF664, SF3269
Cast bronze bracelet, oval in shape. It is decorated with slight knobs with ribs in between (Pl. 4.5, Fig. 4.12). The ribs were originally incised with short horizontal lines, though most of this detail is missing because of corrosion; most of the original surface has been lost. About a quarter of the circumference consists of a separate section, joined to the main part of the bracelet by a hinge joint, pivoted by an iron pin. The terminal is pointed and fits into a hole at the end of the main bracelet (mortice and tenon). The hinged part is longer than the gap and would have to be flexed to fit into the hole, thus ensuring a tight fit.

Inner measurement of bracelet 54 × 43 mm. Thickness 4.5 mm. Average length of knob 3.5–4 mm.

Bracelet 2. SF1101, SF1834
Two fragments (not joining) of a cast bronze bracelet, ribbed around the entire circumference (Fig. 4.12). It was oval in shape though is slightly distorted, probably by wear. It is corroded but with some original surface; this shows that the bracelet has been worn, but the decoration is still

BRACELET 1

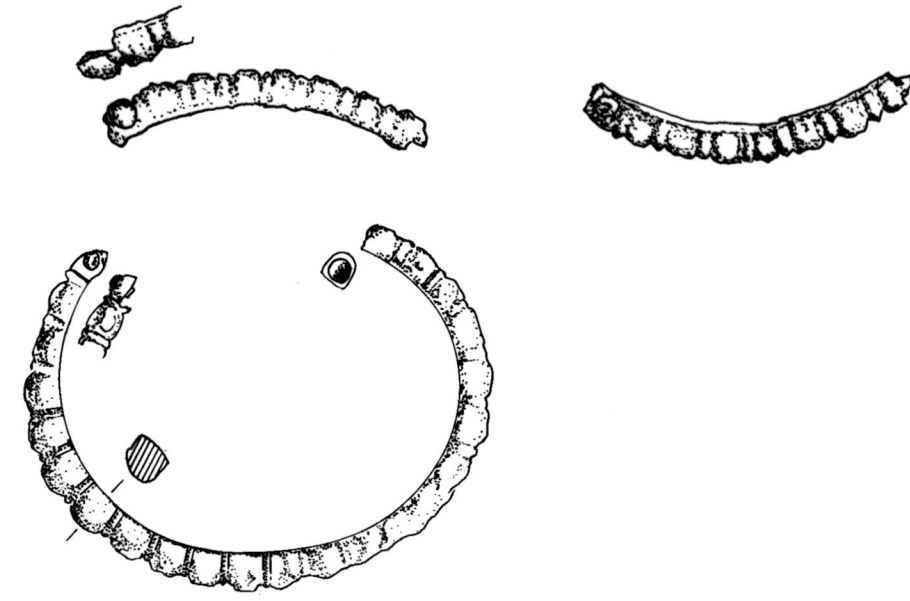

BRACELET 2

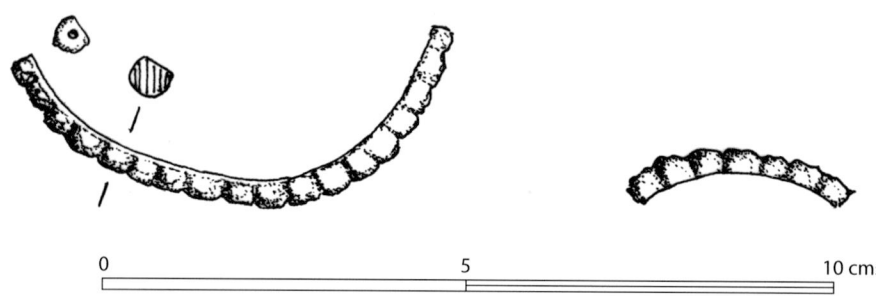

Figure 4. 12 The King's Low bracelets, (drawn by Derek Outram).

distinct. The terminals of this bracelet probably abutted together, although about one quarter is missing and it may have had a fastening like Bracelet 1.

Inner measurement 54 × 43 mm. Thickness 4 mm. Average length of rib 4 mm.

Discussion
These two bracelets belong to a series of early La Tène knobbed and ribbed bracelets widespread in Europe, which developed from massive Hallstatt types. Most, like Bracelet 2, are simple rings with abutting terminals. The majority of British bracelets are from the Yorkshire Arras burials (Stead 1965; 1991), some having mortice and tenon joints but without hinges. The decoration of Bracelet 1 is closest to the bracelet from South Ferriby, Lincs (Stead 1965, 52), knobbed with the ribs between decorated with incised lines. This bracelet, however, has a catch rather than a mortice and tenon joint and is hinged half way around the circumference. A closer parallel is the hinged section from a knobbed and ribbed bracelet that was part of a hoard from Mount Batten, Plymouth (Fox 1958, 14). An armlet from Clynnog, Caernarvonshore, Wales, with simple knobbed decoration, also has the same fastening as Bracelet 1 (Savory 1976, 26, figure 36.1; here it is described as a neck ring but with a diameter of 12 cm is more likely to be an armlet.). This type of fastening is widespread in France, Germany and Switzerland but on torcs rather than bracelets (Dechelette 1927, 721, figure 516, 2). Bronze bracelets in Yorkshire tend to date to La Tène I or early La Tène II (450–200 BC) and the pair from King's Low are probably of that date. Bronze objects from this period are not common in Britain (there are about 50 bracelets from the Early to Middle Iron Age) and it is not possible to say whether these were imported or made locally.

The context of the finds suggests that these bracelets were buried in a grave. Iron Age secondary burials in earlier barrows are extremely rare, probably because they were not recognised as such. The small number of bracelets from the Yorkshire burials (Stead 1991, 90–1) shows that corpses were usually buried with one bracelet, though one burial (Burton Fleming 10) had a bracelet on each arm; the bracelets were similar though not matched exactly. The two bracelets from King's Low have exactly the same inner measurements and were probably seen as a pair, although the decoration was slightly different.

4.4.2 Technical analyses
Peter Northover
Eight items of copper-based metalwork recovered from excavations at King's Low were submitted for metallurgical

analysis. The metalwork came from disturbed subsoil at the top of the mound, none if it having a secure context. The typology of the ribbed bracelets indicates an Iron Age date for at least some of the metalwork (see Foster above).

Sampling and analysis
Samples were taken from the sheet metal either with a jeweller's saw or with sharp scissors, and from the bracelets with a handheld model-maker's electric drill with a 0.9 mm bit. The objects sampled and their sample numbers are as follows:

Ox 453 SF664, Area D		ribbed bracelet fragment (Bracelet 1)
Ox 456 SF3269, Area D		ribbed bracelet fragment (Bracelet 1)
Ox 454 SF1834, Area D		ribbed bracelet fragment (Bracelet 2)
Ox 455 SF1101, Area D		ribbed bracelet fragment (Bracelet 2)
Ox 451 SF3900, Area F		sheet fragment
Ox 452 SF6300, Area H		binding fragment
Ox 457 SF2283, Area B		fused sheet fragment
Ox 458 SF2205, Area A		thin sheet fragment

The samples were hot mounted in a carbon-filled thermosetting resin, ground and polished to a 1:m diamond finish. Analysis was by electron probe micro-analysis using wavelength dispersive spectrometry; operating conditions were an accelerating voltage of 20kV, a beam current of 30nA and an X-ray take-off angle of 40E. Thirteen elements were analysed, as detailed in the table; count times were 20 s per element and detection limits were 100–200 ppm with the exception of 400 ppm for gold.

Three to seven areas, each 30 × 50:m were analysed per sample. The individual analyses, normalised to 100%, with their means are shown in Table 4.6. All concentrations are in weight %.

After analysis the samples were examined metallographically in both as-polished and etched states; the etch used was an acidified aqueous solution of ferric chloride further diluted with ethanol.

The metals
The copper alloy compositions fall into three groups. The largest comprises the complete ribbed bracelet and three ribbed bracelet fragments. These in turn can be divided into two pairs: SF1834 and SF1101 are virtually identical with 11.3% and 11.7% tin and 0.24% and 0.30% lead respectively. Their impurity patterns are in all other respects virtually identical with the exception of a variation in antimony content; the principal impurities are 0.11–0.16% iron and 0.22% arsenic. They could easily be part of the same melt. The second pair, SF664 (the complete bracelet) and SF3269, are a little different in having higher tin (12.8–13.4%) and lower lead (0.00–0.02%) and iron contents (0.06–0.07%). The important feature of their impurity patterns is the content of cobalt and nickel, where cobalt and nickel are low and, within the limits of experimental error, roughly equal with on occasion Co>Ni.

This impurity pattern has been previously recognised by the present writer in a small amount of Iron Age metal work. Bronze with Co>Ni but at significantly higher concentrations than here has been shown to be typical of La Tène period metalwork in southern and south-western England up to the middle of the first century BC (e.g. Northover 1991a; 1991b). If examples with, say, <0.05% cobalt are taken out they also spread through the La Tène period but are rather likely to be associated with the earlier part of the period. For example, the only stratified occurrence at Danebury is in cp3 while about half those from Maiden Castle are in the earliest Iron Age phases. We may also add a small number of relevant unpublished analyses, for example a La Tène I brooch from Hunsbury hillfort, Northamptonshire (Barnes 1985), a sword scabbard from Standlake, Oxfordshire (Jope 2000, No. 48) and a cauldron from Kincardine Moss in Scotland (Jope 2000, No. 306a) which represents the Early Iron Age developing from the bronze cauldrons of Atlantic Europe. Although the other pair of bracelet compositions has rather lower cobalt still, they essentially belong to the same grouping. It may be added that the suggestion of a date range centred on La Tène I would fit well with the proposed dating of the bracelets based on typology (Foster above).

The second group consists of two sheet fragments, one partly fused by heat, SF3900 and SF2283. They are both high tin bronzes with 14.10–14.4% tin and with all impurities at or close to the limits of detection. This composition is not strongly diagnostic as to date since it occurs in more than one period; however these periods are well scattered and two are of particular interest in the context of King's Low. High tin, low impurity bronze is first important in the Early Bronze Age, particularly towards the end in Arreton type bronzes (Northover 1999). It does occur sporadically in the Middle Bronze Age but not in the Late Bronze Age. Its next significant occurrence is in the La Tène Iron Age but almost all known examples belong to phases 6G–H at Maiden Castle. It is unlikely to be Roman, Saxon or Medieval but a more recent date cannot be entirely ruled out.

The final two items must be regarded as relatively recent. The binding, SF6300, is made from an alloy of copper with zinc; it is highly corroded and has suffered from some de-zincification but care was taken to ensure that analyses were made on un-corroded metal. Such alloys do not occur in Britain before the last years of the first century BC. However, what is essentially a gilding metal with 10.7% zinc and low levels of most impurities, especially iron, is not consistent with such an early date. Indeed a date before the Late Medieval period can be ruled out. The last find, SF2205, appears to be a thin sheet of copper. It, too, is badly corroded and it is not impossible that it is the product of the de-zincification of a sheet similar to SF6300. If it was in fact a copper sheet a post-medieval date would seem probable. While copper sheets do exist in earlier periods they are usually considerably thicker.

Metallography
Metallographic examination of the bracelets was precluded by the use of drilled samples. The sheet samples, though, were cut because their structure and condition might give

Table 4.6 Analysis of the copper-based metalwork from King's Low.

Sample	sf no.	Object	Fe	Co	Ni	Cu	Zn	As	Sb	Sn	Ag	Bi	Pb	Au	S
Ox 451/1	3900	Cu alloy sheet	0.00	0.02	0.00	85.44	0.00	0.00	0.00	14.49	0.00	0.01	0.02	0.00	0.01
Ox 451/2			0.01	0.00	0.00	85.24	0.00	0.00	0.00	14.66	0.00	0.05	0.00	0.01	0.02
Ox 451/3			0.01	0.00	0.01	85.78	0.00	0.03	0.00	14.13	0.00	0.02	0.00	0.00	0.01
Ox 451/4			0.01	0.02	0.00	85.86	0.00	0.00	0.00	14.10	0.00	0.01	0.00	0.00	0.00
Ox 451/5			0.00	0.00	0.01	85.50	0.03	0.00	0.00	14.34	0.00	0.04	0.07	0.00	0.00
Ox 452/1	6300	Binding	0.02	0.03	0.06	89.27	10.24	0.18	0.03	0.02	0.12	0.00	0.00	0.00	0.03
Ox 452/2			0.02	0.01	0.03	89.10	10.52	0.16	0.00	0.01	0.05	0.02	0.00	0.10	0.00
Ox 452/3			0.01	0.01	0.06	88.03	11.39	0.25	0.01	0.02	0.07	0.00	0.07	0.07	0.01
Ox 452/4			0.01	0.00	0.04	88.89	10.67	0.20	0.02	0.02	0.04	0.01	0.02	0.01	0.04
Ox 453/1	664	Ribbed bracelet	0.06	0.03	0.06	86.01	0.05	0.20	0.00	13.57	0.00	0.00	0.00	0.00	0.01
Ox 453/2			0.09	0.02	0.02	86.41	0.05	0.18	0.00	13.18	0.00	0.00	0.00	0.00	0.05
Ox 453/3			0.09	0.01	0.00	85.87	0.02	0.16	0.02	13.72	0.00	0.06	0.01	0.00	0.05
Ox 453/4			0.10	0.05	0.01	84.67	0.04	0.17	0.19	14.42	0.00	0.10	0.09	0.08	0.08
Ox 453/5			0.01	0.01	0.03	87.56	0.00	0.18	0.00	12.19	0.00	0.00	0.00	0.00	0.01
Ox 454/1	1834	Ribbed bracelet, fragment	0.22	0.03	0.06	87.49	0.03	0.29	0.04	11.35	0.00	0.00	0.39	0.00	0.10
Ox 454/2			0.18	0.01	0.01	87.70	0.00	0.17	0.04	11.57	0.00	0.03	0.18	0.00	0.11
Ox 454/3			0.14	0.00	0.00	87.42	0.00	0.24	0.08	11.68	0.01	0.06	0.19	0.12	0.06
Ox 454/4			0.14	0.01	0.06	88.11	0.00	0.23	0.05	11.05	0.00	0.08	0.13	0.01	0.13
Ox 454/5			0.11	0.01	0.04	88.07	0.07	0.16	0.04	11.01	0.00	0.00	0.33	0.02	0.15
Ox 455/1	1101	Ribbed bracelet, fragment	0.12	0.00	0.00	87.75	0.00	0.20	0.01	11.51	0.00	0.07	0.33	0.00	0.02
Ox 455/2			0.11	0.04	0.00	87.67	0.00	0.22	0.00	11.46	0.00	0.13	0.25	0.05	0.07
Ox 455/3			0.10	0.01	0.03	87.68	0.00	0.26	0.00	11.61	0.00	0.00	0.25	0.03	0.02
Ox 455/4			0.09	0.00	0.05	86.93	0.07	0.19	0.05	12.18	0.00	0.00	0.35	0.00	0.08
Ox 456/1	3269	Ribbed bracelet, fragment	0.03	0.01	0.04	86.79	0.00	0.18	0.05	12.89	0.00	0.00	0.00	0.00	0.00
Ox 456/2			0.03	0.00	0.05	86.59	0.10	0.22	0.00	12.99	0.00	0.01	0.00	0.00	0.01
Ox 456/3			0.09	0.02	0.05	88.16	0.00	0.14	0.01	11.43	0.00	0.01	0.01	0.01	0.06
Ox 456/4			0.11	0.04	0.03	87.65	0.02	0.20	0.01	11.90	0.00	0.03	0.00	0.00	0.01
Ox 456/5			0.02	0.03	0.03	84.62	0.00	0.22	0.02	14.91	0.00	0.00	0.00	0.14	0.01
Ox 457/1	2283	Fused sheet fragment	0.03	0.00	0.00	86.66	0.07	0.05	0.00	13.16	0.00	0.00	0.01	0.00	0.02
Ox 457/2			0.02	0.00	0.00	86.13	0.00	0.00	0.00	13.78	0.00	0.00	0.00	0.04	0.03
Ox 457/3			0.02	0.01	0.00	85.52	0.04	0.06	0.00	14.32	0.00	0.00	0.00	0.00	0.03
Ox 457/4			0.00	0.00	0.02	85.27	0.03	0.02	0.05	14.58	0.00	0.00	0.00	0.00	0.02
Ox 457/5			0.00	0.00	0.00	85.30	0.00	0.01	0.00	14.64	0.00	0.00	0.01	0.04	0.00
Ox 458/1	2205	Thin sheet fragment	0.01	0.00	0.01	99.30	0.23	0.10	0.00	0.01	0.00	0.05	0.17	0.00	0.12
Ox 458/2			0.01	0.00	0.02	99.80	0.03	0.01	0.01	0.00	0.04	0.01	0.00	0.07	0.02
Ox 458/3			0.03	0.00	0.00	99.75	0.15	0.06	0.00	0.01	0.01	0.00	0.00	0.00	0.00
Ox451	3900	Sheet fragment	0.01	0.01	0.00	85.56	0.01	0.01	0.00	14.35	0.00	0.03	0.02	0.00	0.01
Ox452	6300	Binding	0.02	0.01	0.05	88.82	10.70	0.20	0.02	0.02	0.07	0.01	0.02	0.04	0.02
Ox453	664	Ribbed bracelet	0.07	0.03	0.02	86.10	0.03	0.18	0.04	13.42	0.00	0.03	0.02	0.02	0.04
Ox454	1834	Ribbed bracelet, fragment	0.16	0.01	0.03	87.76	0.02	0.22	0.05	11.33	0.00	0.03	0.24	0.03	0.11
Ox455	1101	Ribbed bracelet, fragment	0.11	0.01	0.02	87.51	0.02	0.22	0.01	11.69	0.00	0.05	0.30	0.02	0.05
Ox456	3269	Ribbed bracelet, fragment	0.06	0.02	0.04	86.76	0.02	0.19	0.02	12.82	0.00	0.01	0.00	0.03	0.02
Ox457	2283	Fused sheet fragment	0.01	0.00	0.00	85.78	0.03	0.03	0.01	14.10	0.00	0.00	0.00	0.02	0.02
Ox458	2205	Thin sheet fragment	0.01	0.00	0.01	99.62	0.13	0.06	0.00	0.01	0.02	0.02	0.06	0.02	0.05
Ox453	664	Ribbed bracelet	0.07	0.03	0.02	86.10	0.03	0.18	0.04	13.42	0.00	0.03	0.02	0.02	0.04
Ox456	3269	Ribbed bracelet, fragment	0.06	0.02	0.04	86.76	0.02	0.19	0.02	12.82	0.00	0.01	0.00	0.03	0.02
Ox454	1834	Ribbed bracelet, fragment	0.16	0.01	0.03	87.76	0.02	0.22	0.05	11.33	0.00	0.03	0.24	0.03	0.11
Ox455	1101	Ribbed bracelet, fragment	0.11	0.01	0.02	87.51	0.02	0.22	0.01	11.69	0.00	0.05	0.30	0.02	0.05
Ox451	3900	Sheet fragment	0.01	0.01	0.00	85.56	0.01	0.01	0.00	14.35	0.00	0.03	0.02	0.00	0.01
Ox457	2283	Fused sheet fragment	0.01	0.00	0.00	85.78	0.03	0.03	0.01	14.10	0.00	0.00	0.00	0.02	0.02
Ox452	6300	Binding	0.02	0.01	0.05	88.82	10.70	0.20	0.02	0.02	0.07	0.01	0.02	0.04	0.02
Ox458	2205	Thin sheet fragment	0.01	0.00	0.01	99.62	0.13	0.06	0.00	0.01	0.02	0.02	0.06	0.02	0.05

further clues as to history. The sample from the copper-zinc alloy binding, SF6300, shows a deformed re-crystallised grain structure with annealing twins heavily penetrated by corrosion with considerable areas of de-zincification. The thin sheet fragment, SF2205, is also heavily corroded. Apparently sound areas of copper show a twinned structure but that this is the result of the growth of re-deposited copper during corrosion cannot entirely be ruled out.

The two bronze fragments, SF3900 and SF2283, have very similar structures. They both exhibit fully re-crystallised equiaxed grain structure with annealing twins but both have very large grain sizes of 250:m or more. Neither shows any coring but some un-dissolved eutectoid remains; there are some slip traces by they could represent damage during post-depositional disturbance. The structures are not typical of normal wrought bronze structures but they are to be expected in bronze that has undergone prolonged heating. There are no signs of internal oxidation either in the surviving metal or preserved in the corrosion product so it is probable that the heating was under reducing conditions.

Given the suggestion made above about a late Early Bronze Age date for the metal it would be not unreasonable to connect these fragments with the cremation associated with the Collared Urn. If so, the metal was probably placed on the body which would burn with a reducing flame, but did not fall into the body cavity which might have been too cold.

Conclusions

The eight metal small finds examined fall into three groups on the basis of composition and structure:

1. One large and three smaller fragments of two ribbed bracelets. Metallurgical and archaeological data concur in placing these at the start of the La Tène Iron Age.
2. Two fragments of heated, wrought sheet bronze; these have a composition which could date them to the latter part of the Early Bronze Age. They could be associated with a cremation, possibly that recovered with the Collared Urn.
3. Two thin sheets of metal of uncertain age.

5 King's Low and Queen's Low: a wider discussion

Gary Lock

> ... let it be remembered that archaeological evidence is essentially our creation, that is, the objects that we study only acquire their specific character because we apply the techniques of archaeology to them. The men who raised barrows, wielded battle-axes and long daggers, ... did not think of their tools and weapons [and] structures as potential archaeological evidence. These things are only such because we record, classify, and analyse them in order to extract from them the knowledge of the prehistoric past. (Ashbee 1960, 16).

5.1 Background and antiquarian interest

It is implicit within the quote above that the understanding of round barrows has changed considerably since their first being described and catalogued by John Leland, William Camden, John Aubrey and other antiquarians from the 16th century onwards. From being initially thought of purely as grave mounds that provided artefacts when dug into, barrows are now seen as complex structures with their own internal sequential biographies that can say something about the identities of the deceased and their wider social relationships. The current position is epitomised by the title of a recent book offering new perspectives on barrows – *Beyond the Grave* (Last 2007a). In this chapter we will discuss some of the past and recent developments in barrow studies and position King's Low and Queen's Low within them.

Both Last (2007b) and Ashbee (1960, ch. 1) give accounts of the early development of barrow studies from the 16th century as part of an antiquarian understanding of prehistoric monuments more generally and the first national surveys and how they tied in with the development of chronologies. By the early 19th century these earlier works were used within a series of more local, often county-based, surveys such as Sir Richard Colt Hoare and William Cunnington in Wiltshire (Colt Hoare 1812 and 1821). These two, often seen as the pioneers of barrow research based on excavation, dug into 379 barrows around the Stonehenge area, their findings being published within a framework of contemporary 'objectivity' ('we speak from facts not theory' they claim in the Introduction) which became the model for other barrow diggers.

While this national background is obviously important for establishing the intellectual atmosphere for barrow exploration, it is activities more local to King's Low and Queen's Low that we will focus on here. Of importance are the father and son team of William and Thomas Bateman who, with Samuel Carrington and James Ruddock, in the ten years from 1848 dug into over 400 barrows in Derbyshire, Staffordshire and Yorkshire (Bateman 1861). It was Carrington who worked in Staffordshire although this was in a limited area within 10 km of his home in Wetton, North Staffordshire, within which he investigated 122 barrows (Barnatt 1996a, 13). His area of interest did not extend as far south as King's Low and Queen's Low, approximately 40 km away from Wetton as the crow flies, confirmed by a lack of reference in Gunstone's gazetteer of Staffordshire barrows (1965, 49). This is perhaps not surprising being as Bateman and his colleagues were focussed on the Peak District monuments, as has been much recent work by John Barnatt (Barnatt and Collis 1996). Barnatt's corpus of barrows in the Peak District (1996b) divides the area into zones, the southern most of which, Zone 17: Staffordshire, includes ten extant sites and nine destroyed or lost although, again, this does not reach as far south as King's Low and Queen's Low. The higher density of barrows in the Peak District compared to the rest of Staffordshire is shown in the background section of this report (Ch. 1, Figs 1.4 and 1.5).

It is clear from this that because King's Low and Queen's Low fall beyond the Peak District grouping of barrows they, and the area they are in, appear to have been neglected both by antiquarians and modern researchers alike. Their isolation from the main concentration of barrows to the north is illustrated on the map of prehistoric and Roman sites in Greenslade and Stuart's (1965, 11) *History of Staffordshire,* and in Thomas and Gunstone's *Introduction to the Prehistory of Staffordshire* (1964, figure 1), where the two dots stand in clear isolation. Even so, as shown in Chapter 1, the two barrows were certainly recognised by at least 1780 and written about by William Camden in 1806, with the indication of a third barrow by Clifford and Clifford in 1817. Erdeswick's Survey of Staffordshire published in 1844 actually refers to two 'remarkable' tumuli, and they were located and named on maps from 1831/2, the first by Henry Teesdale. All of this indicates that during the period of intense antiquarian interest in barrows both King's Low and Queen's Low were known and, therefore, it would not be surprising if they were dug into. Garwood (2007b, 139) has commented on the rarity of 'antiquarian dedicated field work' in Staffordshire outside the Peak District although there was certainly some activity in the area, not least by William Molyneux who dug into five barrows in the Stoke-on-Trent area between 1869 and 1878 (Molyneux 1878). The closest to King's Low and Queen's Low is only three miles away near Brocton in the Sherbrook Valley (*ibid.*, 12; Gunstone 1965, 32, Baswich 1), 'a mound of bunter pebbles with three layers of burnt bone, with coarse brown British pottery at the base' (Robinson 1974). Within a mile or two of that barrow is another at Spring Hill (Gunstone 1965, 33, Baswich 2) described as either a saucer barrow, which would be very unusual in this area, or as 'having the centre lowered through digging'. The other four barrows are all in the parish of Swynnerton closer to Stoke-on-Trent, one at Bury Bank Camp (Gunstone 1965, 48, Swynnerton 3/5; Molyneux 1878, 8) yielding charcoal and human bones. At Monument Hill (Gunstone 1965, 48, Swynnerton 7; Molyneux 1878, 9) there was a gravel mound with stone cist and human bones, and at Trentham Park (Gunstone 1965, 49, Swynnerton 8; Molyneux 1878, 10) the mound was destroyed but an urn found. Most detailed evidence came from the barrow at Northwood Farm (Gunstone 1965, 49, Swynnerton 9; Molyneux 1878, 9) which had a primary stone cist containing the burnt remains of two people and at least three or four secondary burials in a variety of cinerary urns with a series of flints. Antiquarians were not always so fortunate, however, as shown by the earlier investigations into what turned out to be a natural feature at nearby Camp Hills, Maer, Newcastle-under-Lyme (Shaw 1798).

Despite this activity in the area, the evidence for antiquarian interest in both King's Low and Queen's Low is lacking. At the former there was no evidence to suggest that any digging reached the lower parts of the barrow (the phase 1 turf mound and the Collared Urn burial) although any investigation into the upper parts of the mound would probably not be identifiable due to subsequent podsolisation and rabbit activity that has severely altered the deposits. At Queen's Low, where truncation due to agricultural activity had virtually removed the whole mound, there was evidence of disturbance which appeared to post-date the flattening of the mound. An approximately square hole had been dug into the highest point as witnessed by an existing hollow and two old wooden pegs in the ground. This probably dates to during or after World War II and it is not known who is responsible and whether they found anything.

5.2 Barrows in the landscape

Woodward has suggested that the two main themes of recent barrow studies have been 'complexity' and 'context' (2000), both of which apply to their internal structuring but also to their landscape setting and spatial relationships with each other including their occurrence in groups or 'cemeteries'. An interest in the landscape setting of barrows dates back to the antiquarians as shown by Colt Hoare's early 20th century Wiltshire volumes in which he and his surveyor Philip Crocker pioneered the accurate mapping and recording of barrows. This included not just the development of scale maps and plans but novel three-dimensional representations of barrow groups justified by

> a large group of twenty-seven tumuli, which, being so thickly clustered, could not be numbered sufficiently distinct on the general map: I have therefore had them engraved on a separate plate, which will explain, better than any verbal description, the different forms of the barrows which compose this group. (Colt Hoare 1812, 121)

It is from the accumulation of antiquarian's and subsequent field worker's evidence that total numbers of barrows have been estimated. Not least in the 20th century is the work of Leslie Grinsell (1941; 1953) who visited and recorded over 10,000 barrows mainly in central and southern England continuing the importance of field-based observation. Calculations of total numbers of barrows are still somewhat imprecise, Ashbee (1960, 24) for example, states that within the 'well explored area of Wessex' there are some 6,000 barrows and probably 18,000 in the British Isles. A more recent estimate (Parker Pearson 2005) gives the figure of 30,000 within Britain, of varied size with the largest ones up to 50 m diameter. He goes on to note that densities of barrows vary considerable and they can occur within groups of between four and 40, within 3 km of Stonehenge, for example, there are 260 barrows. Obviously of more interest when thinking about King's Low and Queen's Low in terms of density, landscape setting and chronology are regions closer than Wessex. Even in these less dense areas, however, there are problems in arriving at precise numbers, as shown by Barnatt (1996a, 7) in the Peak District where due to problems of destruction and mis-identification he can only estimate there being between 518 and 670 sites. For Staffordshire itself Gunstone's gazetteer of barrows (1965) includes over 270 possible barrows although his summary (Thomas and Gunstone 1964) states a 'minimum estimate' of 119. Arriving at a precise number of barrows for Staffordshire is complicated further by Vine (1982) who has catalogued sites and artefacts from the Neolithic and Early Bronze Age for the Middle and Upper Trent Basin which includes Staffordshire. He lists 86 'proved' barrows and 209 'possible' sites (*ibid.* Maps AE and AF), based largely on Gunstone's gazetteer but with additions. The picture is further confused by Richards (1984) who lists 41 barrows within a ten mile radius of Newcastle-under-Lyme although they are not cross referenced with Gunstone and it is difficult to establish how many are additional to the gazetteer.

Two important recent pieces of work which will be referred to in more detail below are relevant to King's Low and Queen's Low. The first is that of Dave Mullin (2003; 2007) to the north-west of our area, in the low-lying Cheshire Basin where he has catalogued 212 barrows, most in a 'poor state of preservation' mainly due to agricultural damage. His survey includes the north-western parts of Staffordshire, not including the Peak District, which incorporates 20 barrows (although some may be natural features) and includes King's Low and Queen's Low. The second is related to the West Midlands Regional Research Framework and in particular the results of its archaeological resource assessment seminar (Garwood 2007a). This identifies the 'archaeologically neglected' area of the West Midlands, including central and north-western Staffordshire and recognises the considerable potential within the region. The work of Paul Garwood is particularly relevant here who in a first attempt to review the region in its entirety, has identified over 900 barrows (and ring ditches), roughly half of which have surviving mounds (Garwood 2007b, 134), with concentrations in North Staffordshire and the valleys of the Rivers Trent, Severn and Avon. He also records over 250 'investigations' into barrows, most importantly at least 64 having been excavated since 1960, including King's Low and Queen's Low, which together with the identification of ring ditches have 'transformed' our knowledge of this region (*ibid.*, figures 10.1 and 10.2, 140).

It has been recognised almost since the beginnings of barrow studies that they often occur in groups or 'cemeteries' displaying different spatial configurations. The classification by Ashbee (1960, 34) into 'linear, nuclear and dispersed' is still generally used, he also recognised that dispersed cemeteries are 'mainly a North Country phenomenon' indicating striking differences with Wessex. Fleming (1971) refined this model for Wessex suggesting 'nucleated and linear' cemeteries with distances between barrows less than 100 m, 'dispersed' cemeteries where barrows are 100 m to 150 m apart and 'area' cemeteries which contain many barrows 200 m to 400 m apart. More recently Garwood has convincingly argued (2007d) that understandings of cemeteries, their spatial relationships and temporal development, is severely limited by the lack of a detailed chronological scheme which he goes a long way towards providing. He identifies noticeable differences between Wessex and other regions from *c.*1800 cal BC onwards in terms of barrow groupings, an important one being that in areas to the north of Wessex barrows tend to occur in 'dispersed groupings of single mounds, occasionally paired, or small clusters of three or four' (*ibid.*, 45). A possible reason for the difference between Wessex and other parts of the country, he argues, could be the movement into previously unoccupied areas. In these new areas barrows are erected in monument free landscapes for a range of possible reasons. Perhaps to symbolise the group's presence, to establish a landscape marker and to provide focal points which initiate a sense of history based in the landscape, they are in effect community resources in the sense of creating a sense of community and mutual belonging. This contrasts with Wessex where by this time there has been a long period of barrow construction creating dense distributions and barrows with fancy forms and rich grave-goods which are more to do with the power and identity of individuals and established lineages. Of the 212 barrows in the Cheshire Basin (Mullin 2003), less than a quarter occur in cemeteries, mostly are in pairs or singly, a similar situation to the Peak District (Barnatt 1996a, 67). This dispersed grouping of single mounds, also typical of the West Midlands, seems to apply to King's Low and Queen's Low which are approximately 1 km apart and even if the third barrow did exist (Ch. 1), it is still a low density cemetery if that term can be applied at all.

The danger of over simplifying the chronological, structural and social elements within groups of barrows, even the less dense 'non-Wessex' groups, have been shown by two large-scale studies of dispersed cemeteries carried out to modern excavation standards: the Brenig Valley in Denbighshire (Lynch 1993) and the The Raunds Project in Northamptonshire (Harding and Healy 2007). Both show a great deal of complexity within, and difference between, individual barrows with a diversity of forms and longevity of use for the group as a whole. In the Brenig Valley a range of different barrow types span a period of at least 400 years and seem to be centred on an initial barrow which may be Neolithic. It was shown by Kinnes (1979) that round barrows started in the Neolithic and within the complex of monuments excavated at Raunds a whole series of round barrows started in the Late Neolithic and continued through the Early Bronze Age. Interpreting the varied evidence for the adoption of single burial, beneath a barrow, is complex as shown in detail by Bradley (2007, ch. 3). He discusses the implied social changes and establishes that although single burial started earlier in the Neolithic its effects were short lived and when reintroduced 'between 2500 and 2000 cal BC it had a lasting impact' (*ibid.*, 89). Underlying these arguments is a reliance on good regional chronologies although this is problematic for the West Midlands as Garwood (2007b) has shown. Of over 70 barrows that have produced artefacts in the region only 23 are in stratigraphically secure primary locations (*ibid.*, 143). Reliable radiocarbon dates are equally scarce, of the 27 dates from 15 sites, 11 from 7 sites have no stratigraphical context leaving 13 dates possibly related to monument construction, of these five dates from five sites have either a standard deviation which is too large to be useful or the stratigraphical relationship is uncertain. This leaves just four sites with reliable dating for all of the West Midlands and just two in Staffordshire, Low Bent (Wilson and Cleverdon 1987) and King's Low, as Garwood states this is 'no basis for a regional chronology' (Garwood 2007b, 144; appendix 10.1; appendix 10.3).

The whole concept of 'single' and individual' burial has been questioned by Bradley (2007, 158), who emphasises the differences between the earlier Beaker barrow burials with a single inhumed burial and the later barrows which often contain a whole series of cremations. One aspect to emerge from this work is the recognition and importance of these 'cemetery barrows' (Woodward 2000, 22–28), which become the norm in some areas from *c.* 2000 cal BC. These individual mounds attract burials over a long period of time in contrast to the single burial barrows (Mullin 2003, 19). Bradley (2007) and Barrett (1994) see this as symbolising the changing relationships between the dead and the living so that a single burial has a primary relationship with the living who are involved in the burial activities and building the mound, whereas multiple cremations over a period of time also have genealogical relationships with other people buried within the mound. In addition, this long term focus on a particular mound suggested to Lynch (1993) that ceremony based on the mound was more important than the actual burials contained within and Garwood (2007d, 207) sees this as a 'monument focussed expression of cultural identity'. This he argues through larger scale distributions of Neolithic and Early Bronze Age monument types including the Cotswolds, Upper Thames Valley and the Peak District albeit with the warning that 'these simple spatial models need to be treated with great caution'.

It has also been recognised that barrows may have links to the past in that they often seem to be located at places where there is evidence of earlier interest and activity, a long term focus on an area which pre-dates the eventual barrow building. This may take the more obvious form of barrows being built close to Neolithic or earlier sites or the more subtle form of earlier material being incorporated into the mounds even though there is no other evidence for related activity as noticed by Ashbee (1960, 55) suggesting 'deliberate admixture during building'. For the latter, Woodward (2000, 51) suggests the possibility of barrows being built over 'closed habitation sites', perhaps the mounds incorporating midden material, a practice which may have its roots in the 'closing' of Neolithic long barrows. Certainly the mound at King's Low contained sherds of Neolithic Grooved Ware pottery which Gibson (Ch. 4) estimates to date from between 3000 and 2400 cal BC on typological grounds, Beaker sherds as well as Mesolithic, Early Neolithic, Later Neolithic and Beaker lithics. Queen's Low, again from mound material, produced Beaker sherds and Later Neolithic lithics. While these are not large quantities of material, remembering Garwood's (2007b, 201) claim for the 'rarity of Beaker monuments and burials' in the West Midlands, they are enough to require an explanation: either the sherds and lithics were being curated and then intentionally incorporated into the mounds when they were constructed, or more likely they are debris in the soil from earlier activity which was then used for mound construction. It is of interest that at the other recent excavation in the area, both of the barrows Low Bent and Low Farm, Longnor, approximately 40 km north of King's Low and Queen's Low, produced Late Neolithic Grooved Ware (Wilson and Cleverdon 1987). Both Ray (2007) and Woodward (2007) have shown that there is considerable evidence for Neolithic occupation within the West Midlands area. The area of the Tame-Trent confluence (Fig. 1.2), the Catholme/Whitemoor Haye, Staffordshire ceremonial complex, for example, is of national importance (Buteux *et al.* 2007) where there is a possible henge, other enclosures, pits and ring ditches on the dry gravel terraces. At Alrewas and Mavesyn Ridware beside the River Trent north of Lichfield, are two possible causewayed enclosures, both egg shaped with three ditches (Ray 2007, 58). Even without such impressive evidence the excavation of individual barrows often produces earlier material either incorporated into the mound or on the pre-mound surface.

Interpretations of the landscape settings of barrows, and cemeteries, have changed over the years from the rather more pragmatic whereby they are seen to act as visible markers of social groups, perhaps related to 'territories' as with Renfrew's (1973) arguments for the Neolithic and Fleming's (1971) for round barrows, to the more spiritual and phenomenological integration within a natural setting (Tilley 1994). As emphasised by Woodward (2000, ch. 3) the recent research focus has been on the locations of barrows not being on high, visible places but in low-lying situations often close to water. This preference for low-lying locations close to water is widespread through areas of Britain, the three barrows at Cossington, Leicestershire for example (Thomas 2008) lie on the gravel terrace less than 1 km from, and overlooking, the confluence of the Rivers Wreake and Soar. In Cheshire, Mullin (2003, 19; 2007, figure 2.7) shows that most barrows are on the low-lying sides of hills and close to rivers and streams, even though highly visible locations are available they are ignored. He concludes from this that visual connections between barrows were not important and that physical proximity was in the form of being next to a settlement, a known locale and the proximity to other people in the same barrow all contributing to a form of social and genealogical history that was important to individuals and groups. In terms of views these barrows existed within small-scale localised clearance in woodland with short range views, something else that is in contrast with Wessex cemeteries which often had wide vistas across the relatively open chalk down lands and views of other barrows and monuments. Woodward and Woodward (1996) show this convincingly for three major concentrations of Wessex barrows, the South Dorset Ridgeway, Stonehenge and Avebury, concluding that proximity to major monuments together with subtle relationships with local topography, rivers and ridges, structure the positioning of barrows and cemeteries. In the Peak District the size of the mound may be related to visibility, on the limestone plateau with more open views mounds are generally 10 m to 20 m in diameter compared to larger ones in lower areas with more restricted views where they are between 5 m and 50 m (Barnatt and Collis 1996, 26–32). In Staffordshire there are seven exceptionally large mounds, all in low lying areas, which Garwood (2007b, 142) has suggested could be to 'enhance monument visibility and/or expand vistas by creating viewing platforms'. Analysing the topographical settings of the barrows of the Weald in south-eastern England, Field (1998) has shown that despite considerable variation in the size of cemeteries, from two to three barrows to over 30, there is a distinct preference for them being located on low ridges. These are often false crests so that the barrow is visible from afar but not from the low land nearby (*ibid.*, 316). He goes on to build on Grinsell's (1941) early observations concerning a preferred riverine distribution for many barrows being 'set back from rivers, on the valley margins, usually 0.5 km to 1 km from the river'. The suggestion is that the barrows were located on the marginal land at the edge of land holdings so as not to interfere with 'agricultural and other activities'. Over time the number of barrows would increase through different communities sharing these boundary zones thus resulting in the high numbers sometimes seen.

The barrows in North Staffordshire other than the Peak District group, certainly display a preference for riverine locations (Ch. 1 Fig. 1.4). Low Farm and Low Bent, on the edge of the Peak District but important for being excavated in modern times, are two of a widely spaced linear group of four, which together with the nearby Sheen group of four are 3 km from each other at the junction of the River Manifold and the Blake Brook. Of these eight, five are low-lying on the valley slopes while the other three are on a low ridge overlooking the rivers (Wilson and Cleverdon 1987, fig. 1). To the north-west of King's Low and Queen's Low are dispersed and small groups of barrows along the valleys of the Rivers Sow and Trent and their tributaries. Within 5 km to the east are two ring ditches, Bishton and Shugborough Park, both close to the River Trent while further along the river's course, towards its confluence with the River Mease, is a greater density of barrows which together with the evidence for ring ditches suggests considerably more occupation than around King's Low and Queen's Low (Vine 1982).

The locational arguments outlined above certainly seem to apply to King's Low and Queen's Low with both being on higher land overlooking the valley of the Rivers Penk and Sow just over 1 km to the south, both probably easily accessible as the gradient is gradual. The settlements of the people who built and used King's Low and Queen's Low are unknown although this is not unusual for the Early Bronze Age where settlements are acknowledged to be 'fluid and impermanent' (Parker Pearson 2005, 83) yielding 'little evidence' (Mullin 2003, 720). It is not until the Middle Bronze Age, *c*. 1500 cal BC onwards, that settlements, field systems and evidence for landscape organisation becomes widely available although in the Peak District, Barnatt (1999) has identified earlier settlements and fields, some being integrated into landscapes with a variety of burial monuments including barrows and cairns. Garwood (2007b, 196) comments on the limited evidence for Early Bronze Age forest clearance and settlement throughout the West Midlands region, and perhaps not until the mid 2nd millennium BC for the upper Trent and its tributaries. As shown in Chapter 1, the evidence for Early Bronze Age activity around King's Low and Queen's Low is sparse although the HER records a small number of Late Bronze Age artefacts within *c*. 5 km and slightly further away to the south-east is a concentration of burnt mounds (Welch 1990). It has been noticed that burnt mounds, of which there are 18 known in Staffordshire, tend to be in different areas to barrows, perhaps being associated with animal related activities and, therefore, associated with pastoral areas rather than the more fertile soils (Welch 1997). A Middle to Late Bronze Age date, radiocarbon dates cluster around 1400–1200 cal BC, is now generally accepted for these still poorly understood sites (Barfield and Hodder 1989). The burnt mound excavated at Milwich, less than 10 km from King's Low and Queen's Low, was thought to have originally been an island within the Milwich Brook and comprised 80% burnt stones and charcoal the date range being 1880–1400 cal BC to 1510–1170 cal BC (Welch 1997) showing a long period of periodic use.

The environmental evidence from the Sow floodplain (Ch. 3, Sugden and Outram) suggests clearance from the Middle Bronze Age onwards although pollen from King's Low does show some clearance and human activity earlier than this and before the mound was built. Mullin (2003, ch. 5) indicates the limitations of the environmental evidence for this area, and the limited usefulness for Staffordshire of the North West Wetlands Survey which lacks ^{14}C dates and relationships with human activity (Leah *et al.* 1998). Within the immediate area the pollen sequence from the King's Pool (Bartley and Morgan 1990), *c*. 3 km away from King's Low, is important and is fundamental to the stages of clearance suggested by Greig (2007, 47, table 4.2) with clearance starting between 2800 and 2000 cal BC (although possibly on a smaller scale from as early as the Mesolithic based on the presence of charcoal perhaps from fire used to create small clearances) and then increasing from 2000 cal BC onwards together with pastoralism and a warmer climate. It seems likely, therefore, that the higher ground where King's Low and Queen's Low are located was partially cleared at the time of their construction with extra clearance immediately around the barrows. Assuming settlements were nearby, they are perhaps more likely to have been on the slopes towards the river rather than on the floodplain in the lower valley, to provide better opportunities for small scale agriculture and some hunting. It does seem that this represents an increase in population within the area from the sparse Later Neolithic and earlier groups, and although still small numbers of people they are laying claim to the area by building barrows, the first monumental structures.

5.3 The construction and use of barrows

The traditional classification of round barrows (Grinsell 1953) sees bowl barrows as by far the commonest form either ditched or not ditched varying in size from '30 feet in diameter to giants of 150 feet or more, as little as 3 or 4 feet in height to as much as 20 feet' (Ashbee 1960, 24). The 'Wessex' or 'fancy' barrows including bell, bell-disc, disc, pond and saucer, are far fewer in number, 'about five hundred' according to Ashbee (*ibid.*), and as the name suggests limited in distribution. In the West Midlands area most, if not all are bowl barrows with ditches common in lowland areas but not in the Peak District where the mounds tend to be stone cairns rather than earthen (Garwood 2007b, 142). The danger in paying too much attention to this over-simplistic classification based on outward form is that it masks the complexity of construction now shown through the excavation of many barrows (Last 2007c). While the final form of barrows, especially after 4,000 years, may look similar it is the constructional sequences of individual barrows that provide insights into the lives of the people who built and used them. As Owec (2007, 115) has shown it is the constructional process in the form of a particular order of integrated 'fabricative and ritual activities' that modify natural materials into culturally meaningful structures. For the Cheshire Basin, Mullin (2003, 16) has identified a sequence of 'commonalities' in barrow construction:

- The area is de-turfed.
- A primary burial of a single individual usually a cremation in a pit.
- A mound constructed over the primary, secondaries inserted into it often over a lengthy period, funerary pyres may be associated with mound.
- The final enlargement of the mound ends the funerary activity associated with it, domestic debris (pottery, flints etc) may be incorporated into mound material.
- Further secondary burials may occur around the outside of the mound.

As suggested in the opening paragraph of this chapter, barrows can be seen as primarily burial monuments although they were not just 'places to put dead bodies' (Parker Pearson 1999) but symbols of status, power and group identity. The act of burying individuals involving complex social rituals and activities would create that person's place within the genealogical framework of the group, but in the longer term when the memory of dead individuals fades, it is the physical presence of the barrow that ensures continuance. In Gosden and Lock's (1998) account of 'prehistoric history' they suggest a difference between shorter-term genealogical history based on named and remembered dead individuals and a much deeper mythological history triggered by landscape features which act as historical mnemonics. Even though the majority of excavated barrows have produced a primary burial, a small number have not and it has been suggested these are 'cenotaph barrows', perhaps markers for individuals that could not be buried for some reason. Church Lawton South, Cheshire, (McNeil 1982), for example, is a complex structure with a rectangular turf and daub 'mortuary house' at the centre of a setting of glacial boulders *c.* 25 m in diameter (dated to 2300–1650 cal BC) and although there is no evidence for a burial the whole lot is then sealed beneath a sand mound. At West Heath, Harting, West Sussex, of the nine barrows excavated (Drewett *et al.* 1988), only two contained human remains. The point here is that once the immediacy of the burial ceremony has faded the monument itself 'transcends time', 'becomes timeless' and represents the 'immortality of the community' (Parker Pearson 1999, 144).

In the following discussion we will concentrate on King's Low simply because the evidence has survived more fully than at Queen's Low although the ritual activity surrounding the burials and subsequent mound construction could have been equally complex at both sites. Garwood (2007d) has shown that during the final period of barrow building, i.e. *c.* 1850–1500 cal BC, cremation is the normal burial rite, often deposited in urns, with evidence for the cremation pyres being close to the point of final deposition for the primary burials. This appears to be the case at King's Low although the primary burial had been removed at Queen's Low so if there was one, details are lacking. It can be argued that cremation is a more complex burial rite than inhumation as it involves the construction of the funeral pyre, burning the body (with or without pyre goods), collecting the remains (and artefacts) and then burying the remains (perhaps in a container, with or without grave goods). The technology of cremation, the required construction of the pyre, the temperatures reached and the times involved in maintaining those temperatures along with the archaeological patterns left from a burnt pyre with body, have all been explored through experimentation by McKinley (1997). As she points out 'burial comprised a small part of the funerary rites attendant on cremation, somewhere towards the end' (*ibid.*, 130). The more difficult to reconstruct social context and implications of cremation are evoked by Barrett (1994) who shows the possible range of meanings that could have been embedded within the extended process of cremation and burial and how it relates to mound construction. When discussing the cremation and burial at Newford, Ireland, discussed below, Wilkins (2010) draws on anthropology to suggest a difference between primary and secondary burial rites as representing physical and social death. In this the actual cremating of the body symbolises the physical death of the person and the subsequent deposition of bone, sometimes only small amounts, in pits, under barrows and in other contexts with associated ritual and ceremonial is the social death. This final act in what can be a long process represents the incorporation of the person into the world of the ancestors, the building of the barrow becoming an eternal symbol of that world and its connections with the everyday. This is similar to Barrett's (1988) argument that funerary ritual is a process rather than an event, perhaps the notion of a rite of passage taking a tripartite structure (Jones 2008, 190) so that the body is removed from the living community, enters a stage of transformation and is then incorporated into the world of the dead.

One of the things that Barrett (1994) discusses is the idea that raised platforms could be used as architectural components incorporated into the final mound but also as places where the 'theatre' of the ceremony and ritual could take place and be viewed by people attending the activities. At King's Low the first structural component was a sand platform constructed from scraped-up material and it was upon this platform that the burial activities were performed, although probably not the pyre. Associated with this are the two deep stake holes, close together, possibly holding wooden stakes that were driven deep through the platform and into the natural sub-soil. While their function is unknown, Last (2007c) has shown that it is not unusual to find evidence for posts, stakes and stones beneath barrows representing a range of pre-barrow activities and structures. The possible complexity is shown by barrow Amesbury G71, Wiltshire (Christie 1967) where various configurations of stakes, some decayed *in situ* and some removed, were then covered by a low turf mound which appears to have been used as a platform upon which was a burnt area, in this case possibly including the pyre.

Many barrow excavations have produced what has been interpreted as evidence for the actual cremation pyre although it is important to establish whether this is *in situ* or pyre debris, i.e. pieces of charcoal and bone that have been moved from the pyre. It would seem that in most cases it is the latter based mainly on the small quantities found even though some individual pieces can be large, as at King's Low. Evidence for an actual *in situ* cremation pyre is rare although one of the sites excavated as part of the N6 road scheme in Ireland provided an insight into the required size and structure needed to dispose of a human body (Wilkins 2010). At Newford, a Late Bronze Age (1,000 to 800 cal BC) pyre was excavated in its entirety and consisted of a pit 3.5 m long, 2 m wide and 0.75 m deep, thought to be for up-draught and aiding firing, over which the logs were stacked with the body placed on top. Parker Pearson (1999, 49) has estimated that it would take a ton of (preferably dry) timber to dispose of an adult corpse. After firing at Newford, the whole collapsed into the pit from where 700 g of bone were recovered and being as an adult human cremation produces on average 3,000 g of bone this suggested to the excavators that some, but by no means all, bone had been removed from the pyre to be deposited elsewhere. Small amounts of cremated bone, *c.* 15 g, were found within several small pits around the pyre although in total this does not account for the whole amount taken from the pyre. The Newford pyre evidence is of extremely good, and unusual, quality although the location of a pyre can be claimed based on much less, sometimes just an area of burning and charcoal pieces. At Eagleston Flat in Derbyshire (McKinley 1994b) the pyre consisted of an area of charcoal *c.* 1.5 m by 2.0 m, 'consistent with the size one would expect of a pyre site', and appears to have been used several times. Pyre material was re-deposited into nearby pits while still hot as indicated by scorching on the pit sides. There may have been a variety of ways of constructing a pyre and burning a corpse, at Sproxton, Leicestershire (Clay 1981, 19) it was suggested that the pyre was built above the body resulting in only partial burning and the burial of poorly calcined and still articulated bone. Even so, as MicKinley has pointed out (1997, 132), over 10,000 cremation burials have been excavated (implying 10,000 actual cremations) and less than 100 pyre sites are claimed. Of these many are from old records, poorly recorded and probably represent pyre debris rather than an actual pyre site.

The evidence from King's Low suggests a pyre deposit with over 100 fragments of charcoal including 11 large pieces and one piece of a radially split 'plank', the majority are oak (Ch. 3, Challinor). Considering that this was a substantially deforested landscape, based on the pollen evidence, there must have been considerable effort invested in the collection and preparation of timber for the pyre. Challinor comments on the lack of evidence for brushwood which would be required to start the pyre fire and suggests this shows selection of larger pieces from the pyre to scatter over the surface of the sand platform. This must have happened after the digging of the pit and deposition of the Collared Urn containing the charred bone and the filling of the pit as the charcoal is spread over the top of the pit fill. Assuming this is the primary, i.e. initial burial, at King's Low, the burnt bone of the 9–11 year old sub-adult was collected very carefully from the pyre so that the majority of the body was represented, and put into the pot with a minimal amount of charcoal. The quantity of bone recoverable from a modern adult cremation is 1600–3600 g, with an average of 3000 g (McKinley 1989, 66) and here the weight was 957 g which is a high proportion of the original body compared to typically between 40% and 60% being collected for burial. There is evidence for pyre goods with ten pieces of unworked burnt flint and two worked tools, a fabricator and a backed blade, as well as the spherical faience bead, showing evidence for intense burning. It is not clear whether these objects were placed on the top of the bone in the pot or placed on the surface of the platform with the charcoal pyre pieces as they were all found in subsequently disturbed contexts and the top part of the pot and its contents were also disturbed by rabbit action. The most fully represented cremation burial from Queen's Low comprises only 409 g of an adult, 45+ years, so appears to be partial selection from the pyre, a practice that is widespread, for example at Newford, above. Indeed, at Queen's Low there are three other small discrete concentrations of cremated bone (12 g, 62 g and 99 g in weight), one of them containing three fragments of sheep/goat bone indicating another widely recognised practice that of burning parts of animals on the pyre with the human corpse. There are also burnt flints and the possibly burnt quoit-shaped faience bead from Queen's Low, perhaps pyre goods although found in insecure contexts within the mound material. The occurrence of a single faience bead at both sites is interesting and the chemical analysis suggests links between them, perhaps even being made by the same person (Ch. 4, Tite and Shortland). Woodward (2000, 117) remarks that beads found in barrow burials are usually 'remnants of necklaces' not complete necklaces, mostly found in groups of less than eight and are just as common with Collared Urns as in the 'rich' Early Bronze Age graves of Wessex. Even so, faience beads are rare in general and certainly in this part of Britain as shown by Barnatt's (1994, 335) discussion of the two found with a cremation at Eagleston Flat, Derbyshire, the closest to King's Low and Queen's Low.

Scattered throughout the mound of King's Low due to the effects of rabbit action is a large amount of cremated human bone all of which must have originated from cremation burials within unknown locations and contexts. By this period cremation is the most common burial rite and although this can occur in a range of urn types, Collared Urns being the commonest (Parker Pearson 2005), un-urned cremation burials are also often identified. In Mullin's study area of the Cheshire Basin (2003), including central and western Staffordshire, from 40 excavations there are 17 Collared Urns from burial contexts but the same number of un-urned cremation burials. It is perhaps worth noting that although mainly represented by small numbers of sherds, there are 10 different Collared Urns at King's Low and seven at Queen's Low. Whether these all originally contained cremations is unknown although secondary burials within barrow mounds are common-place perhaps showing a changing focus from the now sacrosanct centre of the mound containing the primary to edges of the mound which take on added significance. Secondary burials around the edges of barrows suggests that being within the mound is not of prime importance, for example at Barton-under Needwood about 30 km east of King's Low and Queen's Low where excavations have revealed a cremation cemetery just outside a barrow ditch with 22 individual cremation burials, three within pots and 17 uncontained (Martin and Allen 2001). The average weight of bone for the urned burials was 1236 g whereas for the un-urned deposits it was only 0.268 g suggesting that these were 'token' burials. It is also worth mentioning here the recent salvage excavations at Hints Quarry near Lichfield, where an un-urned cremation within a pit has been dated to 1540–1410 cal BC, adding to the few dates for Staffordshire, although it isn't clear whether this was a barrow or not (Kraviec *et al.* 2010). Further afield, at Barrow 1 Cossington, Leicestershire (Thomas, 2008, 15) a cremation cemetery of at least 11 burials, some in urns, were deposited within 5 m of the barrow ditch around its south-eastern flank. Being buried close to others from your lineage, either within the mound or around it, appears to be important and Parker Pearson (1999, 115) has suggested that within that importance is the order of deposition. He notes that often if the primary burial is male secondaries can be of either gender and any age, whereas if the primary is female secondaries tend to be also female and also include children and adolescents. This, he suggests, shows a patrilineal framework of succession and is a 'ritual representation of kinship and the ordering of life'.

After the construction of the sand platform at King's Low, the construction and firing of the pyre presumably not far away, the collection of the bone and artefacts, the digging of the pit, deposition of the pot containing the bone, the filling of the pit, the placing of the charcoal and perhaps artefacts on the surface of the platform, came the construction of a low turf mound to cover the whole platform area. Turf as a building material for barrows has been recognised for a long time, and is generally accepted as being 'a cut piece of land including surface humus, rooting zone and mineral soil beneath, which may not be of regular size or thickness' (Dimbleby 1985, 71). To Ashbee and Dimbleby (1976, 17) the use of turf in barrows shows that Bronze Age people were 'used to breaking up pasture and heathland with spades' and this contributed to the creation of a patchwork of small, short-lived clearances, by which forests were slowly degraded to heath and scrub woodland. Estimates have been made of the amount of turf needed to construct a barrow, for example at King Barrow Ridge, near Stonehenge (Cleal and Allen 1994), there are turf mounds within several large bell and bowl barrows. Here there was intensive grazing of the area just before barrow construction, perhaps to prepare the ground, and then large areas of turf cut. It is estimated that a minimum of 3 acres in area are needed for one barrow, 18 acres for the 6 main barrows. This could have taken place over several generations and it is suggested that the use of turf is not just pragmatic but a symbolic act representing the incorporation of an already sacred place. In a rather less precise estimate, at West Heath, Harting, West Sussex, eight of nine barrows excavated (Drewett *et al.* 1988) had turf stacks requiring 'extensive areas of heath and turf' to provide enough material.

Depending upon the post-construction conditions, turf is often very distinctive and can be easily recognised visually, especially from heathland where the soil is the A horizon of a podzol and strongly bleached, forming a good colour contrast with the humus layer, an extremely good example being the Dudsbury Barrow, Dorset (Ashbee 1960, plate VIa). Dimbleby (1985, 108) has shown that the pollen within the vegetation of a turf can be extremely illuminating, for example in telling which way up a turf is laid as for the barrow at Minsted, Sussex, where it was shown that an inverted turf lay on the original ground surface and it was cut from not far away. At Snail Down, Wiltshire (Thomas 2005) it was shown through the differences in the thickness of buried soils beneath two barrows that one was built on already de-turfed ground while the other was not and used turf cut from around it.

These elements of cremation burial, mound structure and the use of turf come together in various ways over large geographical areas. For example, Moor Green Barrow, West End, Hampshire (Ashbee and Dimbleby 1976), from the well-studied Wessex chalk down lands, a barrow 23 m diameter and 2.1 m high stands as one of a group of five on a low gravel spur overlooking streams. There was a primary cremation in a Collared Urn within a burial pit containing pyre debris of oak charcoal from large timbers. The first phase mound, about 1.5 m high, was built from turf shown by palynological evidence to have come from different areas all nearby in woodland probably recently cleared by fire. The turves were a light sandy soil covered by a darker sooty black humic layer, averaging 9 cm to 10 cm thick, cut and carried with the subsoil attached, most were 25 cm to 30 cm long, some were up to 75 cm long these perhaps used to stabilise the mound, all of which would have required careful cutting and rolling (*ibid.* 10). The first layer was laid turf downwards on a pre-barrow soil where the turf had been removed, over the filled burial pit to create a flat-topped cone-shaped mound with gently sloping sides. A mantle of clay and sand about 1 m thick covered the turf mound, the material being dug from a surrounding ditch. It is interesting to note here that the excavators noticed iron pan deposition at the base of this second phase mound together with wispy feint horizontal veins of iron infiltration throughout mound and turf and pre turf soil (*ibid.* 12, plate 4), the result of percolating soil water and impeded drainage. Similar areas of horizontal veining were recognised throughout much of the lower areas of King's Low.

Nearer to King's Low and Queen's Low, two barrows have been excavated at Fawfield Head, Longnor, Staffordshire (Wilson and Cleverdon 1987), which despite being close together show very different constructional biographies. Neither had evidence for a ditch but Low Farm had no evidence for pre-mound activity and was a single phase mound whereas Low Bent was multi-phase with much activity before the mound was built. Low Farm had a single primary cremation burial of bone wrapped up in a hide, the excavators thought this had been prepared at the pyre and then carried to the pit for burial as there was no soil mixed with the bone, just calcined flints (*ibid.*, 2). There were possible secondary cremation burials but due to extensive disturbance these could not be clarified. The mound had three components but was probably a single phase as no turf formed between them, an initial turf stack *c*. 1.5 m high (radiocarbon dated to 2270 bc +/-80), extended with less well cut turves and clay and then a final capping of clay. The other barrow, Low Bent, was also very damaged not least by Bateman digging there in 1848 and removing what is assumed to be the primary inhumation. Considerable pre-mound activity is represented by a 5 m by 3.6 m rectangular area defined by a trench, possible a temporary mortuary enclosure, and two thin layers of deposit that are cut by the burial pit. Charcoal from the mound is radiocarbon dated to 1680 bc +/- 100, and a secondary cremation within the mound to 1830 bc +/- 110.

The other relatively recent excavations in the area are the two barrows at Church Lawton in Cheshire (McNeil 1982; Mullin 2003). Church Lawton South has been mentioned above as having a pre-mound possible mortuary house (2300–1650 cal BC) which was sealed beneath a sand barrow lacking a primary burial. Church Lawton North has a complex two-phase sequence, phase 1 comprised an empty central rectangular pit with a wooden lid (2040–1600 cal BC) cut into the de-turfed subsoil covered by a barrow 16 m in diameter with a ditch (charcoal from the ditch dated to 2140–1730 cal BC). In the mound were 18 cremation burials clustering in the south-western quadrant representing adults, children and infants in Food Vessels and a Biconical Urn but without any grave goods. Phase 2 saw an enlargement of the mound to *c.* 30 m diameter with dumped sand capped with turf, there was one possible cremation burial but the main activity was three bowl shaped pits cut into the sides of the mound, surrounded by stake holes and filled with ash and charcoal. These are thought to be fire pits for cremating de-fleshed disarticulated bones which were then buried elsewhere, two pits have been dated to 1890–1510 cal BC and 1770–1400 cal BC.

Although neither King's Low nor Queen's Low showed any evidence for a surrounding ditch one of the important elements of the latter site is the partial presence of a kerb of stones. Surviving are twelve stones around the south and south-western areas, with evidence of being placed in sockets and it seems likely that the kerb would have originally surrounded the whole mound and the presence of sockets without stones suggests so (Ch. 2). Kerbs are rare in this area, Garwood (2007b, 143) cites only one other than Queen's Low in the whole West Midlands, that being Low Bent also in Staffordshire (Wilson and Cleverdon 1987). Here, in the first phase, are parts of a kerb of small stones around a possible pit although relationships are unclear and it does appear to be of a small diameter and quite different in character to that at Queen's Low. The other similarity with Queen's Low is the presence of cup marks on some of the stones, at Low Bent there is one cup-marked stone within the kerb and three others incorporated within the later turf and stone mound, these have ten, two and a single cup mark on them (*ibid.*, figure 8). Rock art is rare in the Peak District and surrounding areas (Barnatt and Reeder 1982, 33) of which Queen's Low and Low Bent can be seen as outliers together with one of the barrows at Sheen near Low Bent excavated by Carrington (Bateman 1861, 177–8). Sheen contained two stones with single cup marks, one a small triangular stone which appeared to have been cut to shape with a cup mark on one face similar to one found within the Low Bent mound. In Vine's survey of the Neolithic and Early Bronze Age in the Middle and Upper Trent Basin he lists and illustrates six examples of stones with cup marks from the whole area (1982, 65 and figures on pages 409 and 410). At Ramshorn, about 20 km northeast of Queen's Low in the foothills of the Peak District, a single slab with at least five cup marks was discovered in a farmyard during the laying of a drain (Guilbert *et al.* 1997). It is unclear whether this was originally part of a barrow although there are barrows within 1 km of the find on the Weaver Hills. Guilbert *et al.* (*ibid.*, 19) suggest that from the few examples of rock art in Staffordshire the distribution is on the sandstone foothills surrounding the limestone heartland of the Peak District and this applies to Queen's Low. They also point out that rock art is usually on natural outcrops but if within a barrow or cist, then the art often faces towards the centre suggesting a secondary use, i.e. the slabs have been removed from bedrock with the art in situ and incorporated into the monument so that the art isn't visible. This could have been the case at Queen's Low as discussed by Derek Outram in Chapter 2.

The continuing significance of King's Low as a recognised physical and cultural feature is suggested by a possible Iron Age burial within the mound. While Iron Age activity is shown in the area by the range of sites and finds (Ch. 1 Figs 1.8 and 1.9), burials are rare. King's Low contained the parts of two copper-alloy bracelets, a pair probably dating to La Tène I or early La Tène II, 450–200 BC (Ch. 4, Foster). There is no evidence for the grave itself although with the extensive rabbit damage in the upper levels of the mound this is not surprising and assuming it was an inhumation the acidity of the soil would not enable survival of the bone. Iron Age secondary burials within Early Bronze Age burial mounds are extremely rare and although not suggesting a burial, at Low Bent (described above) a sherd of haematite-coated carinated bowl, dating to the early Iron Age, 7th to 5th centuries BC was found in the subsoil (Wilson and Cleverdon 1987). Further afield at Cossington, Leicestershire, an Iron Age settlement was established around the still extant mound of Barrow 3, as well as pottery deposited within it although not with a burial (Thomas 2008, 122), and the excavator argues that memory and myth would have ensured the continuing importance of monuments to later people. The lasting significance of King's Low as a place associated with burial, or at least death, could have continued for much longer with the erection of the stone cross probably in the early 19th century as a marker for the nearby assassination of a locally important person (Ch. 2). It is not known whether the people who erected the cross knew that it was upon a burial mound as this was before the period of major antiquarian investigations, but even so it was obviously recognised as a prominent landscape feature.

Appendix 1 King's Low context description list

Note: The complex nature of the deposits due to disturbance, mainly rabbit and roots, and alteration through podsolisation and other geo-chemical action, has resulted in over recording. This is a simplified context list where layers considered to be the same in stratigraphic terms have been amalgamated. Only layers (and groups of layers of stratigraphical equivalence) that are of stratigraphical significance are listed.

Features that are considered to be of archaeological significance are separated from those of indeterminate character.

Contexts are shown on the main N–S and W–E sections, Figures 2.3 and 2.4. The original context sheets are in the site archive.

Significant Layers (and layer groups)

Context number: (1)
Same as: (201), (301), (307), (309), (401), (501)
Location: all areas.
Description: Brown/black loam, very disturbed by rabbits and roots, infrequent pebble inclusions. Over whole site, thickness varies to a maximum of c. 15 cm.
Interpretation: Topsoil.
Confirmed relationships: Above (3)

Context number: (3)
Same as: (6), (13), (56), (203), (256), (303), (403), (503), (1049)
Location: all areas.
Description: Brown/red/grey firm sand, patches of various coloured podsolisation including hard black patches and nodules, very disturbed in places by rabbits and roots, few small pebbles. Patches of colour become gradually more frequent towards the base of the context as it merges into (10). Very occasional blocks of (10) and (32) are 'floating' within (3). Thickness varies to a maximum of c. 1.5 m, thicker on the flanks of the mound. Context (13) is part of thicker flank material, hard/very hard black hard panning of sand, thicker towards the edges of the mound, seen mainly in Area A.
Interpretation: Heavily leached mound material, podsolised, hardpan (13) around the edges.
Confirmed relationships: Below (1), above (10), (17), (24), (32), (42), (43), (44), (53),

Context number: (10)
Same as: (29), (30), (210), (254), (410), (510)
Location: Areas A, B, D, E, and C.
Description: Red/orange mottled and patchy sand, soft 'creamy' texture, occasional small pebbles, occurs mainly as blocks 'floating' within (3) above (32). Thickness varies to a maximum of c. 70 cm.
Interpretation: Degraded context (32), altered through podsolisation and rabbit action.
Confirmed relationships: Below (3) and (1), above (32), within (3).

Context number: (17)
Same as: (14), (18), (21), (22), (1068)
Location: All areas.
Description: Bright orange/red hard sand, containing many water worn cobbles and pebbles c. 2-8 cm in size sometimes forming layers or 'surfaces'. Stones thin out towards the bottom of the layer. Thickness variable, up to 30 cm.
Interpretation: Natural, glacial sand, OGS in places where (44) has been removed.
Confirmed relationships: Below (3), (3/13), (42), (44), above (24).

Context number: (24)
Location: All areas.
Description: Red/orange firm sand, occasional clay patches and small pebbles, pieces of broken red sandstone bedrock included.
Interpretation: Deep undisturbed natural.
Confirmed relationships: Below (17), (3), (3/13).

Context number: (32)
Same as: (40), (240), (414), (415), (432), (449), (511), (532), (1007)
Location: Areas A, B, D, E
Description: Colourful sand, pink/orange/peach patches with dark red lines and patches, some charcoal flecks, soft and 'creamy' texture, occasional 'greasy' silver/purple patches (40). Some blocks of (32) 'floating' within (3) and merging into (10). Thickness varies to a maximum of c. 1.1 m.
Interpretation: Stacked turfs forming a mound, some individual turves are identifiable and average 35 × 20 cm in size.
Confirmed relationships: Below (3), (10), above (51), (53), (42), (44) within (3).

Context number: (42)
Location: Areas A, B, D and E.
Description: Uniform pink/orange sand, occasional dark orange lines (but no definite turfs as in (32)), firm, charcoal flecks and small pieces. Thickness varies to a maximum of c. 35 cm.
Interpretation: Pre-barrow laid surface, a sand 'platform'.
Confirmed relationships: Below (3), (32), (51), (53), above (17), (44), cut by (245).

Context number: (43)
Same as: (243), (443), (460)
Location: Areas A, B, D, E, F, N, M, K, C, G.
Description: Very clean orange sand, firm. Thickness varies to a maximum of c. 35 cm.
Interpretation: Addition to Phase 1 turf barrow, unconfirmed whether this was just around the edges or over the top of the turf barrow.
Confirmed relationships: Below (3), (3/13), (10), above (17) and (44).

Context number: (44)
Same as: (255)
Location: All Areas.
Description: Clean orange sand, occasional charcoal flecks, soft and 'creamy', depth varies to a maximum of $c.\,25\,\mathrm{cm}$.
Interpretation: Natural but disturbed, Late Neolithic/Early Bronze Age soil and OGS.
Confirmed relationships: Below (3), (3/13), (32), (42) and (43), above (17).

Context number: (51)
Same as: (253), (550), (1012), (1013), (1014), (1016)?, (1017)?, (1030), (1031), (1035), (1036), (1038), (1043), (1055), (1069), (1070)
Location: Areas A, B, D and E.
Description: Hard, red sand, occasional purple/brown patches, even consistency, containing charcoal pieces with concentrations, about 1.5 cm thick. Some large pieces of charcoal on the surface of (51), especially (1016) and (1017), which may have spread from (53).
Interpretation: Basal layer of turf mound containing charcoal possibly originating from the cremation pyre.
Confirmed relationships: Below (32), above (42), abuts (53).

Context number: (53)
Same as: (252), (452), (1015), (1016)?, (1017)?, (1019), (1039), (1041), (1042), (1045), (1047), (1048), (1050)
Location: Areas B and D.
Description: Patchy grey/purple/silver sand, hard dark red lines around charcoal and grey areas, charcoal pieces, some large with heavy concentrations.
Interpretation: material associated with the cremation pyre, may be *in situ* or re-deposited, if the latter probably not far.
Confirmed relationships: Below (32), (3), abuts (51), above (245), (1027), (42).

Significant Features

Context number: (245) (cut)
Same as: (445).
Location: Areas B and D, centre 31.8, 20.9.
Description: irregular shape averaging 0.8 m west to east, 1.2 m north to south and approximately 30 cm deep.
Interpretation: A pit.
Confirmed relationships: Cuts (42), filled by (1027), overlain by (53).

Context number: (1027) (fill)
Same as: (1028), (347)
Description: mottled brown/orange sand containing charcoal lumps up to 3 cm in size and small pieces of clay.
Interpretation: Single fill of pit (245).

Context number: (1029) (cut)
Location: Areas F and G, centre 35.9, 13.6.
Description: Approximately 1.0 m square in size, 0.70 m deep but edges very indistinct.
Interpretation: socket hole for medieval cross.
Confirmed relationships: Cuts (3), below (1), filled by (1029a).

Context number: (1029a) (fill)
Description: Pale sand, layered in its upper fill suggesting small pieces of turf, small pieces of the stone cross within it.
Interpretation: Fill of (1029)
Confirmed relationships: Fill of (1029), below (1), contains (39).

Context number: (1044) (cut)
Location: Area B, centre 30.8, 20.2.
Description: circular, $c.\,5\,\mathrm{cm}$ diameter at the top, $c.\,1\,\mathrm{m}$ deep, pointed bottom (seems to stop at the interface with red sandstone).
Interpretation: Stake hole.
Confirmed relationships: Below (51), cuts (42), (17) and (24), filled by (1044a).

Context number: (1044a) (fill)
Location: Area B.
Same as: (1053), (1054)
Description: grey sand with black 'organic' material towards the bottom and around the edges in places for the whole depth.
Interpretation: fill of stake hole.
Confirmed relationships: Fill of (1044), overlain by (51).

Context number: (1051) (cut)
Location: Area B, 30.95, 20.19.
Description: circular, $c.\,3.5\,\mathrm{cm}$ diameter at the top, $c.\,1\,\mathrm{m}$ deep (same as (1044) seems to stop at the interface with red sandstone), narrows gradually with depth, pointed at the bottom.
Interpretation: Stake hole.
Confirmed relationships: Below (51), cuts (42), (17) and (24), filled by (1051a).

Context number: (1051a) (fill)
Description: grey sand with black 'organic' material towards the bottom and around the edges in places for the whole depth.
Interpretation: fill of stake hole.
Confirmed relationships: Fill of (1051), overlain by (51).

Context number: (1064) (cut)
Location: Area C, centre 37.15, 21.30.
Description: Approximately circular 35 cm diameter, only $c.\,5\,\mathrm{cm}$ deep, badly damaged by a rabbit burrow, not known what level it was cut from.
Interpretation: A shallow pit cut into the subsoil.
Confirmed relationships: Cuts (17) and (24), filled by (1064a), overlain by (3).

Context number: (1064a) (fill)
Description: grey/orange sand containing small pieces of charcoal and cremated human bone.
Interpretation: A shallow pit cut into the subsoil.
Confirmed relationships: Fill of (1064), overlain by (3).

Indeterminate features

Context number: (25)
Location: Area A, TP3.
Description: Indeterminate, approximately circular, $c.\,11\,\mathrm{cm}$ diameter, $c.\,11\,\mathrm{cm}$ deep tapering to pointed base. Filled with red/grey/brown sand with charcoal inclusions and surrounding small pieces of charcoal.
Interpretation: part of (3).
Confirmed relationships: Within (3).

Context numbers: (7), (8), (9), (11)
Location: Area A.
Description: four $c.\,0.6\,\mathrm{cm}$ diameter holes, close together, filled with grey/brown sand.
Interpretation: Natural, root holes.
Confirmed relationships: Cuts (3) and (10).

Context number: (2), (15), (16), (248)
Location: Area A
Description: Various circularish indeterminate stains, typically 10 to 20 cm in size, pale grey sand, no depth on sectioning.
Interpretation: Natural, rabbit disturbance.
Confirmed relationships: Cuts (3).

Context number: (19), (20), (23), (41)
Location: Area A.
Description: (19) – distinctive 6 × 5 cm dark orange compacted sand, no depth on sectioning. (20) – 18 × 10 cm. (23) – indeterminate, (41) – $c.\,10\,\mathrm{cm}$ diameter.
Interpretation: Natural, possible rabbit disturbance.
Confirmed relationships: Within (10).

Appendix 1 *King's Low context description list*

Context number: (26), (27), (28), (411)
Location: Areas A and D.
Description: Large stones, between 10 and 55 cm dimensions.
Interpretation: Natural.
Confirmed relationships: Within (3).

Context number: (33), (34)
Location: Area A
Description: Annulus, *c.* 14 m, red sand, hard black thin wall around fill. (34) – circular patch of red/mottled sand, *c.* 22 cm diameter.
Interpretation: Natural, (33) root hole with podsolisation, (34) water staining.
Confirmed relationships: Within (10).

Context number: (4), (12), (35), (36), (37), (38)
Location: Area A.
Description: Patches of grey/red/black sand of varying hardness and size.
Interpretation: Natural, indistinct features due to podsolisation.
Confirmed relationships: Within (10) and (32).

Context number: (39),
Same as: (39A), (1046), (1052)
Location: Areas F and G.
Description: Large stones, *c.* 20 cm maximum dimension, some showing worked faces.
Interpretation: Parts of the cross.
Confirmed relationships: Within (3) and (1029).

Context number: (412), (413), (417), (418), (446), (1008), (1024), (1026)
Location: Areas B, D, E.
Description: Lumps of clay with small stone inclusions, typically *c.* 10 cm square.
Interpretation: Variations within the disturbed mound material.
Confirmed relationships: Within (3) and (32).

Context number: (416), (431), (1058), (1060), (1061), (1062), (1065), (1066), (1067)
Location: Areas D, E, F and K.
Description: Patches of light brown to deep red sand, less than 20 cm diameter, dark brown outer ring and some black. No depth on sectioning. (431), black staining.
Interpretation: Natural staining or rabbit disturbance.
Confirmed relationships: Within (3) and (10).

Context number: (657), (658)
Location: Area F.
Description: Grey 'sticky' sand, long patch 3 × 0.75 m, (658) patches of hardpan.
Interpretation: natural due to podsolisation.
Confirmed relationships: Within (3).

Context number: (1001), (1002), (1003), (1004), (1005), (1006), (1009), (1018), (1020), (1025), 1033), (1034), (1040)
Location: Areas B, D and E.
Description: Indeterminate patches of black staining, some associated with other patches of coloured sand especially dark red, some with rabbit disturbance around.
Interpretation: Natural – water staining of mound material, some manganese modules/staining/hard panning sometimes associated with rabbit disturbance.
Confirmed relationships: Within (32), (3) and (10).

Context number: (1021), (1022)
Location: Areas D and A.
Description: Indeterminate possible cut features first noticed when re-drawing section 17, subsequently disregarded.
Interpretation: Natural – probable rabbit disturbance of mound material.
Confirmed relationships: Within (3) and (32).

Context number: (1010), (1011), (1057), (1063)
Location: Area A
Description: Brown/grey linear typically *c.* 15 cm wide, may contain artefacts and charcoal.
Interpretation: Natural, filled in rabbit burrows.
Confirmed relationships: Within (3), (10) and (32).

Context number: (1023)
Location: Area A
Description: Orange sand with darker orange wispy lines (may be degraded (32/10), some black staining.
Interpretation: Natural, deep rabbit disturbance.
Confirmed relationships: Below (51), within (42).

Context number: (1037)
Location: Area D
Description: Circular block of turf (32), c. 10 cm diameter, curious because it seems to have 'slumped' down into and below (51).
Interpretation: A block of turf at the very base of the mound on/into the surface (51), perhaps into a hollow in the ground?
Confirmed relationships: Below (51) in places.

Appendix 2 Queen's Low context description list

Note: This is a simplified context list where layers considered to be the same in stratigraphic terms have been amalgamated. Only layers (and groups of layers of stratigraphical equivalence) that are of stratigraphical significance are listed.

Features that are considered to be of archaeological significance are separated from those of indeterminate character.

The areas excavated were given identifiers A, B, C, D, E, F, G, H, J, K,L, M, Western Extension (WX), Northern Extension (NX), Eastern Extension (EX), Southern Extension (SX).

Contexts are shown on the plans and sections Figures 2.21, 2.23, 2.24 and 2.27. The original context sheets are in the site archive.

Significant Layers (and layer groups)
Context number: (1)
Location: All areas.
Description: Grass and brown/grey sandy loam.
Interpretation: Turf.
Confirmed relationships: Above (2), (3)

Context number: (2)
Location: Areas A, B, L.
Description: Brown/grey sand, hard patches. Very mixed contents including brick, glass, 18th century pot and flints.
Interpretation: Hard core for a path or track. This is visible on the resistivity plot Figure 2.20.
Confirmed relationships: Below (1), above (4).

Context number: (3)
Location: All areas.
Description: Brown sandy loam. The thickness of contexts (3) and (4) together is 25 to 30 cm
Interpretation: Upper modern plough soil.
Confirmed relationships: Below (1), above (4)

Context number: (4)
Same as: (16).
Location: Areas A, B, C and D.
Description: Brown sandy loam, with orange/yellow small sandstone fragments (from plough hitting bedrock).
Interpretation: Lower modern plough soil.
Confirmed relationships: Below (2) and (3), above (5).

Context number: (5)
Same as: 25.
Location: All areas.
Description: Orange/yellow sandstone of very variable hardness, from tough sandstone through fragmented sandstone to compact sand.
Interpretation: Natural, bedrock with band of differing compaction.
Confirmed relationships: Below (3), (4), (6), (7), (8), (10), (11), (17), (18), (19), (22), (28), (39), (41), (46), (48)

Context number: (6)
Same as: 27.
Location: Areas A, B, E, G, H, J, WX and SX.
Description: Grey/brown sand with mottled yellow/orange patches.
Interpretation: Found in association with the kerb, but could be rabbit disturbed.
Confirmed relationships: Below (3), (4).

Context number: (10)
Location: Areas B, E, F and SX.
Description: Reddish mixed sand and clay with patches of grey sand.
Interpretation: Ploughing feature (probably 19th century marled agriculture).
Confirmed relationships: Below (4), (6), above (41). Some of the displaced kerb stones (1 and 2) and other stone fragments lie on top and/or within this context.

Context number: (18)
Same as: 21.
Location: Areas C and D.
Description: Soft pale cream sand nearly white.
Interpretation: Weathered sand possibly indicating edge of mound. This was striped with darker material which clearly represented ploughing.
Confirmed relationships: Below (3) above (5).

Context number: (19)
Location: Areas C.
Description: Piece of bone and charcoal in soft pale cream sand nearly white.
Interpretation: Weathered sand possibly indicating edge of mound. This was striped with darker material which clearly represented ploughing. Probably represents tiny part of plough disturbed cremation.
Confirmed relationships: Below (3), within (18), above (5).

Context number: (21)
Location: Areas C.
Description: Piece charcoal in soft pale cream sand nearly white.
Interpretation: Weathered sand possibly indicating edge of mound. This was striped with darker material which clearly represented ploughing. Probably represents tiny part of plough disturbed cremation.
Confirmed relationships: Below (3), within (18), above (5).

Context number: (22)
Location: Area D.
Description: Mixture of ash, charcoal and cremated bone.

Interpretation: Secondary cremation burial disturbed by rabbit action but a small amount probably in original position.
Confirmed relationships: Below (3), above (5).

Context number: (28)
Same as: (29), (30), (34), (35).
Location: Areas SX, E.
Description: Grey sand.
Interpretation: Stake holes.
Confirmed relationships: Below (3), above (5).

Context number: (39)
Location: Area B.
Description: Scattered charcoal and bone in grey sand matrix (6).
Interpretation: The bone find SF665 has a black core and has been established as sheep or goat. It was positioned close to a stone hole of the kerb.
Confirmed relationships: Below (4), within (6).

Context number: (41)
Same as: (13), (76).
Location: Areas B, E, F, G, H, WX and SX.
Description: Blotchy mixture of yellow, brown and grey sand, with some hard panning. Grit and pebble inclusions.
Interpretation: Material probably removed from the mound and re-deposited outside the kerb stones.
Confirmed relationships: Below (4), (10), above (5).

Context number: (48)
Same as: (47) although this is disturbed.
Location: Area G.
Description: Grey sand containing a quantity of charcoal and cremated bone.
Interpretation: Cremation in a rectangular cut hole (26 by 31 cm) into sandstone context (5).
Confirmed relationships: Below (4), above and cuts (5).

Context number: (86)
Location: Area SX.
Description: A linear spread of pot and charcoal within a layer of blotchy mixture of yellow brown and grey sand (41).
Interpretation: The pot was the remains of the upper part of a Bronze Age Collard Urn representing the whole of the rim and other decorated shards.
Confirmed relationships: Within (41).

Significant Features
Stones and stone holes of kerb (recorded clockwise from the Southern extention)

STONE 1
Context number: (84)
Same as: (33).
Location: Area SX.
Description: Stone with cup mark on underside.
Interpretation: A displaced stone from the kerb (40 × 30 cm).
Confirmed relationships: Within (41).

STONE 2
Context number: (85)
Location: Area SX.
Description: Stone.
Interpretation: A displaced stone from the kerb (60 × 43 cm).
Confirmed relationships: Within (41).

Start of a continuous four metre long section of 9 kerb stones (stones 3 to 11), more or less, in their original positions.

STONE 3
Context number: (65)
Location: Area E.
Description: Stone.
Interpretation: A stone in the kerb (40 × 28 cm).
Confirmed relationships: Below (3), (4) above (66).

Context number: (66)
Location: Area E.
Description: Dark grey sandy loam.
Interpretation: Rabbit disturbed material.
Confirmed relationships: Below (65) above (5).

STONE 4
Context number: (67)
Location: Area E.
Description: Stone.
Interpretation: A stone in the kerb.
Confirmed relationships: Below (3), (4) above (68).

Context number: (68)
Location: Area E.
Description: Mainly brown sandy loam with patches of white sand.
Interpretation: Fill of stone hole, slightly disturbed by rabbit activity.
Confirmed relationships: Below (67) above (5).

STONE 5
Context number: (70)
Location: Area E.
Description: Stone.
Interpretation: A stone in the kerb with a worn concave area on the north (inner) face.
Confirmed relationships: Below (3), (4) above (5), (71).

Context number: (71)
Same as: (37).
Location: Area E.
Description: Stone.
Interpretation: A stone which supported stone (70).
Confirmed relationships: Below (70) above (5), (72)

Context number: (72)
Location: Area E.
Description: Mainly brown sandy loam with patches of white sand.
Interpretation: Fill of stone hole, slightly disturbed by rabbit activity.
Confirmed relationships: Below (70), (71) above (5).

STONE 6
Context number: (77)
Location: Area E.
Description: Stone.
Interpretation: A stone in the kerb.
Confirmed relationships: Below (3), (4) above (80).

Context number: (80)
Location: Area E.
Description: The area beneath the stone (77). A mixed area with a small (10 cm) stone on the west. Centrally beneath the kerb stone was an area of compressed yellow sand surrounded by an area of brown sandy loam. Interpretation: The small stone was probably a packing stone. The brown sandy loam was probably caused by rabbit disturbance.
Confirmed relationships: Below (77) above (5).

STONE 7
Context number: (78)
Location: Area E.
Description: A stone.
Interpretation: A stone in the kerb.
Confirmed relationship: Below (3), (4) above (79).

Context number: (79)
Location: Area E.
Description: The area beneath the stone (78). A mixed area with 2 small stones (15 × 10 cm), one to the west and the other to the east. These were surrounded with brown sandy loam.
Interpretation: The two stones were probably packing stones. The brown sandy loam was probably caused by rabbit disturbance.
Confirmed relationships: Below (78) above (5).

STONE 8
Context number: (75)
Location: Area E.
Description: A small broken stone resting on stones 7 and 9.
Interpretation: A stone broken from the kerb by ploughing left against the kerb.
Confirmed relationships: Below (3), (4) above (78), (73).

STONE 9
Context number: (73)
Location: Area E.
Description: Stone.
Interpretation: A stone in the kerb.
Confirmed relationships: Below (3), (4) above (74).

Context number: (74)
Location: Area E.
Description: Mainly yellow sand and sandstone with some brown sandy loam.
Interpretation: Mainly the same as context (5) but with slight rabbit disturbance.
Confirmed relationships: Below (73) above (5).

Context number: (81)
Location: Area E.
Description: Circular area of dark sandy loam (15 cm diameter 10 cm deep) with a 2 cm diameter hole at the base continuing a further 5 cm The feature was close to north west of (73) and north east of (63) two of the stones of the kerb.
Interpretation: Probably a rabbit disturbed area (originally thought to be a possible post hole). It may originally have been a stake hole the top of which was rabbit damaged.
Confirmed relationships: Below (4) above (5).

STONE 10
Context number: (63)
Location: Area E, F.
Description: Stone.
Interpretation: A stone in the kerb.
Confirmed relationships: Below (3), (4) above (64).

Context number: (64)
Location: Area E, F.
Description: Yellow sand and sandstone but surrounded by dark brown sandy loam.
Interpretation: Mainly the same as context (5) surrounded by probable rabbit disturbance.
Confirmed relationships: Below (63) above (5).

Context number: (27)
Location: Area E.
Description: A narrow strip (about 10 cm wide) of brown sandy loam touching the northern sides of stones 3 to 10.
Interpretation: The once upright kerb stones have been pushed over towards the south. This left a gap which has been filled with the sandy loam. Later rabbit activity has further altered the shape and fill of the feature.
Confirmed relationships: Below (4) above (5).

STONE 11
Context number: (61)
Same as: (26)
Location: Area F.
Description: Stone.
Interpretation: A stone in the kerb.
Confirmed relationships: Below (3), (4) above (62).

Context number: (62)
Location: Area F.
Description: Mixed Context (5) immediately beneath the stone to the north, the rest, brown sandy loam.
Interpretation: when upright the stone sat directly on the natural. Rabbit disturbance formed round the stone. Ploughing caused the stone to tilt to the south pressing on the rabbit disturbance.
Confirmed relationships: Below (61) above (5).

STONE HOLE 11A
Context number: (6)
Location: Area F.
Description: An isolated area of brown sandy loam immediately to the west of stone 11.
Interpretation: Probably a stone hole for a kerb stone on the edge of a continuous section of kerb stones. Thought to be affected by rabbit disturbance.
Confirmed relationships: Below (4) above (5).

Gap in the kerb of just over 2 metres.

STONE 12
Context number: (59)
Location: Area F.
Description: Stone.
Interpretation: A stone in the kerb.
Confirmed relationships: Below (3), (4) above (60).

Context number: (60)
Location: Area F.
Description: An area of yellow sand and sandstone.
Interpretation: Bottom of stone 12 (59) sat directly onto natural (5).
Confirmed relationships: Below (59) above (5).

STONE 13
Context number: (57)
Location: Area F.
Description: Stone.
Interpretation: A stone in the kerb.
Confirmed relationship: Below (3), (4) above (58).

Context number: (58)
Location: Area F.
Description: A patch of yellow sand with pieces of bed rock (5) was in contact with the stone (57). Round the yellow sand was brown sandy loam.
Interpretation: The area beneath the stone (57). Suggesting the stone rested directly on the natural yellow sand with possible rabbit disturbance round it.
Confirmed relationship: Below (57) above (5).

Gap in the kerb of just over 1 metre with just a possible small packing stone in position.

STONE 14
Context number: (44)
Location: Area B.
Description: Stone.
Interpretation: A stone in the kerb.
Confirmed relationship: Below (3), (4) above (42).

Appendix 2 *Queen's Low context description list*

Context number: (42)
Location: Area B.
Description: A patch of yellow sand with pieces of bed rock (5) was in contact with the stone (44). Round the yellow sand was brown sandy loam.
Interpretation: The area beneath the stone (44) but extending west probably represented the fill of the stone hole but also indicating the position of a second missing stone to the west. The area of brown sandy loam is thought to be rabbit disturbance.
Confirmed relationships: Below (44), (4), above (5).

Context number: (43)
Location: Area B.
Description: Elliptical (55 × 19 cm) shallow but well defined area.
Interpretation: Cut for stone (44) and perhaps an adjacent (lost) stone of the kerb.
Confirmed relationships: Below (42) above (5).

STONE HOLE 14A
Context number: (45)
Location: Area B.
Description: Circular area of dark sandy loam (23 cm. diameter 8 cm. deep) close to north east of (53).
Interpretation: Probably a rabbit disturbed area (originally thought to be a possible post hole).
Confirmed relationships: Below (4) above (5).

Context number: (53)
Location: Area B.
Description: Two aligned elliptical areas (together measuring 33 × 6 cm) of pinkish sand surrounded by a mixture of yellow sand (to the north) and brown sandy loam. A small stone to the west (20 × 10 cms) and a circular area to the east (45).
Interpretation: The fill of one or possibly two stone holes of stones missing from the kerb. The stone to the west could have been a packing stone or a broken part of a kerb stone.
Confirmed relationships: Below (4) above (5).

Context number: (54)
Location: Area B.
Description: Two aligned elliptical areas (together measuring 33 × 6 cm) of pinkish sand about 2 cm. deep.
Interpretation: The cut for one or 2 missing stones of the kerb.
Confirmed relationships: Below (53) above (5).

STONE 15
Context number: (46)
Location: Area B.
Description: Circular area of dark sandy loam (25 cm diameter 7.5 cm deep) close to north east of stone 15 (87).
Interpretation: Probably a rabbit disturbed area (originally thought to be a possible post hole).
Confirmed relationships: Below (4) above (5).

Context number (83)
Location: Area B.
Description: Circular dark sandy loam.
Interpretation: Fill of context (46).
Confirmed relationships: Below (4) above (5).

Context number: (87)
Location: Area B.
Description: Stone.
Interpretation: A stone from the kerb.
Confirmed relationships: Below (3), (4) above (55).

Context number: (55)
Location: Area B.
Description: A mixed area of yellow sand (5) surrounded by brown sandy loam.
Interpretation: Area beneath stone 15, the fill of the cut for this stone. The stone sat on natural yellow sand (5) surrounded by rabbit disturbed material.
Confirmed relationships: Below (87) above (5).

Context number: (56)
Location: Area B.
Description: Irregular feature approximately circular 30 cm diameter.
Interpretation: The cut for the stone 15 (87) much affected by rabbit disturbance, only 2 cm deep at the maximum.
Confirmed relationships: below (55) above (5).

Gap in the kerb of 1 metre.

STONE HOLE 15A
Context number: (39)
Location: Area B.
Description: An elliptical area (60 × 30 cm) of mottled sand patches in grey sand (as context (6)) with a scatter of charcoal and cremated bone (the bone has a black core).
Interpretation: A stone hole of a missing stone from the kerb. With an animal cremation placed within the cut for the stone on the northern side of the stone.
Confirmed relationships: Below (4) above (5).

Gap in the kerb of 5 metres. However there is a secondary cremation site (47), (48) in this gap suggesting that the kerb did exist in this area.

STONE HOLE 15B
Context number: (49)
Location: Area G, H.
Description: A group of small pieces of sandstone forming a rough circle round a patch of grey sand. There were 2 larger sandstone fragments (30 cm) to the south west.
Interpretation: A stone hole with possible packing stones and fragments of stone possibly from the kerb.
Confirmed relationships: Below (4) above (5).

Context number: (51)
Location: Area G, H.
Description: An elliptical area of grey/brown sandy loam (60 × 20 cm).
Interpretation: The fill of a stone hole for a missing stone from the kerb. The fill material is identical to context (6).
Confirmed relationships: Below (4) above (5).

Context number: (50)
Location: area G, H.
Description: Ellipse (60 × 20 cm) about 5 cm deep.
Interpretation: The cut of a stone hole from the kerb.
Confirmed relationships: Below (4) above (5).

Gap in the kerb of 6 metres.

STONE HOLE 15C
Context number: (52)
Location: Area J.
Description: An elliptical area (43 × 28 cm up to 11 cm deep) of grey brown sandy loam (context (6)).
Interpretation: A possible stone hole for a missing stone from the kerb.
Confirmed relationships: Below (4) above (5).

This is the last recognisable feature of the kerb.

Other contexts associated with the kerb
Context number: (24)
Location: Area E.
Description: Stones 3 to 10 from the kerb.

Excavations at King's Low and Queen's Low

Context number: (36)
Location: Area F.
Description: Stones 11 to 13 from the kerb.

Context number: (31)
Location: Area SX.
Description: Stones 1 and 2 displaced from the kerb.

Other contexts possibly associated with the kerb, being broken pieces of sandstone to the south of the known kerb

Context number: (82)
Same as: (69).
Location: Area F.
Description: Broken stones up to 20 cm across.
Interpretation: Broken stones well to the south of stones 12 and 13 ((59) and (57)) which may have been part of the kerb before being broken and displaced.
Confirmed relationships: Below (4), within (10) and above (41).

Indeterminate features

Context number: (7)
Location: Area A.
Description: Squarish break in the sandstone about 1 metre across, of brown sandy loam with pieces of orange/yellow sandstone pieces in it.
Interpretation: A shallow plough cut into the sandstone filled with plough soil (4).
Confirmed relationships: Below (4) above (5).

Context number: (8)
Location: Area A.
Description: Squarish area in sandstone (5) about 50 cm across, containing upright fragments of broken sandstone.
Interpretation: An area of plough disturbed sandstone.
Confirmed relationships: Below (4) above (5).

Context number: (14)
Location: Area A.
Description: A collection of upright broken sandstones.
Interpretation: The fill of (8), plough disturbed sandstone fragments.
Confirmed relationships: Below (4) above (8).

Context number: (15)
Same as: (9).
Location: Area A, B.
Description: A group of broken sandstones.
Interpretation: The fill of (11) and (12), plough disturbed sandstone fragments.
Confirmed relationships: below (4) above (5).

Context number: (11)
Same as: (12).
Location: Area A, B.

Description: Vaguely rectangular area in sandstone (5) about 2×1 m, containing fragments of broken sandstone.
Interpretation: An area of plough disturbed sandstone.
Confirmed relationships: Below (4) above (5).

Context number: (17)
Location: Area EX.
Description: A linear feature of blackish sandy loam oriented north south cutting through the yellow sandstone (5). 30 cm wide narrowing to 7 cm at a depth of 30 cm.
Interpretation: A cleft in the bed rock (5) naturally filled with sandy loam.
Confirmed relationships: Below (4) above (5).

Context number: (32)
Location: Area F.
Description: An indistinct linear feature of dark sandy loam.
Interpretation: Loam filled animal hole.
Confirmed relationships: Below (4) above (5).

Context number: (40)
Location: Area F.
Description: indistinct area of dark sandy loam.
Interpretation: Probably a series of mole holes filled with sandy loam.
Confirmed relationships: Below (4).

Contexts from test pits outside the described excavations

Context number: (20)
Location: (65, 64).
Description: Mixed plough soil 35 cm deep.
Confirmed relationships: Standard sequence of Top (3) above (4) which was above (5).

Context number: (23)
Location: (65, 41).
Description: Mixed plough soil 70 cm deep.
Confirmed relationships: Standard sequence of Top (3) above (4) which was above (5).

Context number: (38)
Location: (53, 31).
Description: Mixed layer 70 cm deep with 30 cm of brown sandy loam above 20 cm of red clay and sandy loam, which is above a further 20 cm of brown sandy loam. At this point the natural orange/ yellow sand is met.
Interpretation: The top 30 cm represents modern ploughing. The lower 50 cm represent earlier ploughing with clay introduced. The depth of plough soil is a good indication the material from the destruction of the mound was re-deposited to the south of the mound, raising the ground surface.
Confirmed relationships: Sequence of top (3) above (10) which was above more (3). The bottom being the natural sand and bedrock (5).

Bibliography

Abrams M. D. 1992, Fire and the development of oak forests, *Bioscience* 42, 346–353.

Agren, J. and Zackrisson, O. 1990. Age and Size Structure of *Pinus sylvestris* populations on mires in Central Northern Sweden, *Journal of Ecology* 78, 1049–62.

Ashbee, P. 1960. *The Bronze Age round barrow in Britain*. London: Pheonix House.

Ashbee, P. and Dimbleby, G. W. 1976. The Moor Green Barrow, West End, Hampshire: excavations, 1961. *Proceedings of the Hampshire Field Club and Archaeological Society*, Volume 31 for 1974, 5–18.

Aspinall, A., Warren, S. E., Crummett, J. G. and Newton, R. G., 1972. Neutron activation analysis of faience beads, *Archaeometry*, 14.1, 27–40.

Barber, K. E. 1976. History of vegetation, in S. B. Chapman (ed), *Methods in Plant Ecology*. Oxford: Blackwell Scientific, 5–83.

Barclay, A. 2002. Ceramic lives, in J. D. Hill and A. Woodward (eds), *Prehistoric Britain: the ceramic basis*, Oxford: Oxbow Books, Prehistoric Research Group Occasional Paper 3, 85–95.

Barclay, A. Gray, M. and Lambrick, G. 1995. *Excavations at the Devil's Quoits, Stanton Harcourt, Oxfordshire, 1972–3 and 1998*. Oxford: Thames Valley Landscapes: the Windrush Valley 3.

Barclay, A. and Halpin, C. 1999. *Excavations at Barrow Hills, Radley, Oxfordshire. Volume 1: The Neolithic and Bronze Age monument complex*. Oxford: Thames Valley Landscapes 11.

Barfield, L. and Hodder, M. 1989. Burnt mounds in the West Midlands: surveys and excavations, in Gibson, A. (ed) *Midlands Prehistory*. British Archaeological Reports British Series, 204, 5–13.

Barnes, I. 1985. The non-ferrous metalwork from Hunsbury Hillfort, Northants. Unpublished dissertation for Postgraduate Diploma in Post-Excavation Studies, University of Leicester.

Barnatt, J. 1994. Excavation of a Bronze Age unenclosed cemetery, cairns, and field boundaries at Eaglestone Flat, Curbar, Derbyshire, 1984, 1989–1990. *Proceedings of the Prehistoric Society*, 60, 287–370.

Barnatt, J. 1996a. Barrows in the Peak District: a review and interpretation of extant sites and past excavations, in J. Barnatt and J. Collis, 3–94.

Barnatt, J. 1996b. Barrows in the Peak District: a corpus, in J. Barnatt and J. Collis, 171–263.

Barnatt, J. 1999. Taming the land: Peak District farming and ritual in the Bronze Age. *Derbyshire Archaeological Journal* 119, 19–78.

Barnatt, J. and Collis, J. 1996. *Barrows in the Peak District. Recent research*. Sheffield: J. R. Collis Publications.

Barnatt, J. and Reeder, P. 1982. Prehistoric rock art in the Peak District, *Derbyshire Archaeological Journal*, 102, 33–44.

Barrett, J. C. 1988. The living, the dead and the ancestors: Neolithic and Early Bronze Age mortuary practices, in J. C. Barrett and I. A. Kinnes (eds) *The archaeology of context in the Neolithic and Bronze Age: recent trends*. Sheffield: University of Sheffield.

Barrett, J. C. 1994. *Fragments from Antiquity*. Oxford: Blackwell.

Bartley, D. D. and Morgan, A. V. 1990. The Palynological Record of the King's Pool, Stafford, England. *New Phytologist* 116, 177–19.

Bateman, T. 1861. *Ten years digging in Celtic and Saxon grave hills in the counties of Derby, Stafford and York*. London and Derby. (Reprinted by Moorland Press, 1978).

Beckensall, S. 1999. *British Prehistoric Rock Art*. Stroud: Tempus.

Behre, K. E., 1981. The interpretation of anthropogenic indicators in pollen diagrams. *Pollen et Spores* 23(2), 225–245.

Behre, K. E. (ed.). 1986. *Anthropogenic Indicators in Pollen Diagrams*. Rotterdam: Balkema.

Bennett, K. D, 1984. The post-glacial history of *Pinus sylvestris* in the British Isles, *Quaternary Science Reviews* 3, 133–155.

Bengtsson, L. and Enell, M. 1986. Chemical Analysis, in B. E. Berglund (ed), 473–483.

Berglund, B. E., (ed.). 1986. *Handbook of Holocene Palaeoecology and Palaeohydrology*. London: John Wiley and Sons.

Bowman, S. G. E., Leslie, K. A., Sheridan, J. A., Eremin, K. and Wilthew, P. T. 2012. The faience quoit bead from Cefn Cwmwd, in R. Cuttler, A. Davidson and G. Hughes, *A corridor through time: the archaeology of the A55 Anglesey road scheme*. Oxford: Oxbow Books, 145–49.

Bowman, S. G. E. and Stapleton, C. P. 1997. The faience ornament fragment: its technology and provenance, in I. Greig, Excavation of a Bronze Age settlement at Varley Halls, Coldean Lane, Brighton, East Sussex, *Sussex Archaeological Collections*, 135, 44–7 and 56–8.

Boycott, A. E, 1936. Habitats of freshwater mollusca in Britain. *Journal of Animal Ecology*, 5, 116–136.

Boyd, W. E. 1988. Methodological problems in the analysis of fossil non-artifactual wood assemblages from archaeological sites, *Journal of Archaeological Science*, 15, 603–619.

Boyer, P. 1992. The contents of the urn, in R. Young and A. T. Welfare, Fieldwork and excavation at the Crawley Edge cairnfield, Stanhope, Co. Durham. *Durham Archaeological Journal* 8, 43–44.

Boyle, A. 1999. Human remains, in A. Barclay and C. Halpin, *Excavations at Barrow Hills, Radley, Oxfordshire. Volume 1: The Neolithic and Bronze Age Monument Complex*. Oxford: Oxford Archaeological Unit Thames Valley Landscapes 11, 171–183.

Boyle, A. In preparation. The human remains, in *Maidenhead, Windsor and Eton flood alleviation scheme: Neolithic and Bronze Age activity on the floodplain*. Oxford: Oxford Archaeology.

Bradley, R. 2007. *The prehistory of Britain and Ireland*. Cambridge: Cambridge University Press.

Bradley, R., Chowne, P., Cleal, R. M. J., Healy, F. and Kinnes, I. 1993. *Excavations on Redgate Hill, Hunstanton, Norfolk and at Tattershall Thorpe, Lincolnshire*. East Anglian Archaeology Report 57.

Briard, J. 1984. *L'Age du Bronze en France – 3: Les Tumulus d'Armorique*. Paris: Picard.

Britnell, W. J. 1982. Two Round Barrows at Trelystan, Powys. *Proceedings of the Prehistoric Society*, 48, 133–201.

Britton, J. 1807-26. *The architectural antiquities of Great Britain*. London.

Brothwell, D. R. 1981. *Digging up bones. The excavation, treatment and study of human skeletal remains*. Oxford: Oxford University Press and The British Museum of Natural History.

Brown, A. G., 1982. Human Impact of the former floodplain woodlands of the Severn, in M. Bell and S. Limbrey (eds.), *Archaeological Aspects of Woodland Ecology*, British Archaeological Reports International Series 146, 93–105.

Brown, A. G., 1988. The Palaeoecology of *Alnus* (alder) and the Postglacial history of floodplain vegetation: Pollen percentage and influx data from the West Midlands, United Kingdom. *New Phytologist* 110, 425–436.

Brunning, R. A. and O'Sullivan, A. 1997. Wood species selection and woodworking techniques, in N. Nayling and A. Caseldine, *Excavations at Caldicot, Gwent: Bronze Age Palaeochannels in the Lower Nedern Valley*. York: Council for British Archaeology Research Report 108, 163–187.

Buckland, P. and Edwards, K. J. 1984. The longevity of pastoral episodes or clearance activity in pollen diagrams: the role of post-occupation grazing. *Journal of Biogeography* 11, 243–249.

Burgess, C. B. 1986. "Urnes of no small variety": Collared urns reviewed. *Proceedings of the Prehistoric Society*, 52, 339–51.

Buteux, S., Chapman, H. and M. Hewson, 2007. *Where rivers meet – the Catholme ceremonial complex and the archaeology of the river gravels: research at the confluence of the Trent and Tame rivers in Staffordshire*. London: English Heritage.

Camden, W. 1806. *Britannia, or, a chorographical description of the flourishing kingdoms of England, Scotland and Ireland, and the islands adjacent: from the earliest antiquity*. Second Edition translated and enlarged by R. Gough. London: printed for J. Stockdale.

Campbell, G. 2007. Cremation deposits and the use of wood in cremation ritual, in Harding and Healy, 30-33.

Cantrill, T. C. 1911. A flint factory in South Staffordshire, *The Antiquary*, 47, 229–230.

Cartwright, C. R. 1982. Charcoal, in P. L. Drewett, Later Bronze Age downland economy and excavations at Black Patch, East Sussex, *Proceedings of the Prehistoric Society*, 48, 390.

Cartwright, C. R. 1985. Charcoal, in P. M. Christie, Barrows on the north Cornish coast: wartime excavations by C. K. Croft Andrew 1939–44, *Cornish Archaeology*, 24, 106.

Challinor, D. 2010. The Wood Charcoal, in Framework Archaeology, *Landscape Evolution in the Middle Thames Valley, Heathrow Terminal 5 Excavations, Volume 2*, Section 15, Framework Archaeology Monograph 3.

Chambers, F. M. and Price, S. M. 1985. Palaeoecology of *Alnus* (alder): Early Postglacial rise in a valley mire, North-west Wales. *New Phytologist* 101, 333– 344.

Clapham, A. R, Moore, D. M. and Tutin, T. G., 1987. *Flora of the British Isles* (Third Edition), Cambridge: Cambridge University Press.

Christie, P. M. 1967. A barrow cemetery of the second millennium BC in Wiltshire, England, *Proceedings of the Prehistoric Society*, 33, 336–66.

Clarke, D. L. 1970. *The Beaker Pottery of Great Britain and Ireland*. Cambridge: Cambridge University Press.

Clarke, D. V., Cowie, T. G. and Foxon, A. 1985. *Symbols of power at the time of Stonehenge*. Edinburgh: National Museum of Antiquities of Scotland, HMSO.

Clay, P. 1981. *Two multi-phase barrow sites at Sproxton and Eaton, Leicestershire*. Leicester: Leicestershire Museums Archaeological Report No. 2.

Cleal, R. and Allen, M. 1994. Investigation of tree-damaged barrows on King Barrow Ridge, Amesbury. *Wiltshire Archaeological and Natural History Magazine* 87, 54–84.

Clifford, T. and Clifford, A. 1817. *A topographical and historical description of the parish of Tixall, in the county of Stafford*. Paris. Printed privately.

Clough, T. H. McK. and Cummins, W. A. 1988. *Stone axe studies Volume 2. The petrology of prehistoric stone implements from the British Isles*. London: Council for British Archaeology.

Cockin, T. 2000. *The Staffordshire Encyclopaedia: a secondary source index on the history of the old county of Stafford, celebrating its curiosities, peculiarities and legends*. Stoke-on-Trent: Malthouse Press.

Coles, J. M., Heal, S. V. E. and Orme, B. 1978. The use and character of wood in Prehistoric Britain and Ireland, *Proceedings of the Prehistoric Society*, 44, 1–45.

Colt Hoare, R. 1812 and 1821. *The Ancient History of Wiltshire*. (2 Volumes). Republished 1975 by EP Publishing and Wiltshire County Library.

Cotton, J. and Green, A., 2004. Further prehistoric finds from Greater London, *Transactions of the London and Middlesex Archaeological Society*, 55, 119–151.

Coutts, H. 1971 *Tayside Before History*. Dundee: Museum & Art Gallery.

Cutler, D. F. 1978. Amesbury Barrow 51: Wood remains, in P. Ashbee, Amesbury Barrow 51: Excavation 1960,

Wiltshire Archaeological and Natural History Magazine, 70/71, 56.

Dechelette, J. 1927. *Manuel D'Archologie: Prehistorique, Celtique et Gallo-Romaine IV* Paris: Picard.

Dimbleby, G. W. 1965. Charcoal, in D. Dudley and C. Thomas, An early Bronze Age burial at Rosecliston, Newquay, *Cornish Archaeology*, 4, 17.

Dimbleby, G. W. 1981. The charcoal, in P. Ashbee, Amesbury Barrow: Excavations 1960, *Wiltshire Archaeological and Natural History Magazine*, 74/75, 28.

Dimbleby, G. W. 1985. *The Palynology of Archaeological Sites*. London: Academic Press.

Drewett, P., Rudling, D. and Gardiner, M. 1988. *The South-East to AD 1000*. London: Longman.

Dugdale, W. 1656. *The antiquities of Warwickshire illustrated: from records, leiger-books, manuscripts, charters, evidences, tombes, and armes: beautified with maps, prospects and portraictures*. London : Printed by Thomas Warren.

Edlin, H. L. 1949. *Woodland crafts in Britain: an account of the traditional uses of trees and timbers in the British countryside*. London: Batsford.

Edwards, K. J. 1990. The Mesolithic in Scotland, in P. M. Vermeersch and P. van Peer (eds.), *Contributions to the Mesolithic in Europe*. Leuven: Leuven University Press.

Ekwall, E. 1960. *The Concise Oxford Dictionary of English Place-Names* (Fourth Edition). Oxford: Clarendon Press.

Ellis, A. E. 1969. *British Snails*. Oxford: Clarendon Press.

Engelmark, O., Kullman, L. and Bergeron, Y. 1994, Fire and age structure of Scots pine and Norway spruce in northern Sweden during the past 700 years, *New Phytologist* 126, 163–168.

Erdeswick, S. 1844. *A survey of Staffordshire containing the antiquities of that county*. (Second Edition). London: J. B. Nichols and Son.

Evans, L. 1960. *The story of Margam Abbey*. Gloucester: British Publishing Company.

Fahey, V., Opeskin, K., Silbertstein, M., Anderson, R. and Riggs, C. 1998. The pathogenesis of Schmorl's nodes in relation to acute trauma. An autopsy study, *Spine* 23, 2272–5.

Field, D. 1998. Round barrows and the harmonious landscape: placing early Bronze Age burial monuments in south-east England. *Oxford Journal of Archaeology*, 17 (3), 309–26.

Fleming, A. 1971. Territorial patterns in Bronze Age Wessex, *Proceedings of the Prehistoric Society* 37, 138–66.

Fox, C. 1958. *Pattern and Purpose*. Cardiff: National Museum of Wales.

Gale, R. 1997. Charcoal, in A. P. Fitzpatrick, *Archaeological Excavations on the Route of the A27 Westhampnett Bypass, West Sussex, 1992*. Salisbury: Trust for Wessex Archaeology, Wessex Archaeology Report 12, 253.

Gale, R. 1998. Charcoal, in J. Barnatt and F. Robinson, Excavations of a Bronze Age cremation burial and multi-period artefact scatters at Horse Pastures, Beeley, Derbyshire; 1994, *Derbyshire Archaeological Journal*, 118, 43–45.

Garwood, P. (ed) 2007a. *The undiscovered country. The earlier prehistory of the West Midlands*. Oxford: Oxbow Books. The Making of the West Midlands Volume 1.

Garwood, P. 2007b. Late Neolithic and Early Bronze Age funerary monuments and burial traditions in the West Midlands, in Garwood, P. (ed), 134–65.

Garwood, P. 2007c. Regions, cultural identity and social change, *c*. 4,500–1500 BC: the West Midlands in context, in Garwood, P. (ed), 194–215.

Garwood, P. 2007d. Before the hills in order stood: chronology, time and history in the interpretation of Early Bronze Age round barrows, in Last, J. (ed), 30–52.

Gibbs, A. L. 1989. *Sex, gender and material culture patterning in later Neolithic and earlier Bronze Age England*. Cambridge: unpublished D.Phil. thesis, University of Cambridge.

Godwin, H. 1975. *The History of the British Flora*. Cambridge: Cambridge University Press.

Gosden, C. and Lock, G. 1998. Prehistoric histories, *World Archaeology*. 30.1, 2–12.

Green, H. S. 1980. *The Flint Arrowheads of the British Isles*. Oxford: British Archaeological Reports 75.

Greenslade, M. W. (ed). 1970. *A History of the County of Stafford*, (Volume 3). Oxford: Oxford University Press, The Institute of Historical Research, The Victoria History of the Counties of England.

Greenslade, M. W. and Stuart, D. G. 1965. *A History of Staffordshire with maps and pictures*. Beaconsfield: Darwen Finlayson.

Greig, J. 1982. Past and Present Lime Woods of Europe, in M. Bell and S. Limbrey, (eds.), *Archaeological Aspects of Woodland Ecology*. Oxford: British Archaeological Reports International Series 146, 23–39.

Greig, J. 2007. Priortities in Mesolithic, Neolithic and Bronze Age environmental archaeology in the West Midlands, in Garwood, P. (ed), 38–50.

Grimm, E. C. 1991. *TILIA and TILIA*GRAPH*. Springfield: Illinois State Museum.

Grinsell, L. V. 1941. *The Bronze Age Round Barrows of England*. (Second Edition). London: Methuen.

Grinsell, L. V. 1953. *The Ancient Burial-Mounds of England*. (Second Edition). London: Methuen.

Guilbert, G., Garton, D. and Walters, D. 1997. A cup-marked stone at Ramsor Farm, Ramshorn. *Staffordshire Archaeological and Historical Society Transactions*, XXXVI, 16–20.

Gunstone, A. J. H. 1964. An archaeological gazetteer of Staffordshire: Part 1: Chance finds and sites excluding barrows and their contents, *North Staffordshire Journal of Field Studies*, 4, 11–45.

Gunstone, A. J. H. 1965. An archaeological gazetteer of Staffordshire: Part 2: The barrows, *North Staffordshire Journal of Field Studies*, 5, 20–63.

Harding, J. and Healy, F. 2007. *The Raunds Area Project: A Neolithic and Bronze Age landscape in Northamptonshire*. London: English Heritage.

Havinga, A. J. 1974. Problems in the interpretation of pollen diagrams of mineral soils. *Geologie en Mijnbouw* 53, 449–453.

Henderson, J. (ed.) 1989. *Scientific analysis in archaeology and its interpretation*. Oxford: Oxford Committee for Archaeology, Monograph 19.

Hilton, C. 1979. Bower Farm, near Rugeley, *West Midlands Archaeological News Sheet*, 22, 7.

Hodder, M. A. 1980–1. The prehistory of the Lichfield area, *Transactions of the South Staffordshire Archaeological and Historical Society*, 22, 13–23.

Hooke, D. 1983. *The Landscape of Anglo-Saxon Staffordshire: The Charter Evidence*. Keele: University of Keele, Department of Adult Education.

Jones, A. 2008. How the dead live: mortuary practices, memory and the ancestors in Neolithic and Early Bronze Age Britain and Ireland, in J. Pollard (ed) *Prehistoric Britain*. Oxford: Blackwell, 177–201.

Jope, E. M. 2000. *Early Celtic Art in the British Isles*, 2 Volumes. Oxford: Clarendon Press.

Keepax, C. A. 1976. Report on the charcoal, in F. de M. Vatcher and H. L. Vatcher, The excavation of a round barrow near Poor's Heath, Risby, Suffolk, *Proceedings of the Prehistoric Society*, 42, 292.

Keepax, C. A. 1985. The charcoal samples, in N. Field, A multi-phased barrow and possible henge monument at West Ashby, Lincolnshire, *Proceedings of the Prehistoric Society* 51, 132–3.

Kelly's Directory, 1904. *Kelly's Directory of Staffordshire*. London.

Kelly, M. and Osbome, P. J. 1963. Two Faunas and Floras from the alluvium at Shustoke, Warwickshire. *Proceedings of the Linnean Society of London* 176;1, 37–66.

Kinnes, I. 1979. *Round barrows and ring-ditches in the British Neolithic*. London: British Museum Occasional Papers 7.

Kinnes, I. H., Gibson, A. M., Ambers, J., Bowman, S., Leese, M. and Boast, R. 1991. Radiocarbon dating and British Beakers: the British Museum programme. *Scottish Archaeological Review*, 8, 35–68.

Klemperer, W. D. and R. Barnett, 1993, *Stafford Eastern By-Pass Environmental Assessment: Cultural Heritage Evaluation, Stoke-on-Trent City Museum Archaeology Unit*, unpublished.

Kraviec, K., Edwards, E. and Brickley, M. 2010. A Middle Bronze Age cremation and other prehistoric features at Hints Quarry, Staffordshire. *Staffordshire Archaeological and Historical Society Transactions*, XLIV, 1–7.

Langdon, A. 1997. *Stone crosses in West Penwith*. Cornwall: Federation of Old Cornwall Societies.

Lanting, J. N. and van der Waals, J. D. 1972. British Beakers as seen from the Continent. *Helinium*, 12, 20–46.

Last, J. (ed) 2007a. *Beyond the Grave. New perspectives on barrows*. Oxford: Oxbow Books.

Last, J. 2007b. Beyond the Grave. New perspectives on barrows, in Last, J. (ed), 1–13.

Last, J. 2007c. Covering old ground: barrows as closure, in Last, J. (ed), 156–75.

Leah, M., Chaffer, R., White, R and Cherchali, S.-A. 1998. *The wetlands of Shropshire and Staffordshire*. Lancaster: University of Lancaster Archaeological Unit and English Heritage, Lancaster Imprints 7, North West Wetlands Survey, 5.

Limbrey, S. 1983. Archaeology and Palaeohydrology, in K. J. Gregory (ed.), *Background to Palaeohydrology*. Chichester: John Wiley and Sons.

Limbrey, S. 1987. Farmers and Farmland: Aspects of Prehistoric Land Use in the Severn Basin, in K. J. Gregory, J. Lewm and J. B. Thomes (eds.), *Palaeohydrology in Practice*. Chichester: John Wiley and Sons.

Longworth, I. H. 1984. *Collared Urns of the British Bronze Age in Great Britain and Ireland*. Cambridge: University Press.

Lorimer, C. G. 1985. The role of fire in the perpetuation of oak forests, in J. Johnson (ed) *Challenges in oak management and utilization*. Madison: University of Wisconsin Cooperative Extension Service, 8–25.

Lynam, C. 1878. A visit of discovery to St. Thomas's Priory, Stafford. *North Staffordshire Naturalists Field Club and Archaeological Society*, 58–59.

Lynch, F. 1993. Excavations in the Brenig Valley, a Mesolithic and Bronze Age landscape in North Wales. Aberystwyth: *Cambrian Archaeological Monograph 5*.

Macan, I. I. 1977. *A Key to the British Freshwater and Brackish-water Gastropods* (Fourth Edition). Ambleside: Freshwater Biological Association Scientific Publication No. 13.

Martin, A. and Allen, C. 2001. Two prehistoric ring ditches and an associated Bronze Age cremation cemetery at Tucklesholme Farm, Barton-under-Needwood, Staffordshire. *Staffordshire Archaeological and Historical Society Transactions*, XXXIX, 1–15.

McK. Clough, T. H. and Cummins, W. A. (eds), 1988. *Stone axe studies Volume 2: The petrology of the prehistoric stone implements from the British Isles*, London: Council for British Archaeology Research Report 67.

McKinley, J. I. 1989. Cremations: expectations, methodologies and realities, in C. A. Roberts, F. Lee and J. Bintliff (eds), *Burial archaeology: current research, methods and developments*. Oxford: British Archaeological Reports 211, 65-76.

McKinley, J. I. 1994a. *The Anglo-Saxon cemetery at Spong Hill, North Elmham. Part VIII: the cremations*. Gressenhall: East Anglian Archaeology 69.

McKinley, J. I. 1994b. Cremation burials, in J. Barnatt, 335–40.

McKinley, J. I. 1997. Bronze Age barrows and funerary rites and rituals of cremation, *Proceedings of the Prehistoric Society*, 63, 129–145.

McKinley, J. I. 2000. The analysis of cremated bone, in M. Cox and S. Mays (eds) *Human Osteology in archaeology and forensic science*. London: Greenwich Medical Media, 403–421.

McKinley, J. I. 2004. Compiling a skeletal inventory: cremated human bone, in M. Brickley and J. I. McKinley. *Guidelines to the standards for the recording of human remains*. Reading: Institute of Field Archaeologists Paper No. 7, 14–17.

McNeil, R. 1982. Burial Mound (Church Lawton North). Burial Mound (Church Lawton South). *Cheshire Archaeological Bulletin*, 8, 46–9.

McVean, D. N. 1956a. Ecology of *Alnus glutenosa* (L.) Gaertn; V. Notes on some British Alder populations, *Journal of Ecology*, 44;2, 321–330.

McVean, D. N. 1956b. Ecology of *Alnus glutenosa* (L.) Gaertn; VI. Postglacial history, *Journal of Ecology* 44;2, 331–333.

Mellars, P. 1976. Fire ecology, animal populations and man: a study of some ecological relationships in prehistory, *Proceedings of the Prehistory Society*, 42, 15–45.

Molyneux, W. 1878. *The early history of Trentham*. Newcastle: Staffordshire Newspaper and Printing Co.

Moore, P. D. 1979. Forest Fires, *Nature* 272, 27.

Moore, P. D., Webb, J. A. and Collinson, M. E. 1991. *Pollen Analysis*. Oxford: Blackwell.

Morgan, R. A. 1975. The selection and sampling of timber from archaeological sites for identification and tree-ring analysis, *Journal of Archaeological Science*, 2, 221–230.

Mullin, D. 2003. *The Bronze Age Landscape of the Northern English Midlands*. Oxford: British Archaeological Reports British Series, 351.

Mullin, D. 2007. 'A bit close for comfort': Early Bronze Age burial in the Cheshire Basin, in J. Last (ed), 83–90.

Needham, S. 2005. Transforming Beaker Culture in North-west Europe; Processes of fusion and fission. *Proceedings of the Prehistoric Society*, 71, 171–217.

Newton, R. G. and Renfrew, C. 1970. British faience beads reconsidered, *Antiquity*, 44, 199–206.

Northover, J. P. 1991a. Non-ferrous metalwork and metallurgy, in N. Sharples, *The excavations at Maiden Castle, 1985–6,*. London: English Heritage, 159–165 and microfiche.

Northover, J. P. 1991b. Non-ferrous metalwork and metallurgy, in B. W. Cunliffe, *Danebury: an Iron Age hillfort in Hampshire, Volume 5, The excavations 1979–1988: the finds*. London: CBA Research Report, 73, 407–412.

Northover, J. P. 1999. The earliest metalworking in southern Britain, in A. Hauptmann., E. Pernicka, T. Rehren and Ü. Yalçin (eds), *The beginnings of metallurgy*. Bochum: Deoutsches Bergbau-Museum: *Der Anschnitt*, Beiheft 9, 211–226.

Owec, M. A. 2007. To build or not to build: Bronze Age monument construction as technological practice, in J. Last (ed), 113–26.

Owen, E. 1886. *Old stone crosses of the vale of Clwyd and neighbouring parishes: together with some account of the ancient manners and customs and legendary lore connected with the parishes*. London: B. Quaritch.

Paffard, M. 1996. Staffordshire Place-Names, *Staffordshire Studies*, 8, 1–23.

Page, W. (ed). 1908. *The Victoria History of the County of Stafford*, (Volume 1). London: Archibald Constable.

Pallister, D. M. 1976. *The Making of the English Landscape. The Staffordshire Landscape*. London: Hodder and Stoughton.

Palmer, R. 1976. Interrupted ditch enclosures in Britain: the use of aerial photography for comparative studies, *Proceedings of the Prehistoric Society*, 42, 161–186.

Pape, T. 1935. Gargoyles at Brocton Hall. *The North Staffordshire Field Club. Transactions and Annual Report 1934–5*, LXIX, 72–74.

Parker, F. (ed) 1887. "Chartulary" of the Priory of St. Thomas (A' Becket) near Stafford (founded circa 1173–1175 AD). *Collections for a History of Staffordshire*. Edited by the William Salt Archaeological Society. London: Harrison and Son, 123–201.

Parker Pearson, M. 1999. *The archaeology of death and burial*. Stroud: Sutton Publishing.

Parker Pearson, M. 2005. *Bronze Age Britain*. Stroud: Batsford.

Parry Jones, L. 1981. *Llanynys Church. Past and present.* (Third Edition). Welsh Universal Press.

Patterson, W. A., Edwards K. J. and Maguire, D. J. 1987. Microscopic Charcoal as a Fossil Indicator of Fire, *Quaternary Science Reviews* 6, 3–23.

Peng, B., Wu, W., Hou, S., Shang, W., Wang, X. and Yang, Y. 2003. The pathogenesis of Schmorl's nodes, *Journal of Bone and Joint Surgery (Br)* 85, 879–82.

Pennington, W. 1969. *The History of British Vegetation*. London: The British Universities Press Ltd.

Pevsner, N. 1975. *Staffordshire*. Harmondsworth: Penguin.

Pitts, M. W, and Jacobi, R. M. 1979. Some aspects of change in flaked stone industries of the Mesolithic and Neolithic in southern Britain, *Journal of Archaeological Science*, 6, 163–177.

Rackham, O. 1990. *Trees and woodland in the British landscape*, (Second Edition), London: Phoenix Giant.

Ray, K. 2007. The Neolithic in the West Midlands: an overview, in P. Garwood (ed), 51–78.

Renfrew, C. 1973. Monuments, mobilisation and social organisation in Neolithic Wessex, in C. Renfrew (ed) *The explanation of culture change*, London: Duckworth, 539–58.

Resnick, D. and Niwayama, G. 1988. *Diagnosis of bone and joint disorders*, (Second Edition). Philadelphia: Saunders.

Richards, W. P. 1984. The burial mounds of North Staffordshire. *The North Staffordshire Field Club Transactions 1983–4, New Series*, Volume 9, 10–13.

Riley, H. 1990. The scraper assemblages and petit tranchet derivative arrowheads, in J. Richards, *The Stonehenge Environs project*, London: English Heritage Archaeological Report 16, 225–228.

Robinson, M. 1998. Carbonised plant remains and molluscs, in A. Boyle, D. Jennings, D. Miles and S. Palmer, *The Anglo-Saxon cemetery at Butler's Field, Lechlade, Gloucestershire, Volume 1: prehistoric and Roman activity and grave catalogue*, Oxford: Oxford Archaeological Unit, Thames Valley Landscapes, 10, 25–27.

Robinson, M. A and Lambrick, G. H. 1984. Holocene alluviation and hydrology in the upper Thames basin. *Nature* 308, 809–814.

Robinson, P. H. 1974. The 1862 Excavation by W. Molyneux of Deadman's Barrow, 3 Kings Grave, The Bury, *Staffordshire Archaeology*, 3, 50–1.

Roese, H. E. 1981. Some aspects of topographical locations of Neolithic and Bronze Age monuments in Wales. III. Round cairns and round barrows. *Bulletin of the Board of Celtic Studies*, 29, II, 575–87.

Rogers, J. and Waldron, T. 1995. *A field guide to joint disease in archaeology*. Chichester: John Wiley and Sons.

Rohl, B. and Needham, S. P. 1998. *The Circulation of Metal in the British Bronze Age: the Application of Lead Isotope Analysis*. London: British Museum Occasional Paper 102.

Savory, H. N. 1976. *Guide Catalogue of The Early Iron Age collections.* Cardiff: National Museum of Wales.

Savory, H. N. 1980. *Guide catalogue of the Bronze Age collections.* Cardiff: National Museum of Wales.

Scaife, R. and Burrin, P. I. 1992. Archaeological Inferences from alluvial sediments: some findings from Southern England, in S. Needham and M. G. Macklin (eds.), *Alluvial Archaeology in Britain.* Oxford: Oxbow Monograph 27.

Schweingruber, F. H. 1990. *Microscopic wood anatomy,* (Third Edition). Swiss Federal Institute for Forest, Snow and Landscape Research.

Shaw, S. 1798. The *history and antiquities of Staffordshire,* Volume 1. London: J. Nichols.

Sheridan, J. A. 2001. The National Museums of Scotland Dating Cremated Bones Project, *Discovery and Excavation in Scotland* 2, 129.

Sheridan, J. A. and McDonald, A. 2002. Faience, in I. A. G. Shepherd, and A. N. Shepherd, A Cordoned Urn burial with faience from 102 Findhorn, Moray, *Proceedings of the Society of Antiquaries of Scotland* 131, 110–19.

Sheridan, J. A. and Warren, S. in preparation. *Bronze Age Faience in North-West Europe.* Edinburgh.

Simmons, I., Dimbleby G. W. and Grigson, C. 1981. The Mesolithic, in T. Simmons and M. Tooley (eds), *The Environment in British Prehistory.* London: Duckworth, 82–124.

Smith, A. G. 1970. The influence of Mesolithic and Neolithic man on British Vegetation, in D. Walker and R. G. West (eds.), *Studies in the Vegetational History of the British Isles.* Cambridge: Cambridge University Press, 81–96.

Smith, A. G. (with Grigson, C., Hillman, G. and Tooley, M. I.) 1981. The Neolithic, in T. Simmons and M. Tooley (eds), *The Environment in British Prehistory.* London: Duckworth, 125–209.

Stead, I. M. 1965. *The La Tene cultures of Eastern Yorkshire.* York: Yorkshire Philosophical Society.

Stead, I. M. 1991. *Iron Age cemeteries in East Yorkshire.* London: English Heritage.

Stone, J. F. S. and Thomas, L. C. 1956. The use and distribution of faience in the ancient East and prehistoric Europe, *Proceedings of the Prehistoric Society* 22, 37–84.

Straker, V. 1988. The charcoal, in G. Lambrick, *The Rollright Stones, megaliths, monuments and settlements in the prehistoric landscape,* London: English Heritage Archaeological Report, 6, 102–103.

Taylor, M. 1981. *Wood in archaeology.* Aylesbury: Shire Publications.

Thomas, J. 2008. *Monument, memory and myth: the use and re-use of three round barrows at Cossington, Leicestershire.* Leicester: Leicester University Archaeological Services Monograph 14.

Thomas, N. 2005. *Snail Down Wiltshire: the Bronze Age Barrow Cemetery and related earthworks, in the parishes of Collingbourne Ducis and Collingbourne Kingston: excavations, 1953, 1955 and 1957.* Devizes: Wiltshire Archaeological and Natural History Society.

Thomas, N. and Gunstone, A. J. H. 1964. An introduction to the prehistory of Staffordshire. *The Archaeological Journal,* CXX, 256–63.

Thompson, G. B. 1999. The analysis of wood charcoals from selected pits and funerary contexts, in A. Barclay and C. Halpin, *Excavations at Barrow Hills, Radley, Oxfordshire, Volume 1: the Neolithic and Bronze Age monument complex,* Oxford: Oxford Archaeological Unit, Thames Valley Landscapes, 11, 247–253.

Tilley, C. 1994. *A phenomenology of landscape.* Oxford: Berg.

Tite, M. S., Freestone, I. C. and Bimson, M. 1983. Egyptian faience: an investigation of the methods of production, *Archaeometry,* 25.1, 17–27.

Turner, J. 1962. The Tilia Decline: An Anthropogenic Interpretation. *New Phytologist,* 61, 328–341.

Van Beek, G. C. 1983. *Dental morphology: an illustrated guide* (Second Edition). Bristol: Wright-PSG.

Vandiver, P. 1998. A review and the proposal of new criteria for the production technologies of Egyptian faience, in S. Colinart and M. Menu (eds.), *La couleur dans la peinture at l'émaillage de L'Égypte ancienne.* Ravello: Centro Universitario Europeo, 121–142.

Varley, W. J. 1938. The Bleasdale Circle. *Antiquaries Journal,* 18, 154–71.

Vine, P. M. 1982. *The Neolithic and Bronze Age cultures of the Middle and Upper Trent Basin.* Oxford: British Archaeological Reports British Series, 105.

Wainwright, G. J. and Longworth, I. H. 1971. *Durrington Walls: Excavations 1966-1968.* London: Society of Antiquaries Research Report No. 29.

Welch, C. M. 1990. *Burnt Mounds in S. E. Staffordshire: The Recovery of a Distribution by Sampling.* York: University of York.

Welch, C. M. 1997. A Bronze Age 'Burnt Mound' at Milwich, *Staffordshire Archaeological and Historical Society Transactions* 1994-1995, XXXVI, 1–15.

Wilkins, B. 2010. Excavating death in Galway. *Current Archaeology,* 246, 36–43.

Wilkinson, D. (ed) 1992. *Oxford Archaeological Unit Field Manual.* Oxford: Oxford Archaeological Unit.

Wilson, D. and Cleverdon, F. 1987. Excavations of two round barrows at Low Farm and Low Bent, Fawfieldhead, Longnor, Staffordshire. *Transactions of the South Staffordshire Archaeological and Historical Society* 27, 1–26.

Woodward, A. 2000. *British Barrows. A matter of life and death.* Stroud: Tempus.

Woodward, A. 2007. Ceremonial landscapes and ritual deposits in the Neolithic and Early Bronze Age periods in the West Midlands, in P. Garwood (ed), 182–93.

Woodward, A. and Woodward, P. 1996. The topography of some barrow cemeteries in Bronze Age Wessex, *Proceedings of the Prehistoric Society,* 62, 275–92.

Workshop of European Anthropologists. 1980. Recommendations for age and sex diagnoses of skeletons, *Journal of Human Evolution,* 9, 517–49.

Wymer, J. J. 1977. *Gazetteer of Mesolithic sites in England and Wales,* London: Council for British Archaeology Research Report 22.